The Psychology of Happiness

The Psychology of Happiness

2nd Edition

Michael Argyle

Routledge
Taylor & Francis Group

LONDON AND NEW YORK

First edition published 1987
by Methuen & Co. Ltd.
First edition reprinted 1989, 1993
by Routledge

Second edition published 2001
by Routledge
27 Church Road, Hove, East Sussex BN3 2FA

Simultaneously published in the USA and Canada
by Taylor & Francis Inc
29 West 35th Street, New York, NY 10001

Reprinted 2002

Routledge is an imprint of the Taylor & Francis Group

© 2001 Michael Argyle

Typeset in Bembo by RefineCatch Limited, Bungay, Suffolk
Printed and bound in Great Britain by
Biddles Ltd, Guildford and King's Lynn

British Library Cataloguing in Publication Data
A catalogue record for this book is available from the British Library

Library of Congress Cataloguing in Publication Data
Argyle, Michael.
   The psychology of happiness / Michael Argyle—2nd ed.
      p.   cm.
   Includes bibliographical references and index.
   ISBN 0–415–22664–3 (hbk)—ISBN 0–415–22665–1 (pbk)
   1. Happiness. 1. Title.
   BF575.H27 A74   2001
   152.4′2—dc21
                                          2001018072

ISBN 0–415–22664–3 (hbk)
ISBN 0–415–22665–1 (pbk)

Contents

About the author

Michael Argyle DSc, DLitt, Hon. DScPsych, is Emeritus Reader in Social Psychology at Oxford University, a Fellow of Wolfson College, and Emeritus Professor of Psychology at Oxford Brookes University. Born 1925, he was educated at Nottingham High School and Emmanuel College, Cambridge and was a navigator in the RAF.

He taught social psychology at Oxford from 1952 and his research interests in this area include the experimental study of social interaction and its application to wider social problems. He has lectured internationally, and was a visiting professor at a number of universities in the USA, Canada, and Australia.

He is the author of many books, including *The Social Psychology of Everyday Life* (1992), *The Psychology of Social Class* (1993), *The Psychology of Religious Behaviour: Belief and Experience* (with Beit-Hallahmi) (1997), *The Psychology of Money* (with Furnham) (1998), and *Psychology and Religion: An Introduction* (2000), all published by Routledge.

Acknowledgements

The author and publishers gratefully acknowledge the following for permission to reproduce copyright material:

Academic Press for Figure 6.1 from R. W. Larson (1990) "The solitary side of life: an examination of the time people spend alone from childhood to old age", *Developmental Review*, *10*, 155–183; and Figure 6.2 from C. Walker (1977) "Some variations in marital satisfaction" in R. Chester and J. Peel (Eds.) *Equalities and Inequalities in Family Life* (pp. 127–139).

American Journal of Epidemiology for Figure 6.4 from L. F. Berkman and S. L. Syme (1979) "Social networks, host resistance, and mortality: a nine-year follow-up study of Alameda county residents", *109*, 186–204. Reproduced by permission of Oxford University Press.

American Psychological Association for Figure 3.1 from J. A. Russell (1980) "A circumplex model of affect", *Journal of Personality and Social Psychology*, *39*, 1161–1178; Table 4.6 from P. Brickman et al. (1978) "Lottery winners and accident victims: is happiness relative?", *Journal of Personality and Social Psychology*, *36*, 917–927; Table 4.8 from F. Strack et al. (1985) "Happiness and reminiscing: the role of time perspective, affect and mode of thinking", *Journal of Personality and Social Psychology*, *49*, 1460–1469; Figure 9.3 from M. E. Lachman and S. L. Weaver (1998) "The sense of control as a moderator of social class differences in health and well-being", *Journal of Personality and Social Psychology*, *74*, 763–776; Figure 10.2 from K. M. Sheldon and A. J. Elliot (1999) "Goal-striving, need satisfaction, and longitudinal well-being: the self-concordance model", *Journal of Personality and Social Psychology*, *76*, 481–497; Figure 12.3 from E. Diener et al. (1995) "Factors predicting the subjective well-being of nations", *Journal of Personality and Social Psychology*, *69*, 851–864; Figure 13.2 from S. Lichter et al. (1980) "Increasing happiness through cognitive training", *New Zealand Psychologist*, *9*, 57–64; Table 13.2 'Positive life events: American students' from K. Magnus et al. (1993) "Extraversion and neuroticism as predictors of objective life events: a longitudinal analysis", *Journal of Personality and Social Psychology*, *65*, 1046–1053; Table 13.3 from P. M. Lewinsohn and M. Graf (1973) "Pleasant activities and depression", *Journal of Consulting and Clinical Psychology*, *41*, 261–268. Copyright © 1973, 1978, 1980, 1985, 1993, 1995, 1998, 1999, respectively, by the American Psychological Association. Reprinted with permission.

Blackwell Publishers for Table 10.1 from D. Lykken and A. Tellegen (1996) "Happiness is a stochastic phenomenon", *Psychological Science*, *7*, 186–189, © 1996 American Psychological Society.

BMJ Publishing Group for Figure 7.3 from M. G. Marmot, G. Rose, M. Shipley, and P. J. S. Hamilton (1978) "Employment grade and coronary heart disease in British civil servants", *Journal of Epidemiology and Community Health*, *32*, 244–249. Reprinted with permission.

British Psychological Society for Table 7.1 from P. B. Warr (1982) "A national study of non-financial commitment", *Journal of Occupational Psychology*, *55*, 297–312. Reproduced with permission from *The Journal of Occupational Psychology*, © 1982 The British Psychological Society.

Cambridge University Press for Table 7.5 from M. H. Banks and P. R. Jackson (1982) "Unemployment and risk of minor psychiatry disorder in young people: cross sectional and longitudinal evidence", *Psychological Medicine*, *12*, 789–798.

Elsevier Science for the following material from *Personality and Individual Differences*: Tables 2.2 and 8.1, from P. Hills and M. Argyle (1998b) "Positive moods derived from leisure and their relationship to happiness and leisure", *25*, 523–535; Table 6.2 and Figure 10.1 from M. Argyle and L. Lu (1990) "The happiness of extraverts", *11*, 1011–1017; Table 8.2 from P. Hills and M. Argyle (1998a) "Musical and religious experiences and their relationship to happiness", *25*, 91–102; Table 8.5 from D. Markland and L. Hardy (1993) "The exercise motivations inventory: preliminary development and validity of a measure of individuals' reasons for participation in regular physical exercise", *15*, 289–296; Table 10.2; from P. Hills and M. Argyle (2001) "Happiness, introversion–extraversion and happy introverts", *30*, 595–608. Table 12.4, reprinted from R. Lynn and T. Martin (1995) "National differences for thirty-seven nations in extraversion, neuroticism, psychoticism and economic, demographic and other variables", *19*, 401–406; Also Table 11.3 reprinted from G. W. Comstock and K. B. Partridge (1972) "Church attendance and health", *Journal of Chronic Diseases*, *25*, 665–672. Copyright © 1972, 1990, 1993, 1995, 1998, 2001, respectively. Reprinted with permission from Elsevier Science.

The Gallup Organization for Table 9.2 from G. H. Gallup (1976) "Human needs and satisfaction: a global survey", *Public Opinion Quarterly*, 40, 459–467.

Harcourt for Table 3.1 from *Mood and Personality* by Alden E. Wessman and David F. Ricks, copyright © 1966 by Harcourt, Inc, reproduced by permission of the publisher.

HarperCollins Publishers for Figure 9.5 from D. M. Myers (1992) *The Pursuit of Happiness*, copyright © 1992 by The David G. and Carol P. Myers Charitable Foundation. Reprinted by permission of HarperCollins Publishers Inc.

Harvard University Press for Table 5.1, reprinted by permission of the publisher from *Play* by Catherine Garvey, Cambridge, Mass.: Harvard University Press, Copyright © 1977, 1990 by Catherine Garvey; Table 6.5 from H. Carter and P. C. Glick (1970) *Marriage and Divorce: A Social and Economic Study*.

John Wiley & Sons for Table 6.4 from R. Cochrane (1988) "Marriage, separation and divorce" in S. Fisher and J. Reason (Eds.) *Handbook of Life Stress, Cognition and Health* (pp. 137–160), © 1988 by John Wiley & Sons Limited. Reproduced with permission.

Kaohsiung Journal of Medical Sciences for Figure 8.3 from L. Lu and M. Argyle (1993) "TV watching, soap opera and happiness", *9*, 501–507.

Kluwer Academic Publishers for the following material: Figure 2.1 from F. M. Andrews and S. B. Withey (1976) *Social Indicators of Well-Being*, New York and London: Plenum; Figure 9.1 from E. Diener, E. Sandvik, L. Seidlitz, and M. Diener (1993) "The relationship between income and subjective well-being: relative or absolute?", *Social Indicators Research*, *28*, 195–223; Figure 12.4 from T. E. Jordan (1992) "An index of the quality of life for Victorian children and youth: the Vicy index", *Social Indicators Research*, *27*, 257–277; and Figure 13.1 from B. W. Headey, E. L. Holmstrom, and A. J. Wearing (1985) "Models of well-being and ill-being", *Social Indicators Research*, *17*, 211–234; and Table 12.3 from E. Diener (1995) "A value-based index for measuring national quality of life", *Social Indicators Research*, *36*, 107–127. Reprinted with kind permission from Kluwer Academic Publishers.

Lawrence Erlbaum Associates for Table 4.2 from E. Diener et al. (1985) "The Satisfaction With Life Scale", *Journal of Personality Assessment*, *49*, 71–75; and Table 11.5 from Argyle and Hills (2000) "Religious experiences and their relationships with happiness and personality", *International Journal for the Psychology of Religion*, *10*, 157–172.

Macmillan Ltd for Table 9.3 from S. Harding (1985) "Values and the nature of psychological well-being", in M. Abrams, D. Gerard, and N. Timms (Eds.) *Values and Social Change in Britain* (pp. 227–252), © 1985 Macmillan.

MIT Press for Figure 9.2 from E. Diener and S. Oishi (in press) "Money and happiness: income and subjective well-being across nations" in E. Diener and E. M. Suh (Eds.) *Subjective Well-Being Across Cultures*.

National Centre for Volunteering for Tables 8.4 and 12.2 from P. Lynn and J. D. Smith (1991) *Voluntary Action Research*.

National Council on Family Relations for Figure 6.3 from M. Argyle and A. Furnham (1983) "Sources of satisfaction and conflict in long-term relationships", *Journal of Marriage and the Family*, *45*, 481–493. Copyrighted 1983 by the National Council on Family Relations, 3989 Central Ave. NE, Suite 550, Minneapolis, MN 55421. Reprinted with permission.

Oxford University Press for Table 2.3 from D. Goldberg (1978) *Manual of the General Health Questionnaire*; Figure 8.1 from R. S. Paffenbarger et al. (1991) "Health benefits of physical activity" in B. L. Driver, P. J. Brown and F. L. Peterson (Eds.) *Benefit of Leisure* (pp. 49–57).

PFD for Table 7.3 from M. Argyle and M. Henderson (1985). Reprinted by permission of PFD on behalf of Michael Argyle and Monica Henderson.

Princeton University Press for Table 6.3 from R. Inglehart (1990) *Culture Shift in Advanced Industrial Society*. Copyright © 1990 by PUP. Reprinted by permission of Princeton University Press.

Psychology Today for Table 8.3 from C. Rubenstein (1980) "Vacations", *13* (May), 62–76. Reprinted with permission from *Psychology Today* Magazine, Copyright © 1980 Sussex Publishers, Inc.

Review of Religious Research for Table 11.4 from T. B. Heaton and K. L Goodman (1985) "Religion and family formation", *26*, 343–359.

Routledge for Figure 8.2 from M. Argyle (1996) *The Social Psychology of Leisure*.

Russell Sage Foundation for Tables 4.1 and 6.1 from A. Campbell, P. E. Converse, and W. L. Rogers (1976) *The Quality of American Life*, © 1976 Russell Sage Foundation, New York.

Sage Publications Inc. for Table 6.6 from L. W. Hoffman and J. D. Manis (1982) "The value of children in the United States" in F. I. Nye (Ed.), *Family Relationships* (pp. 143–170); Figure 10.3 from R. Helson and E. C. Lohnen (1998) "Affective coloring of personality from young adulthood to midlife", *Personality and Social Psychology Bulletin*, *24*, 241–252. Copyright © 1982, 1998 by Sage Publications, Inc. Reprinted by permission of Sage Publications, Inc.

Tavistock Routledge for Figure 9.4 from M. Blaxter (1990) *Health and Lifestyle*.

The Sunday Times, London for Table 7.4 from C. L. Cooper (1985, Feb 24) "Survey of Occupations Rated on a Nine Point Scale for Stressfulness, Your Place in the Stress League", *Sunday Times*. © Times Newspapers Limited, London (24 February 1985). Reprinted with permission.

University of Michigan Institute for Social Research for Figure 12.1 from R. Inglehart and J.-R. Rabier (1986) "Aspirations adapt to situations— but why are the Belgians so much happier than the French?" in F. M. Andrews (Ed.) *Research on the Quality of Life* (pp. 1–56); for Table 12.1 from World Values Study Group (1994) World Values Survey, 1981–1984 and 1990–1993.

University of Michigan Survey Research Center for Figure 7.2 from R. J. House (1981) *Work Stress and Social Support*.

US Department of Health and Human Services for Figure 7.1 from R. D. Caplan, S. Cobb, J. R. P. French, R. van Harrison, and S. R. Pinneau (1975) *Job Demands and Worker Health*.

The author and publisher have made every effort to obtain permission to reproduce copyright material throughout this book. If any proper acknowledgement has not been made, or permission not received, we would invite any copyright holder to inform us of this oversight.

Preface

The first edition of this book was published in 1987, when the field of happiness research was quite young. Since then it has expanded enormously. A lot of new work has appeared in the journal *Social Indicators Research*, *The Journal of Personality and Social Psychology* and in *Personality and Individual Differences*. Veenhoven produced a reanalysis of surveys from around the world, *Correlates of Happiness* (1994). Kahneman, Diener, and Schwarz edited their equally massive *Well-Being: The Foundations of Hedonic Psychology* (1999), in which I have a chapter. Happiness and well-being research is now published mainly in psychological journals. However economists have also taken an increasing interest in this topic, through their concern with whether money makes people happy, and the effects of unemployment. Governments too have started to take an interest.

Since the first edition of this book I have been carrying out research and writing on some of the central topics of the present book, and this has helped me to rewrite some chapters. During this period I produced books on *The Social Psychology of Work* (2nd edition) (1989), *The Social Psychology of Leisure* (1996) and *Psychology and Religion: An Introduction* (2000).

I have been greatly helped by Peter Hills, Professor Adrian Furnham and Professor Peter Robinson, who read and commented on the whole manuscript. I am indebted to students, especially at Oxford Brookes University, some of whom have done empirical projects in this area. Two conferences have been very useful, one organised by Kahneman at Princeton in connection with the *Well-Being* book, the other at Nuffield College, organised by Professor Avner Offer and others.

Several libraries have been very helpful, especially the Radcliffe Science Library and the PPE Reading Room, New Bodleian at Oxford.

June 2000
Oxford Brookes University

Chapter 1

Introduction

> We hold these truths to be self-evident—that all men are created equal; that they are endowed by their Creator with certain inalienable rights; that among these are life, liberty, and the pursuit of happiness.
>
> (American Declaration of Independence)

THE PURSUIT OF HAPPINESS

It does not really need to be proved that most people, perhaps all people, want to be happy. However there is data to prove it. King and Napa (1998) found with two American samples that happiness and meaning in life were rated as much more important than money in producing the good life, more than moral goodness and more even than going to heaven (this was done in the mid-West). However, although students thought that money was unimportant, adults thought it was a factor in the good life. Skevington, MacArthur, and Somerset (1997) found with a number of focus groups in England that happiness was rated as the most important component of Quality of Life, greater than money, health or sex for example. The enthusiasm for the Lottery, and TV shows where people can win a lot of money, suggests that many people believe that money would solve their problems and make them happy.

It is sometimes said that we can't or shouldn't pursue happiness, that it is the by-product of hard work or some other aspects of a good life. On the other hand psychologists are quite successful in relieving depression in other people, and the aim is to make them happier. We shall discuss later the possible ways of enhancing the happiness both of others and oneself, and indeed of the whole community.

It is sometimes said that the very concept of happiness is obscure and mysterious. But it is clear that most people know very well what it is. Surveys have asked people what they mean by it, and they say either that it is often being in a state of joy or other positive emotion, or it is being satisfied with one's life. These two components, positive emotion and satisfaction, are often measured, and we shall see that they have somewhat different causes. Often a third component is included—the absence of depression, anxiety or other negative emotions. Happiness has sometimes been measured by the answers to a single question in big surveys, but this has led to some very improbable results, especially on international comparisons. Longer scales are better. We discuss the measurement of happiness in Chapter 2.

It was the great imbalance between the number of psychological books and papers on depression and on happiness, 17:1 in one survey, which motivated some of us to start looking at the neglected positive emotions. Recently the situation has changed and there are now many studies of what has come to be called "subjective well-being", SWB for short, which means exactly the same thing, and I shall use this term as an alternative to happiness. "Well-being" is different, since it usually includes objective variables such as income and health.

It is possible that happiness can take different forms. There is the high arousal kind of happiness of those who enjoy noisy and exciting social events, and the quieter happiness of those who enjoy quieter and solitary activities. This becomes a problem when comparing the happiness levels in different cultures. We shall see how happiness can best be measured in the next chapter.

WHAT DO WE WANT TO KNOW FROM HAPPINESS RESEARCH?

Psychologists want to understand the causes of happiness and the psychological processes that produce it, but what do other people want to know? They too may want to know the causes, because this will tell us how to improve the happiness of self or others. Some causal factors can be manipulated, such as choice of leisure activities. And it is possible to change one's mood by simple methods of positive mood induction. This gives the answer to another question—can happiness be changed? The answer is that it can, even though some of the causal factors such as personality are partly innate and outside our control. We discuss how to do it in Chapter 13.

Psychologists are also interested in fundamental issues, which may have practical consequences when they are solved. Good moods depend on physiological processes, some of which we understand. This enables us to explain the effects of drugs like Prozac, but also of exercise for example. In the end we would like to be able to trace the detailed physiological production of this aspect of happiness. And we want to know is there a biological advantage of happiness; does it lead to survival? We shall suggest some answers to this question (Chapter 3).

Happiness depends partly on objective conditions such as being married and employed, but it is partly in the mind; it depends on how we look at things. Optimism is good, but what about "unrealistic optimism"? Having goals is good, but what if the "goal–achievement gap" is too large? These are some of the cognitive processes behind our judgements of happiness and satisfaction with life (Chapter 4).

Seeing the funny side of things is good for happiness too, and a chapter on humour has been added since the first edition of this book. Humour works in several ways, the most important is that being able to look at events in a second, less serious way, can make negative events less stressful. It is also a means of enjoying social encounters, it is part of sociability and a part of social skills. It can discharge conflicts between people and in society (Chapter 5).

The central part of the book is about the main causes of happiness—which I believe are social relationships, work and leisure. We now know that relationships like romantic love, marriage and friendship are major causes of positive emotion and happiness, and also of other aspects of well-being like mental and physical health. They do this by providing social support, in the form of actual help, emotional support and companionship in pleasant activities. There is a close link between happiness and sociability (Chapter 6).

Work is satisfying and enjoyed by most people, partly because it leads to rewards and other goal-attainment, but also because of intrinsic satisfaction from doing the work, and social satisfaction from relations with work mates. Work can be stressful but is overall good for us. Working conditions have been changing, not always for the better; happiness researchers are keeping a watchful eye on new forms of working. Unemployment is high throughout the industrialised world, and we discuss how the effects of it can be alleviated (Chapter 7).

Leisure is an important cause of happiness, and it is the one that is most under individual control. There are several theories of what motivates leisure activity; it will be shown that the main motivation is often to enjoy social relations, real or imaginary. Psychologists are quite puzzled about the great popularity of TV watching, since those watching report very low levels of satisfaction from it and also say that they are almost asleep when watching. There can be positive effects, however, such as for the socially isolated (Chapter 8).

Does money make people happy? This is a really important question, but it has been very hard to resolve since the findings are contradictory. Many people, and governments, act as if it is so, yet rising incomes have not affected life satisfaction, winning lotteries has negative effects for some, and the rich are no happier than those on middle incomes; those most preoccupied with money are less happy. On the other hand the very poor are less happy, and richer countries have higher levels of reported happiness than poorer countries. There are quite large effects of social class and of education, and both of them have a greater effect in some other countries (Chapter 9).

Psychologists also want to know which kinds of personality are happiest. This was once a focus of controversy, but now it has been well researched and it has been found that there are strong links with certain personality traits such as extraversion and neuroticism. There are some other aspects of personality in the domain of styles of thinking: happy people have more self-esteem, sense of control, optimism, and a sense of purpose derived from having goals. Any findings in this area can be made use of in psychotherapy—to persuade patients to look at things in the best way. There are also age differences in happiness, but could this be due to historical changes? Fortunately there have been some longitudinal studies to find out. Chapter 10 deals with personality.

Does religion make people happier? Yes, but not as much as joining a sports club or getting married. Church members benefit from more specialised aspects of well-being—services produce intense positive experiences, as music does; believers have more existential well-being, less fear of death, can cope with major stresses, and they live longer. This is all partly due to the strong social support of church communities (Chapter 11).

There is great interest in knowing how our country compares with other countries. There is a lot of material on this, and the upshot is that Britain, along with the USA, Australia and Scandinavia, score high on self-reported happiness. However, some of the findings in this area have been questioned—is Iceland really the happiest country in the world, and is Europe unhappy, as single-item surveys tend to find? The differences may be due to social norms about express-ing happiness. If we also look at objective social indicators, a more complex picture emerges. In Chapter 12 we also consider whether there have been historical changes. Over the last 40 years, since surveys started, there has been surprisingly little change, despite great increases in average prosperity in many countries; we shall see that this itself is a further problem to be explained. Meanwhile social changes continue, which may affect happiness, some of them in the wrong direction, such as more unemployment, and more family break-up. Chapter 12 deals with differences between countries.

In Chapter 13 we consider how happiness can be enhanced. It can be done in the lab by mood induction experiments, and in field situations by increasing the frequency of positive events such as exercise. Happiness therapy has consisted of increasing positive life events, and using cognitive therapy and training in social skills training. Elaborate packages built on these have been used with both depressed patients and normals. We shall discuss the effects of Prozac and other happiness drugs, but conclude that a changed lifestyle is the best way of achiev-ing happiness (Chapter 13).

Finally we ask, is happiness good for us? Does it produce better health or mental health, make people more sociable, more helpful, work harder or solve problems better? The answer to these questions may help answer another one, what is the use of happiness? Although, of course, happiness is an end in itself (Chapter 14).

DIDN'T WE KNOW IT ALL BEFORE?

Most people are not aware that there is a large body of happiness research. And when they hear about it they are not always impressed. They say "It's obvious". It can be pointed out that findings like these seem more obvious when they have been found out than before the work was done—when it was certainly not obvious to those carrying out the research. I sometimes avoid this reaction when lecturing on this topic by listing some totally unsolved problems. Many "obvious" theories of course turn out to be wrong. Admittedly some of the findings are not very surprising, for example that being unemployed or divorced makes people unhappy. On the other hand we did not know the details, that is which individuals are and are not made unhappy by these experiences—indeed some are happier. But there are other findings that are a lot more surprising to most of us. For example:

- on the whole money does not make people happy
- winning the lottery makes many people less happy
- happiness is partly innate
- happy people live longer
- so do those who go to church
- having children has no overall effect on happiness (it depends on stage in the family life cycle)
- older people are happier than younger
- watching TV soap operas is beneficial (despite evidence that TV watchers are only half awake).

There is research into what people think will make them happy or unhappy. They are often wrong. For example American students think they would be happier living in California than in the Middle West; there is no difference. Faculty think they will be happier if they get tenure: it made no difference. Soldiers expect more fear doing a difficult parachute jump, and dental patients think that it will hurt more, than actually happens. People say that money is not an important cause of happiness, and they are correct; however, their behaviour suggests that they think money is very important (Loewenstein and Schkade, 1999).

I have mentioned a number of issues where there are still unsolved problems. These include sheer empirical matters such as whether some countries are happier than others, and exactly what effect money has on happiness. There are also more theoretical issues, such as tracing the physiological processes producing joy, explaining exactly why extraverts are happy. And there are applied problems, such as which training packages enhance happiness most.

INSPIRATIONAL AND NON-EMPIRICAL THEORIES OF HAPPINESS

There are several groups who think they know all about happiness, without the need for further research. There are some religious people for example, who think that the secret of life can be found in their sacred book. Muslims think this, and think that research into psychology is unnecessary, since it is all in the Koran. If this was true it would follow that religious individuals would be happier than the non-religious. As we shall see several other causes have a greater effect.

Another group is the authors of self-help books, in the tradition of Norman Vincent Peale's *The Power of Positive Thinking* (1953), and there are many books with the general title of *How to be Happy*. These books however do not make any use of the research enterprise described above, they are a kind of inspirational common sense. They advise people to assert themselves, accept themselves and think positively, sometimes with some religious elements such as love people and forgive them. Recent examples are Holden's *Happiness Now* (1998) and Lindenfeld's *Emotional Confidence* (1997). What such books lack is any evidence that the contents are true or that reading them does you any good. We have seen already that common sense is a very poor guide, since often what seems obvious turns out to be wrong, and many problems are still unsolved. The central component, *think positively*, is really part of happiness, and it is doubtful whether it can be acquired by sheer will-power. These books are also full of strange and unverifiable propositions such as "You are truly happy 100% of the time; your only problem is that you are not always aware of this", and "Making a whole-hearted commitment to being happy is a powerful medicine" (Holden, 1998, pp. 160 and 70). It is probably a mistake to think of these as in any sense empirical propositions; they are inspirational statements, with the intention of changing the way their readers feel about their lives. But in this case there is no way of deciding which of many self-help books is right, or best.

THE HISTORY OF HAPPINESS RESEARCH

This is a very short history since the field emerged quite recently. In the 1960s American survey organisations started asking questions about happiness and satisfaction. This led to some early classics: Cantril (1965), *The Pattern of Human Concerns*, an international survey with 23,875 respondents; Bradburn (1969), *The Structure of Psychological Well-Being*, which used an NORC survey; and Campbell, Converse, and Rogers (1976), *The Quality of American Life*, from the Survey Research Center at the University of Michigan. In 1967 Wilson published a review of the happiness literature in the *Psychological Bulletin*, and in 1984 Diener did the same, updating this in 1999 (Diener et al.). Gallup, MORI, and other survey organisations were carrying out further surveys, and not only in America—in Europe the Eurobarometer surveyed Common Market countries.

The journal *Social Indicators Research* began in 1974, and published a lot of happiness material; *Personality and Individual Differences* published increasing numbers of papers on individual differences in happiness. Psychological journals such as *The Journal of Personality and Social Psychology* also began to publish papers on happiness. In 1999 the *Journal of Happiness Research* started, edited by Veenhoven. In 1994 Veenhoven brought out his massive three-volume *Correlates of Happiness*, reanalysing 630 major surveys from around the world. Kahneman, Diener, and Schwarz edited a large volume, *Foundations of Hedonic*

Psychology (1999) (in which I have a chapter), based on a conference at Princeton, containing chapters on most fields of happiness research.

I found a lot to write about in the first edition of the present book, but since then there has been a great deal more. This field has grown at an astonishing rate, and built up a large volume of research and knowledge. It produces conferences, and part of general psychological conferences. It has not however had much impact on the general field of psychology; it does not yet have a chapter in psychology textbooks, for example.

The practical application of happiness research

What can be done with all this knowledge that other approaches can't do?

1 *Enhancing the happiness of individuals.* There has been follow-up research into the benefits of several kinds of therapy or changes in lifestyle. Such follow-up is essential, since many forms of psychotherapy have been found to have no effect at all. Pleasant activities therapy, and some versions of cognitive therapy, are directly addressed to happiness and have been found to be effective. Social skills training has another aim but is successful with depression and has similar results with normals through improving social relationships. Changed leisure activities, such as increased exercise, have been found to work for depression and for normal individuals too. Leisure in particular is under our own control and can therefore be manipulated to increase happiness.

2 *Enhancing the happiness of communities.* Happiness is not entirely an individual matter, but is partly a property of communities. This is particularly true in collectivist societies. The well-being of communities is partly a function of joint facilities, e.g. for leisure, and of social cohesion. In the case of working organisations, their size (smaller is better) and shape (less hierarchical is better), and amount of participation in decisions are important. When we have found out exactly what is the effect of money it should be possible to advise governments on economic matters too.

3 *International agencies.* These are concerned with the quality of life in different countries. First they considered only economic measures, then they added health and education, and a number of other objective measures can be considered. However, subjective well-being is also important, and is not very closely related to these objective indicators. Therefore SWB needs to be taken into account and it might be a matter of concern by these agencies if any country has a very low level of happiness. But making these comparisons is not easy; some happiness may take a different form in different cultures, and there may also be different ways of answering questions.

Chapter 2

How to measure and study happiness

WHAT IS HAPPINESS?

As we have seen, people seem to understand this term perfectly well, and have a fairly clear idea that it is about positive emotions and satisfaction with life. Many surveys have simply asked respondents how happy they are. We are concerned here primarily with such measures of "subjective well-being" (SWB), the subjective side of well-being, rather than with objective measures of income, health etc., which we shall describe as "social indicators".

A lot of the data on happiness comes from social surveys, often with large numbers of respondents. It is expensive to ask a lot of questions so often there was only one question, of the form "How happy are you?" or "How satisfied are you with your life as a whole?". Andrews and Withey (1976) discovered a single item which was intended to measure the two aspects, affect and satisfaction—"How do you feel about your life as a whole?", from "delighted" to "terrible" with a seven-point scale. Campbell et al. (1976) in a famous study *The Quality of American Life* asked another version of this question: "How satisfied are you with your life as a whole these days?"

Another way of measuring satisfaction is with the Satisfaction With Life Scale (SWLS), which is shown in Table 4.2 (see page 40). Research with these scales shows that most people report that their satisfaction is considerably above average, and that there is quite a wide distribution of satisfaction in the population. Diener and Diener (1996) show that many studies of happiness, satisfaction and other measures of subjective well-being have found this. On average 75–80% are above average. Brandstatter (1991) using experience sampling (to be described shortly) found that the people are in a state of positive emotion 68% of the time.

Fordyce (1988) devised a Happiness Measure consisting of two questions: (1) "In general how happy or unhappy do you usually feel?", from "Extremely happy" (feeling ecstatic, joyous, fantastic), which scores 10, to "Extremely unhappy" (utterly depressed, completely down), which scores 0; (2) "On average what percent of the time do you feel happy?" (or unhappy or neutral). The two scores are combined; the average for the first was 6.9 ("mildly happy"), and for the second 54%.

Single-item measures can be quite successful. Job satisfaction can be measured in this way by asking "All things considered, how much do you like your job?", and questions like this correlate as high as .67 with longer scales (Wanous, Reichers, and Hudy, 1997).

The Fordyce scale has high correlations with much longer scales for happiness. However there are problems with simple one-item measures. One is that they are too obvious, and hence likely to be affected by response biases. Psychologists would not try to measure racial attitudes with an item like "Do you like black people?"; they use less direct items. We shall see later that cross-national surveys using single happiness items have produced some very strange results. The second objection arises because psychologists like to know that a variable has some internal validity, i.e. consists of a number of correlated components, and this means having a look at a longer set of items or measures, of domains that can be sampled, like the questions in an intelligence test. Several studies have taken a variety of measures of SWB, and have found that all of these different measures correlate together and do produce a single factor. For example Compton et al. (1996) gave a series of happiness and mental health questionnaires to 338 students and adults, and obtained a clear first factor with loadings that included those shown in Table 2.1. These measures will all be discussed later. It can be seen that the highest loading was Fordyce's Happiness Measure, followed by Diener's Satisfaction With Life Scale and Bradburn's Affect Balance (Positive affect minus Negative affect)—all well-known and widely used measures. The highest correlation was with a measure of general happiness, the second highest was with satisfaction with life, and the third was with affect balance. Other studies have found the same thing: happiness is a basic dimension of experience, something like a personality trait. For the affect part of it we usually want to know more than a person's mood at this minute, we want their usual mood, how they have been "feeling in recent weeks", rather than "now", for example.

The most widely used measure of satisfaction is the Satisfaction With Life Scale (SWLS), due to Diener et al. (1985), and this will be discussed in Chapter 4.

The Oxford Happiness Inventory (OHI; Argyle et al., 1989) was designed to

Table 2.1 Loadings on Compton's happiness factor

Happiness (Fordyce)	.84
Satisfaction with life (Diener)	.83
Affect balance (Bradburn)	.74
Quality of life (Flanagan)	.69
Optimism (LOT)	.69
Psychological well-being (Fordyce)	.60
Self-esteem (Rosenberg)	.51

Source: Compton et al. (1996).

measure happiness as a whole, and followed the design of the well-known measure of depression, the Beck Depression Inventory (BDI; 1976), using some of the same items reversed, plus others, with the same four-choice format. There are 29 items, and the latest version is shown in Table 2.2. The OHI has been used in most of the research done at Oxford, and has been found to have better test–retest reliability than the BDI, it has been found to correlate with ratings by friends, and has strong and predicted relations with personality dimensions, stress and social support. There are Chinese and Israeli versions.

Joseph and Lewis (1998) devised a general Depression–Happiness scale; they found that it correlated with the OHI at .54 and with the Beck Depression Inventory at −.75. This is further confirmation that there is a single happiness dimension, which has a strong negative correlation with depression.

Does happiness have two, three or four main components?

We have just seen that happiness may have somewhat separate cognitive and emotional parts, which can be elicited by asking about satisfaction or about joy and elation. Andrews and McKennell (1980) used 23 SWB measures with substantial British and American samples. They found clear affective and cognitive factors, and that happiness measures correlated more with the affective factor. The affective and cognitive variables are of course correlated, but only at about $r = .50$, sometimes less than this. Suh et al. (1997) reported data from 43 countries, with 56,661 subjects in all; the average correlation between affect balance and satisfaction was .41, but this was higher for countries rated as individualist, like Britain and the USA at .50 or more, but less in collectivist countries, where it was as low as .20; the reason may be that in collectivist cultures reported satisfaction depends on the state of others as well as oneself. So happiness can be said to have at least two components which are partly independent of each other.

The Fordyce measure described above is mainly a measure of affect. Kammann and Flett's Affectometer (1983) is entirely about affect, while Diener et

Here are some faces expressing various feelings. Which face comes closest to expressing how you feel about your life as a whole?

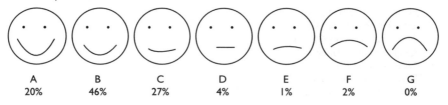

| A | B | C | D | E | F | G |
| 20% | 46% | 27% | 4% | 1% | 2% | 0% |

Figure 2.1 Faces and feelings (Andrews and Withey, 1976).

Table 2.2 The Revised Oxford Happiness Inventory

Below, there are groups of statements about personal happiness. Please read all four statements in each group and then pick out the one statement in each group that best describes the way you have been feeling in the past week, including today. Circle the letter (a, b, c, or d) beside the statement you have picked.

01.	a	I do not feel happy.
	b	I feel fairly happy.
	c	I am very happy.
	d	I am incredibly happy.
02.	a	I am not particularly optimistic about the future.
	b	I feel optimistic about the future.
	c	I feel I have so much to look forward to.
	d	I feel that the future is overflowing with hope and promise.
03.	a	I am not really satisfied with anything in my life.
	b	I am satisfied with some things in my life.
	c	I am satisfied with many things in my life.
	d	I am completely satisfied about everything in my life.
04.	a	I feel that I am not especially in control of my life.
	b	I feel at least partially in control of my life.
	c	I feel that I am in control most of the time.
	d	I feel that I am in total control of all aspects of my life.
05.	a	I don't feel that life is particularly rewarding.
	b	I feel that life is rewarding.
	c	I feel that life is very rewarding.
	d	I feel that life is overflowing with rewards.
06.	a	I don't feel particularly pleased with the way I am.
	b	I am pleased with the way I am.
	c	I am very pleased with the way I am.
	d	I am delighted with the way I am.
07.	a	I never have a good influence on events.
	b	I occasionally have a good influence on events.
	c	I often have a good influence on events.
	d	I always have a good influence on events.
08.	a	I get by in life.
	b	Life is good.
	c	Life is very good.
	d	I love life.
09.	a	I am not really interested in other people.
	b	I am moderately interested in other people.
	c	I am very interested in other people.
	d	I am intensely interested in other people.
10.	a	I do not find it easy to make decisions.
	b	I find it fairly easy to make some decisions.
	c	I find it easy to make most decisions.
	d	I can make all decisions very easily.

continued

Table 2.2 contd

11.	a	I find it difficult to get started to do things.
	b	I find it moderately easy to start doing things.
	c	I find it easy to do things.
	d	I feel able to take anything on.
12.	a	I rarely wake up feeling rested.
	b	I sometimes wake up feeling rested.
	c	I usually wake up feeling rested.
	d	I always wake up feeling rested.
13.	a	I don't feel at all energetic.
	b	I feel fairly energetic.
	c	I feel very energetic.
	d	I feel I have boundless energy.
14.	a	I don't think things have a particular "sparkle".
	b	I find beauty in some things.
	c	I find beauty in most things.
	d	The whole world looks beautiful to me.
15.	a	I don't feel mentally alert.
	b	I feel quite mentally alert.
	c	I feel very mentally alert.
	d	I feel fully mentally alert.
16.	a	I don't feel particularly healthy.
	b	I feel moderately healthy.
	c	I feel very healthy.
	d	I feel on top of the world.
17.	a	I do not have particularly warm feelings towards others.
	b	I have some warm feelings towards others.
	c	I have very warm feelings towards others.
	d	I love everybody.
18.	a	I do not have particularly happy memories of the past.
	b	I have some happy memories of the past.
	c	Most past events seem to have been happy.
	d	All past events seem extremely happy.
19.	a	I am never in a state of joy or elation.
	b	I sometimes experience joy and elation.
	c	I often experience joy and elation.
	d	I am constantly in a state of joy and elation.
20.	a	There is a gap between what I would like to do and what I have done.
	b	I have done some of the things I wanted.
	c	I have done many of the things I wanted.
	d	I have done everything I ever wanted.
21.	a	I can't organise my time very well.
	b	I organise my time fairly well.
	c	I organise my time very well.
	d	I can fit in everything I want to do.

22.	a	I do not have fun with other people.
	b	I sometimes have fun with other people.
	c	I often have fun with other people.
	d	I always have fun with other people.

23.	a	I do not have a cheerful effect on others.
	b	I sometimes have a cheerful effect on others.
	c	I often have a cheerful effect on others.
	d	I always have a cheerful effect on others.

24.	a	I do not have any particular sense of meaning and purpose in my life.
	b	I have a sense of meaning and purpose.
	c	I have a great sense of meaning and purpose.
	d	My life is totally meaningful and purposive.

25.	a	I do not have particular feelings of commitment and involvement.
	b	I sometimes become committed and involved.
	c	I often become committed and involved.
	d	I am always committed and involved.

26.	a	I do not think the world is a good place.
	b	I think the world is a fairly good place.
	c	I think the world is a very good place.
	d	I think the world is an excellent place.

27.	a	I rarely laugh.
	b	I laugh fairly often.
	c	I laugh a lot.
	d	I am always laughing.

28.	a	I don't think I look attractive.
	b	I think I look fairly attractive.
	c	I think I look attractive.
	d	I think I look extremely attractive.

29.	a	I do not find things amusing.
	b	I find some things amusing.
	c	I find most things amusing.
	d	I am amused by everything.

Source: Hills and Argyle (1998b).

al.'s Satisfaction With Life Scale (1985) is of course about satisfaction. Another affect measure is Andrews and Withey's "faces" measure, shown in Figure 2.1. This uses the "life as a whole" question, but the response format makes it into an affect item.

However the emotional part may need to be subdivided further, since it turns out that positive moods are not the opposite of negative moods. Bradburn (1969) asked people about the percentage of the time they had been in positive and in negative moods in the past few weeks; some of the questions were:

> During the past few weeks did you ever feel . . .
> e.g. pleased about having accomplished something

that things were going your way
depressed or very unhappy
very lonely or remote from other people?

His key finding was that these two dimensions were almost totally independent of each other. This issue has been much debated and investigated. The short answer is that PA (positive affect) and NA (negative affect) correlate at about −.43 (Tellegen et al., 1988). We shall explore this further in the next chapter.

Negative affect takes us into the well-charted regions of psychological distress, for which there are several widely used measures, such as the Eysenck Neuroticism scale, and the Beck Depression Inventory. Andrews and Withey (1976) found that their satisfaction measure was fairly independent of measures of both positive and negative affect. This all leads us to the widely agreed conclusion that happiness has three main parts, satisfaction and positive and negative affect—though as we saw earlier all three are correlated with each other. Happiness can be divided up in other ways, but this is the one that has been used most often by research workers so far.

Another way of dividing up emotions in particular is to measure their intensity, or depth, and their frequency. Both influence overall affect, and it is found that frequency is the more important. We shall return to this topic when considering the effect of positive life events, where we will look at the intense ones too.

However, negative affect may need to be subdivided too. Headey and Wearing (1992), in their big Australian study, found that depression (Beck Depression Inventory) and anxiety (Spielberger scale) correlated only at $r = .50$, so these two main forms of negative affect or distress are partly independent. These authors also used Bradburn's negative affect and the General Health Questionnaire, and found that the four measures of negative affect and distress all correlated, but not very highly, between .36 and .50, so there is a case for separating the components of negative affect, and it may be desirable to assess the different negative emotions separately. If two are used, depression and anxiety, this gives us four components of happiness. The relations between these four components found by Headey and Wearing are shown in Figure 2.2.

Lucas, Diener, and Suh (1996) found that different measures of life satisfaction formed a clear factor, correlating tightly together and they were separate from a group of measures of positive emotion, and from the negative emotion factor, also from measures of optimism and self-esteem.

So are optimism and self-esteem parts of happiness? Or purpose in life? There are well-established scales for measuring optimism (the Life Orientation Scale), purpose in life and self-esteem. These can all be looked at as parts of positive thinking and feelings. Or we can keep to a narrower definition of happiness and say that these variables are among the causes of happiness. This is the way most investigators have proceeded. Ryff (1989) took a different approach and has developed a measure of psychological well-being with six factors:

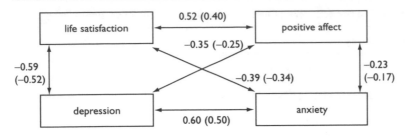

Figure 2.2 Estimates of "true" correlations among sub-dimensions of WB and psychological distress[1] (Headey and Wearing, 1992, p. 45). The reliability estimates (Cronbach alphas) used to disattenuate the observed correlations were: life satisfaction 0.92, positive affect 0.64, depression 0.82 and anxiety 0.85.

- Self-acceptance
- Positive relations with others
- Autonomy
- Environmental mastery
- Purpose in life
- Personal growth.

They also form a single super-factor, though the correlations between them are fairly low. They have somewhat different relations with other variables, and we shall meet several of them again later in this book.

What is the relation between happiness and mental health? Mental health can be assessed in terms of a single factor. The General Health Questionnaire (GHQ) (Goldberg, 1978) is widely used, as is Eysenck's Neuroticism factor (Eysenck, 1976). The short form of the GHQ is shown in Table 2.3. We saw that a single factor of well-being and (good) mental health can be found, as shown in Table 2.1. But we have also seen that positive and negative affect are somewhat independent of each other, so that (absence of) distress, negative affect, depression or anxiety, are better seen as one component of subjective well-being.

Physical health is another matter. It is both a cause and an effect of subjective well-being, and it can be seen as part of a broader concept, Quality of Life. Subjective health is another matter, part of SWB, but not very closely related to physical health; the latter has been measured in recent British studies by the SF-36 scale, which asks about details of how the individual's activities are impaired (Jenkinson and McGee, 1998).

How good are these measurements?

There are several ways of evaluating a psychological test.

1   Does it have internal coherence, that is do the items correlate together? We need to know that there is a variable there to be measured, with components that correlate together, and which have been sampled successfully

Table 2.3 The General Health Questionnaire (GHQ) (12-item version)

Have you recently
  *1 been able to concentrate on whatever you're doing?
   2 lost much sleep over worry?
  *3 felt that you are playing a useful part in things?
  *4 felt capable of making decisions about things?
   5 felt constantly under strain?
   6 felt you couldn't overcome your difficulties?
  *7 been able to enjoy your normal day-to-day activities?
  *8 been able to face up to your problems?
   9 been feeling unhappy and depressed?
  10 been losing confidence in yourself?
  11 been thinking of yourself as a worthless person?
 *12 been feeling reasonably happy all things considered?

Source: Goldberg (1972).

Note
*These items are scored in reverse; 0 means agree strongly.

by the test. This is usually assessed by Cronbach's "alpha". Most of the tests referred to have high scores here, for example Diener's Satisfaction with Life Scale (.84), and the Oxford Happiness Inventory (.85). And these are not narrow scales where all the items are nearly the same.

2   Are the scores stable over time? Most of these tests do very well here too. We have found that the OHI is more stable than the very similar BDI, at .67 over 6 months, and Headey and Wearing (1992) found levels of .5 to .6 for a 6-year interval. The scores are also sensitive to change however, and current hassles as well as past well-being are predictors of current well-being (Chamberlain and Zika, 1992).

3   Are these tests valid? That is do the scores agree with better or more direct measures of happiness? Two kinds of validation have been used. Reports by others correlate at about .5 to .6 with ratings by others who know the subjects, for the OHI, the Delighted–Terrible (D–T) scale and other scales. For example Lepper (1998) with 1500 retired individuals found that ratings of happiness by a significant other correlated as follows:

• happiness .59, .54 (there were two samples)
• positive affect .45, .43
• affect balance .53
• satisfaction .53, .51

They also correlate with daily reports of mood over a period of weeks, a little higher, at .66 for the D–T scale. Sandvik, Diener, and Seidlitz (1993) compared four self-report measures of subjective well-being and a number of non-self-report measures, including ratings by friends and family, daily mood reports, a written interview and cognitive measures. The average correlation between one type of measure and the other was .73, though friends and family only agreed at .44. This is very promising but suggests that the scales are far from perfect.

Another kind of validity is finding out if a test produces the expected pattern of relations with other variables. And here it must be admitted that there are some surprises. Measures of SWB have a lower relation with measures of objective satisfaction than would be expected. In particular the relation with income is very weak: although people in the West are now four times better off than 40 years ago their SWB has not changed at all. And 37% of the American very rich scored below average in happiness (Diener and Suh, 1997a). The explanation of these weak relationships is that satisfaction and other aspects of subjective well-being depend not only on the objective state of their world, but also on people's expectations and other cognitive processes, which are "in the mind". Nevertheless subjective well-being is not entirely subjective, it is a real state, and is indeed "objective" in that it corresponds to actual states of the brain, actual facial expressions, and actual behaviour of various kinds (Diener and Suh, 1997a).

4   Are the scores subject to known biases? One such bias is the effect of immediate mood. Schwarz and Strack (1991) found that individuals reported considerably higher happiness and life satisfaction if the sun was shining or the German football team had won. These effects can be reduced by asking respondents to describe how they have felt "during the past few weeks", rather than now, and of course trying to avoid getting them into an unusual mood.

There is also a danger that respondents will make themselves out to be happier than they really are, either for the benefit of the investigator or themselves. Most people say they are well above average happiness, for example, 6 or 7 on a 9-point ladder (Andrews and Withey, 1976). But most people say they are very happily married in Britain, though half of them will get divorced, and life satisfaction has been found to be correlated with a measure of self-deception (Hagedorn, 1996). On the other hand there seems to be no effect of social desirability response set, the bias towards giving a socially approved answer (Vella and White, 1997). How does this square with the positivity bias described above? Perhaps everyone has a positivity bias. Or perhaps everyone feels happier than average: if they say they are happy we must conclude that they are happy. A serious problem has arisen in connection with international comparisons, to which we now turn.

5   Can the scales be used with different populations? The question of whether some countries or cultures are happier than others is of both practical and theoretical interest. However, to find out requires measures that are valid in more than one culture. We have already seen that the collectivist cultures of the East cause a problem for us, since satisfaction reports are based on the perceived well-being of the group as well as the individual. We have seen that subjective measures produce some questionable results, in particular

sometimes failing to reflect large differences in objective social indicators like income, education and health. There are some other very dubious results such as both France and Italy scoring very low in satisfaction on the Eurobarometer; 10% of them were "very satisfied with their lives in general" compared with 55% of Danes and about 45% in Holland (Inglehart and Rabier, 1986). We shall argue later that this is probably because of different cultural norms about admitting to negative feelings and the desirability of positive ones rather than to enormous national differences in happiness. The solution may be the use of less direct measures.

6   Are there any better measures of happiness? There may be, but they are all likely to be inconvenient and expensive compared to asking people questions. The only one to have been used much is "experience sampling". Here individuals report their mood on a series of occasions, and the scores are averaged. Brandstatter (1991) did this by giving subjects a randomised schedule of times within each of six 4-hour periods per day for 30 days, 180 reports in all. Larson (1978) did it by "paging" them on a number of random occasions. Later a stop watch programmed to go off at certain times was used. There is not enough experience of these methods for us to know yet how many measures are needed or what is the best way of obtaining them, but they have an attractive degree of face validity. These are also self-reports, but they are nearer to experience and make lesser demands for remembering and integrating experiences. Another way of mood sampling might be to obtain measures of facial expression and tone of voice on a number of random occasions. This too is attractive but is quite impractical.

Another method is asking friends to make ratings of those to be assessed, preferably several friends to get a large sample. This avoids the self-report bias described above, but introduces new ones, in particular the problem that their rating may reflect their relationship with the subject. This method is quite feasible and not expensive, but has not been used much.

Finally it may be possible to obtain some physiological measures, of serotonin and the other chemicals that control mood, or left frontal cortex activity, this being where good moods are located, though the method of extraction might reduce happiness. However, these methods have yet to be developed.

SOCIAL INDICATORS

There are clearly some problems about measuring happiness by asking people questions. An alternative is to use objective social indicators. This is most often done to compare cities or nations, using such indices as average income, years of education and length of life. The method can also be used to study historical changes in well-being.

The main difficulty with this approach is deciding which indicators to include. The British government in 1999 announced that it was going to monitor and promote 13 social indicators, including variety of birds and river pollution, as well as more familiar ones like income, education and unemployment. Does having a lot of birds make people happy, or would some other aspects of life be more important? We may have to go back to subjective measures, so that if variety of birds for example doesn't make people happier we might leave them out. Another problem is that the same indicator may be measured differently in different places, and in the case of weather, how can it be decided which temperature or which range of temperature is best?

We shall look at the effects of money and some other objective factors in the course of this book, and we shall return in Chapter 12 to the use of objective indicators for the study of national differences.

It is possible to use objective indicators for individuals as well as countries—using their income, education etc. This approach has been used in assessing quality of life from the point of view of health, not by asking people how well they feel, but finding out what they can do, how much their life is restricted (Jenkinson and McGee, 1998). Other approaches to the well-being of patients assess how successfully they are functioning physically, psychologically, socially and economically (Raphael et al., 1996).

Objective versus subjective indicators

Both are useful. The main weakness of objective indicators is that we don't know which to choose, and there is also the problem of finding equivalent measures in different countries. The main weakness of subjective measures is that they are affected by cognitive biases, such as the effects of expectations and adaptation, so that we don't know how far to believe the scores. Diener and Suh (1997a) suggest that they should be used together in some way, and it is certainly illuminating to have both sets of data. In their study comparing well-being in 40 nations SWB correlated .57 with their Quality of Life Index. There were some large discrepancies; for example Austria and Nigeria had the same level of subjective satisfaction but Austria scored 71 and Nigeria 30 on Quality of Life. So if we wanted to improve people's lives here we might well ignore the subjective happiness scores. The Scandinavian countries always score high on subjective measures, higher than would be expected from objective measures. There may well be similar problems in comparing the young and old, males and females and different personalities.

RESEARCH METHODS

Social surveys

This was the first method of studying happiness to be used, and a large number of surveys have now been carried out. Some of these were on a very large scale, with 160,000 respondents in one case; this means that some good statistical analyses can be made. At first the interest was mainly in the percentage of individuals who were happy or unhappy. Then there were many surveys investigating the statistical relationship of self-reported happiness and other variables, such as age, being married, being employed and so on; Campbell et al. (1976) was an influential early example. Then it was realised that some of these variables were correlated with one another so that one might really reflect the influence of another. Multiple regressions became popular with sociologists to show the independent effect of different variables. We referred earlier to the 630 studies, many using these methods, which were re-worked by Veenhoven (1994). We learn for example that race has little effect on SWB if income, education and similar variables are taken into account.

There are other ingenious designs to test theories about the causes of well-being. Clark and Oswald (1996) for example found that satisfaction with income had no relation with actual income; however, satisfaction was greater for those who expected less, on the basis of their age, education, job etc. What pleased them was doing better than they expected, probably better than they had done in the past or better than other people, though these are further matters to be investigated.

However this still does not show the true direction of causation—people might be happy because they are married, or perhaps happy people are more likely to get married. In some cases there is no problem, for example age can only be a cause not an effect, but for other variables there is often real doubt, and there is no way of finding out from a single collection of data at one point in time; for that we turn to longitudinal and experimental designs.

Longitudinal designs

Most of these take the form of a "panel study" where the same individuals are tested twice, with an interval of some months or years between these occasions. It is then possible to carry out a multiple regression to predict well-being at time 2, from well-being at time 1 and possible causal variables like marriage, employment and personality. Banks and Jackson (1982) tackled the question of whether being unemployed is bad for mental health or whether those in poor mental health are simply less likely to have jobs. They gave several hundred school leavers the GHQ before leaving school and at intervals of 2 and 4 years afterwards. Their scores at the two times are shown in Table 7.5 (see page 104). For those who did not get jobs GHQ scores increased, i.e. their mental health became worse. Causation was in both directions, but was stronger in the direction unemployment–mental health.

A procedure which has been used in the mental health field is the use of "high risk" groups, for example with high risk of becoming depressed. The nearest to this in the happiness field so far is studies of those with high risk of getting married or falling in love, such as first year students; they have shown that love is a major source of mental health (see page 79).

Experiments

This is the traditional preferred way of finding out what causes what, but it has been little used in this field. The main use has been in "mood induction" experiments, in which the moods of subjects are enhanced for example by playing them cheerful music or showing them amusing videos. It is found that subjects can certainly be made happy in the laboratory this way, but the effect is usually rather short-lived, such as 10–15 minutes. Many such experiments have been carried out and these will be reviewed in Chapter 13.

There are two great merits of laboratory experiments—the direction of causation is clear, and many variables can be held constant. This makes it possible to test quite sophisticated theories through the predictions that can be made. The main weakness of such laboratory work is that the studies tend to be artificial or use scaled-down and therefore weaker versions of the real thing—as required by ethics committees. Nevertheless quite positive emotional states can be produced—and there is less objection to these than to the generation of negative emotions.

Correlations with personality traits

An important issue in this field is the impact of personality on happiness. The question is which traits contribute to happiness and how much. So extraversion for example has been found to have quite a strong correlation in many studies, sometimes as high as .5. It is desirable to hold constant such variables as age and sex. Since traits like extraversion are known to be partly innate, very stable and have a known physiological basis, they have been assumed to be the cause of happiness rather than vice versa. However, happiness too is partly innate, stable and may have a definite physiological basis; in some studies extraversion has been found to behave like a dependent variable, and found to be increased by enjoyable social experiences and a high level of well-being (Headey, Holstrom, and Wearing, 1984). So the issue of direction of causation is not clear-cut. At first it was not known which personality traits would correlate with SWB, but now we know, since there have been so many investigations.

THE EFFECTS OF WELL-BEING ON BEHAVIOUR

The other direction of causation concerns the *effects* of happiness. It can be studied by the same designs used for finding the causes of happiness. It can be done by laboratory experiments in which subjects are put in good, neutral or bad moods, to see how some aspect of their performance is affected. Something can be done with big surveys, holding many variables constant, to see for instance whether happy people live longer. We shall see, in Chapter 14, that happiness and even good moods have impressive effects—for health and length of life, mental health, sociability, and for helpfulness and altruism. Good moods have several effects on thinking—they lead to more creativity but less hard thinking.

CONCLUSIONS

Happiness is found to be a single factor of experience, but it consists of at least three partly independent factors—satisfaction with life, positive affect and negative affect. All of these can be measured by single questions but there are advantages in using longer scales.

These are good measures, in that they have high internal consistency, are stable over time and valid against other measures. They are however affected by certain biases, such immediate mood, and national comparisons have been influenced by local customs of appearing to be more or less happy than is the case.

An alternative means of assessing well-being is by social indicators, but it is hard to decide which ones to use; there are some inconsistencies between objective and subjective measures.

Social surveys have been widely used, together with longitudinal designs such as "high risk" studies, experiments and correlations with personality traits. Experiments have been the main method for studying the effects of positive moods.

Chapter 3

Joy and other positive emotions

As we saw in the last chapter, experiencing joy is one of the commonest ways in which people define happiness. Research finds that it is one of the three main components of happiness—together with satisfaction with life and the absence of negative affect. Joy is the emotional side of happiness, in contrast to satisfaction—the cognitive side. We want to know how many positive emotions there are, how they are expressed, by face and voice, and the situations and activities that arouse them. This takes us into the field of experimental mood induction, an important method of happiness research. It also takes us to the physiological processes responsible, to what is going on inside the brain, the brain areas involved, the neurotransmitters, and how drugs can enhance positive moods.

THE EXPERIENCE OF POSITIVE AFFECT

People have a number of negative moods (anger, anxiety, depression etc.), but really only one positive mood, commonly described as "joy". I shall treat moods as relatively enduring emotional states. Research on positive moods and emotions has found that they consist of feelings of enjoyment, relief and self-confidence, and in one study they consisted of a high level of joy, a moderately high level of interest and a smaller level of surprise (Izard, 1977). The dimension of joy–depression can be measured on a scale such as that of Wessman and Ricks (1966), given in Table 3.1.

However, there are some different varieties of positive affect, perhaps due to the cognitions accompanying a basic physiological state. One kind is "exhilaration", a temporary state of cheerful excitement, as in laughter. Ruch (1993) produced a 19-item cheerfulness scale. Another kind of high intensity joy is experienced when pursuing dangerous sports; those doing it tend to be "sensation seekers" who crave the excitement, though for some the positive mood comes when they have safely landed, perhaps due to relief or to excitement (Zuckerman, 1979). The opposite of this is a relaxed positive mood, as when watching TV; Kubey and Csikszentmihalyi (1990) found that this was a

Table 3.1 A joy–depression scale

How elated or depressed, happy or unhappy did you feel today?
10 Complete elation. Rapturous joy and soaring ecstasy.
9 Very elated and in very high spirits. Tremendous delight and buoyancy.
8 Elated and in high spirits.
7 Feeling very good and cheerful.
6 Feeling pretty good, "OK".
5 Feeling a bit low. Just so-so.
4 Spirits low and somewhat "blue".
3 Depressed and feeling very low. Definitely "blue".
2 Tremendously depressed. Feeling terrible, miserable, "just awful".
1 Utter depression and gloom. Completely down. All is black and leaden.

Source: Wessman and Ricks (1966).

The average scores on this scale for American students were 6.0 for males, 6.14 for females, but there was quite a lot of daily variation: plus and minus nearly half a scale point each day.

pleasant state but so relaxed that watchers are only just awake, sometimes asleep. Then there is "depth" of joy, not quite the same as "intensity". Csikszentmihalyi (1975) has described the state of "flow", or absorption, giving profound satisfaction, when people are tackling challenging tasks with enough skill to do them, as in rock climbing. Argyle and Crossland (1987) asked people to group positive emotions from a number of activities on the basis of similarity of feelings; four dimensions were found in this way, one of them a depth dimension, of emotions produced for example by powerful music, close relations with others, and the joys of nature. Waterman (1993) found a dimension of items such as "feeling really alive", and "this is who I really am", which were somewhat separate from measures of pleasure. Several other investigators have located a similar aspect of positive emotion, for example Maslow (1968) with his "peak experiences". The characteristics of these peak experiences include:

- absorption, focused attention
- awareness of power
- intense joy, value and meaning
- spontaneity, effortlessness
- integration and identity (Privette, 1983).

These different varieties of positive affect can be placed on two dimensions. Figure 3.1 shows the two dimensions found by Russell (1980) from multidimensional scaling of emotion words. The horizontal dimension is happy–sad, and the vertical dimension is from aroused, tense or excited to relaxed or sleepy. Bungee jumping comes top right, and watching TV bottom right. Using a single happy–sad, or positive–negative emotion dimension is in conflict with

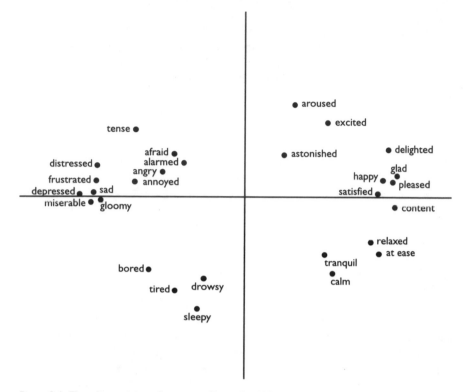

Figure 3.1 Two dimensions of emotion (Russell, 1980).

the idea that positive and negative emotions are somewhat independent of each other. This issue has been much debated. Diener and colleagues have found that the inverse relation between positive and negative emotions is greater when emotions are stronger, and when a shorter period of time is used (e.g. Diener and Larsen, 1984). Russell and Carroll (1999) conclude that there is such a strong negative correlation between them that they can be regarded as a single dimension.

There has been a lot of research interest in the vertical, or intensity dimension, which describes strong moods, both positive and negative. Larsen and Diener (1987) constructed the Affect Intensity Measure (AIM), a 40-item scale, and found that it acted as a stable measure of personality. This scale has been criticised on the grounds that it is not only about intensity, but also includes items referring to the frequency of positive moods. Bachorowsky and Braaten (1994) produced a different version, the Emotional Intensity Scale (EIS), which measures intensity but not frequency, and has scales for positive and negative intensity. The positive intensity scale correlated with extraversion (.41) and the negative intensity scale with neuroticism (.64).

An alternative solution is to use positive affect (PA) and negative affect (NA), which represent a rotation of the previous factors by 45 degrees, combining positive and negative affect with intensity. PA correlates with extraversion, NA with neuroticism (Thayer, 1989). Gray (1972) also favours two dimensions at 45 degrees to the previous ones. He maintains that in rats at least there are two neural systems, one generating approach behaviour and positive emotions, the other producing avoidance behaviour and anxiety: the "behavioural activation system" (BAS) produces arousal and sensitivity to rewards; the "behavioural inhibitory system" (BIS) sensitises to punishment. These two systems have been found to be related to activation of different parts of the brain—approach and rewards with the left hemisphere, withdrawal and punishment with the right (Davidson, 1993). Carver and White (1994) developed scales for these two systems; those with high scores on the BAS scale were happier. Extraverts score highly on the first, neurotics on the second. Psychopaths score low on the BIS scale. There seems to be general research agreement on this two-dimensional space, but it can be represented in two different ways.

How are these emotions related to happiness? Larsen and Diener (1987) used the AIM and reports of how much of each day subjects felt in a positive mood. In a series of studies it was found that frequency correlated about .50 with happiness and intensity about .25 (Diener et al., 1991). This group argue that intensity is of less importance because "extremely positive affect" was only reported on 2.6% of days. (We shall dispute this later, page 207.) They also presented evidence that positive events were often preceded by negative ones, and that there could be negative consequences, such as one extremely positive experience lowering the level of satisfaction for others, through comparison. However, the effects of even moderately intense experience can last for the whole day (Lewinsohn and Graf, 1973), and we have found that the effects of vigorous sport can carry over to the next day (Argyle, 1996).

Furthermore it is possible to amplify the impact of positive (or negative) events. We have found that both thinking about and talking to others about positive events produces positive moods (Argyle and Martin, 1991). And Langston (1994) has shown how people capitalise on positive events by telling others about them, celebrating them or by just thinking about them, and that this increases positive affect and life satisfaction.

THE EXPRESSION OF POSITIVE AFFECT

Emotions consist partly of their expression, in the face, tone of voice and in other ways; this is an important part of what emotions are, in addition to their underlying physiological state and the way they are experienced. Why do emotions need this expressive component?

1   Some of them are direct physiological reactions, not intended to communicate anything, for example disgust when something nasty has been eaten or smelt, and states of drowsiness or excitement.

2   Some expressive signals have been developed in the course of evolution as social signals, now sent spontaneously by animals and men. The evolutionary history of some signals has been traced, as we shall see, and it can be seen to be adaptive for animals to communicate states of anger, dominance or submission for example. It is difficult to see what advantage is given by showing states of anxiety or depression, however, and in some cultures such as that of the Japanese they are concealed. Even though the initial expression is spontaneous there may be deliberate attempts to conceal it thereafter.

3   Other emotional expressions are clearly social signals and are sent deliberately, and not sent if there is no-one there to see them; however, these signals may be different in some ways from spontaneous ones. In fact they are, and it is now known that spontaneous smiles of joy or affection take the form of the "Duchenne smile", which involves activation of the region of the eyes and upper face as well as the mouth, as shown in Figure 3.2. When people are just pretending to be happy the top part of the smile expression is often missing.

Figure 3.2 The Duchenne smile (Ekman and Friesen, 1975).

The sequence of events when an emotion is aroused is as follows:

1　Usually some external event arouses the emotion, creating some inner state of the brain. Internal events can do it too, such as childhood memories.
2　This activates the facial nerve and other nerves that control muscles that produce emotional expression. Other nerves are also affected, such as heart rate and skin conductance, but these are less visible.
3　The actual expression shown is modified by other nerves that exert control from cognitive processes.
4　There may be feedback from the face for example to the brain, affecting the emotional experience obtained.

The main place where emotions are expressed is the face. It can express a number of emotions, but only seven emotions can be reliably discriminated by others in most cultures; one of these is happiness. There may be another one, interest, according to Izard (1977), though this seems to be partly a tilted head position. It is also possible to study the dimensions of facial expression, at least in the minds of those who see them. Different studies here have agreed that there is a pleasant–unpleasant dimension, and an intensity dimension (Ekman, 1982), which is in agreement with the dimensions found for emotional experience.

The facial signal for happy is of course smiling, though this also means friendly, and other positive social signals. Facial expressions are produced by facial muscles which can move the facial skin, for example the *zygomatic*, which draws up the corners of the mouth in smiling, and the *corrugator* which draws the eyebrows together in frowning. These muscles are activated by the facial nerve which has five main branches for the main areas of the face. It emanates from the *pons* in the brainstem, which is controlled by the hypothalamus and the amygdala. But when someone poses or otherwise controls a facial expression, a different route is used, and impulses come from the motor cortex. The first route is derived from innate process resulting from evolution, the second from the effects of social learning from the culture.

There are several kinds of evidence that there are innate facial expressions: (1) similar expressions are found in non-human primates, the "play face" corresponding to smiling; (2) smiles occur in babies by the age of 2 months, and can also be recognised at this age; monkeys reared in isolation can recognise happy versus angry; (3) smiles and the other basic emotions are found in all cultures that have been studied, and are regarded as the sign for happy in all cultures. It is an increasingly widely held view that there is a limited number of basic emotions, perhaps seven, each with its own innate, hard-wired structure in the brain (Ekman, 1982). It is believed that facial expressions have emerged during evolution, for example an angry face is a reduced version of showing the teeth, smiling is a relaxed face with teeth covered; both convey valuable signals.

The social learning aspects of facial expression are shown by the demonstration that there are "display rules" about the facial expression, which may be shown on different occasions. Friesen (1972) found that both Japanese and American subjects looked disgusted when shown a film of a sinus operation, but only the Americans looked disgusted when interviewed about it later. The Japanese smiled—in Japan there is a rule about not showing negative faces in public. Research on children has shown how they learn to produce the correct facial expression, whether they feel that way or not, for example looking pleased when given an unsuitable present (Saarni, 1979). This control of facial expression is not always successful, and there may be "leakage" of the true feeling. However, we manage to control our faces very well, and there is little leakage into the face. Display rules govern whether a face is shown or not, but do not lead to new kinds of expression.

So facial expression partly expresses what people are feeling, and partly what they want others to think that they are feeling. It then feeds back and influences the emotion felt through the phenomenon of "facial feedback". A series of experiments has been carried out in which subjects are asked to arrange their faces in various ways and then given mood manipulations. It is found that smiles and frowns lead to enhancement of the corresponding moods. And this can be done by asking people to contract specific facial muscles, confirming the theory that there are a number of innate emotional systems (Camras et al. 1993).

Facial expressions may express emotions, but their real purpose may be to communicate with others. Kraut and Johnston (1979) found that at the bowling alley very few players smiled at the skittles, but many smiled at their companions, 42% when they hit and 28% when they missed. Facial expressions occur when people are alone, for example when they watch TV, but they are much weaker; the Friesen (1972) disgusting film experiment gives an example of these. Fridlund (1991) believes that such expressions may be directed to imaginary companions. He found that people smiled at an amusing film more if someone else was watching, and also if someone else was believed to be watching it in the next room. Their zygomatic and corrugator muscles were activated just by forming images of social situations. Facial expressions for emotion may be part of an innate system, but whether or not it is activated depends on the social situation.

A similar story can be told about the expression of emotion in the voice. Animals do this a lot by barks, grunts and shrieks; we do this occasionally but more by the tone of voice in which words are spoken. The same range of emotions found in the face can also be expressed in the voice, but a larger number of different voices are distinguished. Just as facial muscles control the face, so throat and mouth muscles control the voice. The effect on speech can be measured physically, for example when feeling fear the pitch is greatly raised. Scherer and Oshinsky (1977) studied the voices used for different emotions by generating a large variety of sounds from a Moog synthesiser and asking raters to decode them. Joy and elation were found in raised pitch, raised speed, varied pitch with gentle changes, fairly loud and fairly fast; others have found a pure tone, contrasted with the harsh tone of anger. Depression is expressed by a low pitch and pitch range, little intonation, slow speed and weak intensity.

The accuracy of communicating emotions by the voice is similar to that for the face. Davitz (1964) found a range of 23% to 50% for different speakers, asked to produce 14 kinds of emotion. Anger and joy were the easiest to decode. These voices are produced by muscles in the throat; tensing these muscles produces a higher pitch, and arousal produces greater loudness. Further aspects of voice quality can be recorded on a speech spectrograph, such as harsh versus pure, caused by further settings of the vocal chords. Pleasant feelings produce an open and relaxed mouth and throat, whereas disgust produces a closed mouth and nose, with direct effects on voice quality (Scherer, 1986). The evolutionary origins of these vocalisations have been traced, and apes and monkeys use about 13 different calls.

The voice is leakier than the face, it is less well controlled. It follows that to know what someone is really feeling it may be better to listen to their voice than to watch their face. Men tend to do this, whereas women look at faces and receive the messages that others intend them to receive, so that women have been called "polite decoders" (Rosenthal and DePaulo, 1979). The possible reason for this is that the male sub-culture is more competitive and less trusting than the female sub-culture.

The body also expresses emotions, but the main one it expresses is aroused–relaxed, and it also expresses dominant and submissive attitudes to others, but there is no particular body posture corresponding to joy. Similarly gestures can signal anxiety, hostility and some other emotions and attitudes, but there seem to be no obvious joy gestures (Argyle, 1988).

THE AROUSAL OF POSITIVE EMOTIONS

There are several ways of studying the causes of joy. One is to carry out surveys asking people when they last had this emotion and what caused it. Scherer et al. (1986) did this with a student sample in five European countries. The most common cause was said to be relationships with friends (36%), success experiences (16%) and the basic physical pleasures of food, drink and sex (9%). We shall report several other surveys of the causes of positive emotion in Chapter 13.

Yet another method is to study the relations between different classes of life events and overall happiness. Frequency of contact with friends, and of sexual intercourse, come out strongly related to happiness (Veenhoven, 1994). Or we can look at "mood induction" experiments to see which methods produce positive moods successfully. The best have been found to be exercise, music and "success" (i.e. at laboratory tasks). We shall describe this mind of work in Chapter 13, where we shall also discuss increasing the number of positive life events as a method of happiness therapy.

Putting together the results of studies of these different kinds it is easy to compile a list of the most common sources of joy. They are:

- Eating
- Social activities and sex
- Exercise and sport
- Alcohol and other drugs
- Success and social approval
- Use of skills
- Music, the other arts and religion
- Weather and environment
- Rest and relaxation.

These are not the only things which cause joy, but they are the most common. And often a joyful event will contain more than one of these. Dancing for example involves music, exercise and social interaction with friends. Playing in a team may involve exercise, success, cooperation and of course winning.

It is a very interesting list, theoretically. It disposes of one theory of joy, that it is due to the decrease in excitement or stress; only the last on the list fits this. Satisfaction of biological needs is only one source of joy, the first on the list. Indeed some of the sources do not relate to the satisfaction of any known need. By far the most common source of joy is relations with other people, especially in friendship and love. We will look briefly at this and the other causes of joy. Most of them are dealt with in more detail in other chapters.

Eating

We have seen that this is one of the most common sources of pleasure, it is the one source based on biological needs; if it was not enjoyable people wouldn't bother to do it. It is enhanced by elaborate cooking, which stimulates the taste cells, and the social occasions in which eating usually occurs.

Social activities and sex

These are the most common sources of positive emotions. Why? Responding positively to others means smiling and giving other positive social signals; this rewards the other, and strengthens the relationship; the others in turn respond with smiles and other signals, but also with real help and cooperation. Positive moods and sociability are closely linked. Infants have the innate capacity to look and smile at adults, which encourages the adults to care for them (Tomkins, 1962). Similar social signals lead to sexual relationships and further rewards and biological advantages. We discuss this further in Chapter 6. In Chapter 5 we discuss humour as a source of positive emotion; this is mainly a social phenomenon also, for example discharging tensions between people, and the experience of shared emotions.

Exercise and sport

This is the easiest and most powerful way of inducing positive moods under experimental conditions, and is also shown by other methods of research. The effect is so clear that exercise is sometimes described as an "anti-depressant" (Thayer, 1989), and it is indeed used in the treatment of depressives. The effect is partly due to the physiological effect of exercise on releasing endorphins, generating feelings of euphoria, power and control, where the body seems to perform on its own (Browne and Mahoney, 1984). There are also social aspects of exercise, since it is usually done in the company of others, as partners or opponents, but in any case involving close interaction, sometimes bodily contact. It also affects self-esteem, not only when winning, but by performing at a reasonable level of competence. Social life and sport are forms of leisure, and we shall discuss leisure as a source of happiness in Chapter 8.

Alcohol and other drugs

Drugs can induce positive moods, and relieve negative ones, through activating neurotransmitters in the brain. Alcohol and Prozac are familiar examples. We describe the actions of these and other drugs later in this chapter.

Success and social approval

As we showed in Chapter 2, self-esteem is closely connected with happiness, and surveys find that success is one of the commonest sources of joy. Success, and social approval are very important to us; self-esteem depends partly on the reactions of others, partly on successful performance. Some other kinds of "success", like winning the lottery, are less effective, as we shall see in Chapter 9. Negative reactions of others produce strong negative emotions such as shame, damaging the self-image. Izard (1977) thought that shame has an important function in promoting conformity and service to the community.

Use of skills

Job satisfaction depends partly on the use of skills, and on recognition and achievement. This is not just for the rewards received, but there is also "intrinsic satisfaction" from carrying out skilled work. The same applies to sport and some other kinds of leisure; people enjoy activities like swimming, skiing and the rest by exercising the skills involved. This fits Csikszentmihalyi's ideas (1975) on the satisfaction derived from challenges, given the necessary skills. However, it is found that people prefer situations where their skills are more than enough for the challenges, and they also spend a lot of time in very unchallenging activities such as watching TV (Argyle, 1996). We discuss work in Chapter 7.

Music, the other arts and religion

One of the easiest methods of inducing positive moods in the lab is to play cheerful music, such as part of a Haydn trumpet concerto. This doesn't satisfy any biological needs, nor does listening to music have much survival value. Part of what music does is to simulate the human voice, and it may be produced by the human voice, in different emotional states. An individual in a good mood speaks in a special way—for example with raised pitch, pure tone, gentle pitch changes, whereas a depressed person speaks with lowered pitch, speed, intensity and pitch range. Music elaborates on this in other ways, as will be described in Chapter 8. Music is usually made on a social occasion with a group of perform-ers and an audience. It can produce emotions of intensity and depth. Religion creates similar emotional states, and there can be great joy from reading a good book. Kubovy (1999) groups music, humour and the satisfaction of curiosity as "pleasures of the mind".

Weather and environment

People are in a better mood when the sun is shining, it is warm but not too warm, and humidity is low (Cunningham, 1979). The sun is important to us, and is worshipped in primitive religions; the lack of it can produce depression. Rain is also important, for watering the crops, and may be prayed for, but oddly rain does not normally cheer us up—probably since there are no immediate benefits, rather the reverse. There seems to a high degree of adaptation to the weather, because there is no evidence that people who live in more favourable climates are any happier, if anything the reverse is the case (see Chapter 12). There are some exceptions in the case of climates that are extremely hot or cold, and there is more Seasonal Affective Disorder in the Scandinavian countries during the dark winter.

People also have strong positive feelings in the countryside, and in wild, natural settings, such as on a mountain, whereas Americans like the "wilder-ness" of their state parks. Even seeing a video of the wilderness lowered blood pressure and produced other signs of relaxation in one experiment (Ulrich et al., 1991). Environmental psychology research shows that people appreciate settings most where there is vegetation, water, depth of view, and that they prefer the natural to the artificial. There may be an evolutionary origin for these preferences (Altman and Wohlwill, 1983).

Rest and relaxation

We saw that joy can be of low intensity as well as high. Leisure research shows that low intensity leisure is very popular. Watching TV is the most obvious example; it is now the third biggest use of time in the modern world after sleeping and working—over 3 hours a day for most. Yet the state of mind it produces has been found to be a deep form of relaxation, "somewhere between being awake and asleep" (Kubey and Csikszentmihalyi, 1990). One of the main motivations for holidays is "relaxing in the sun", though others seek adventure or excitement (Pearce, 1982).

POSITIVE EMOTIONS AND BRAIN CENTRES

Are there "pleasure centres" in the brain? Olds (1958) found that if an electrode was inserted into a certain part of a rat's brain, the rat would press a bar for up to 1,000 times an hour for hours on end; presumably the rat found the stimulation of this area very rewarding. This experiment has opened up a whole field of work. Rolls (1999) carried out many studies with monkeys. He found a number of sites that produced rewarding self-stimulation; some of them were neurons, which are also activated by food. Sem-Jacobsen (1976) applied electrical stimulation to 2639 neural sites in 82 human subjects and found that some of the sites evoked pleasant smells or tastes, i.e. were food related, some produced sexual responses, but more produced positive moods. In this study a number of different moods were generated at different neural sites: (1) well-being and relaxed, (2) enjoyment and smiles, (3) laughter and wanting more stimulation.

Several different parts of the brain are involved.

1   The hypothalamus is a major area for rewarding self-stimulation in monkeys, and it contains the neurons associated with food rewards.
2   The amygdala is the link between stimuli and learned reinforcement; it is the centre of neural links with inputs from the thalamus, neocortex and hippocampus, and outputs to the autonomic nervous system. It has been described as the "emotional computer" for the brain since it works out the emotional implications of sensory inputs. It is responsible for joy from stimuli or activities that have become associated with positive rewards (LeDoux, 1993).
3   The frontal cortex is involved in the expression of emotions. Davidson (1993) and others have found that the left anterior cortex is activated when people are in a happy mood, or making an approach; pointing with the

right hand by a small child is an example. The right cortex is activated at times of depression and other negative emotions and withdrawal. This work was done mainly by studying EEG and the effect of lesions.

NEUROTRANSMITTERS AND DRUGS FOR POSITIVE EMOTIONS

The different parts of the brain are linked by sets of synapses between neurones. For example areas representing visual sensations are linked to areas of cognitive processes, which in turn are linked to motor areas, controlling action. Whether these synapses will transmit messages is made more or less likely by the action of neurotransmitters. These are chemicals whose release is controlled by neural links from central brain areas like the amygdala and activate or inhibit synaptic neurones at different points of the brain. At least 50 different neurotransmitters are now known (Bradford, 1987), and there are several which lead to positive emotions, by affecting the activation of certain brain areas.

Serotonin is the most important of these, for positive moods; it induces alertness, positive mood and sociability, and counters depression, but leads to mania if there is too much. It is released in a number of brain centres which are stimulated by a region of the hypothalamus. There are low levels of natural serotonin in depressed and suicidal patients, high levels in high status persons and animals, and it can be increased by serotonin–inducing drugs.

Dopamine has been found to be important in electrical self-stimulation experiments, it is part of the reward system. Rolls (1999) thinks that dopamine activates the links between the amygdala and the frontal cortex, which connect stimuli and reinforcement, and hence controls rewards. Dopamine is normally produced by eating, sex, or working for food rewards. It has a low level in depressed patients, but can be elevated by anti-depressant drugs like Prozac (without eating, or working for it).

Endorphins are like opium in reducing pain, but also lead to feelings of euphoria. This may explain the attraction of long-distance running and other strenuous exercise. Bortz et al. (1981) found the highest levels of endorphins recorded in a group of 34 marathon runners who ran 100 miles up and down mountains in California. Such runners may become addicted because of the morphia-like properties of "runners' high", which is very rewarding and also makes them unaware of cuts, bruises or other damage at the time (Steinberg and Sykes, 1985).

There are many other neurotransmitters, some of them important for positive moods. GABA is a general inhibitor, whose action is enhanced by barbiturates and minor tranquillisers such as Valium. Noradrenaline is involved in arousal, closely associated with positive affect, and enhanced by amphetamines.

Some drugs like alcohol have a long history, and were discovered and used because they produced positive emotions or inhibited negative ones. Some, like mescaline, were discovered quite recently, in this case by Mexican Indians, and used for the religious experiences that it produces. Drugs have the effects they do by releasing, blocking or promoting the action of neurotransmitters. Others have been discovered by pharmacologists and are used to relieve mental disorders or other sources of negative experience.

Alcohol acts as a "depressant" of the central nervous system probably by reducing the release of most neurotransmitters. At low doses it promotes the action of the neurotransmitter GABA, and hence also reduces anxiety. It leads to some loss of inhibition and increased social intimacy, hence more fun and more sex. Larson et al. (1984) found that alcohol produced positive emotions along all the scales they used—happy, sociable, excited, free etc.

Prozac is one of several antidepressants, which can produce positive moods, euphoria, and relieve depression. This is mainly through promoting the effect of serotonin, and indirectly affecting endorphins and dopamine. As far as is known it is not addictive and does not have bad long-term consequences. We shall discuss research on the effects of Prozac later (see page 214).

Amphetamines, as in benzedrine and pep pills, act as stimulants, by releasing dopamine and also noradrenaline. They produce general arousal of the central nervous system, less fatigue, more alertness. Coffee and nicotine also act by arousing the central nervous system via these and other neurotransmitters.

Tranquillisers like Valium promote the action of the neurotransmitter GABA, which inhibits the central nervous system and results in more calmness, less tension and anxiety. This is certainly a positive mood for those suffering from anxiety.

All drugs (apart from medicines) that are widely used give pleasure or prevent pain, that is why they are used. However, with what have been called "drugs of abuse" there are problems—they lead to addiction and sometimes to a life of crime to pay for it. Cocaine and heroin can produce powerful positive effects of well-being, exhilaration, energy and peace, but later there may be very unpleasant experiences of depression or anxiety and bodily effects such as vomiting and exhaustion. *Cocaine* gives energy and other positive feelings, reduces hunger and fatigue, and is very addictive because of its bad withdrawal symptoms. Cocaine addicts may take the drug every 15 minutes for 24 hours, if they can afford it, which is another problem.

Hallucinogens like LSD, ecstasy, psilocybin and mescaline produce feelings of calm and contentment, but also hallucinations and other kinds of loss of contact with reality. Some have religious experiences, others have experiences of terror and disorientation. These drugs do this by interaction with serotonin and dopamine systems. *Marijuana* has complex effects including euphoria, anxiety, lassitude and general well-being. Larson et al. (1984) found that it produced strong feelings of freedom and excitement but not much positive affect.

"Ecstasy" (MDMA) is an example of a "recreational drug", intended to

produce enjoyable experiences. In fact it does produce positive moods without hallucinations or anxiety, but it also produces unpleasant and disturbing effects later, such as depersonalisation, loss of body control, and insomnia (Vollenwieder et al., 1998)

Some of these drugs also have long-term effects that are less desirable. The effects of alcohol and nicotine are well-known. Some of the others, such as cocaine, heroin and LSD, are worse and may result in brain damage, accidents and death. But why are they so addictive? Addiction comes about when there is adaptation to the drug so that more and more is needed to give the same benefits. One theory of addiction is that these drugs give so much pleasure, are so rewarding, that there is craving for more pleasure. However, there is little relation between the amount of pleasure produced and the difficulty of stopping. Cigarettes give quite a low level of pleasure, as does heroin, while amphetamines may produce terror.

WHY ARE THERE POSITIVE EMOTIONS?

Theories of emotion have been based on negative emotions like anger and fear. The general explanation of these is that they direct and motivate specific action tendencies, such as fight or flight. This does not fit positive emotions at all, since they are not specific, and no new action is required. So why are there positive emotions at all? Fredrickson (1998) proposed an interesting solution to this problem, by examining some positive emotions. Joy she argues, is a part of happiness, leads to play and fooling about, resulting in development of physical, social and intellectual skills. Interest leads to exploration and increase of knowledge. Contentment is linked with doing nothing, but also with feeling at one with the world, and a more integrated view of self and the world. Love of course leads to strengthening social bonds. The biological benefit in each case is the building of resources, physical, intellectual or social.

> The adaptive problem that human ancestors faced that appears to have been solved by positive emotions, is when and how should individuals build resources for survival? The answer is to build resources during satiated moments by playing, exploring, or savoring and integrating.
>
> (Fredrickson, 1998, p. 313)

There is more to the benefits of positive emotions than resource building. Positive emotions are the subjective side of rewards, given when biologically valuable activities are performed. To take the most obvious examples, sex and eating are essential to life, and hence they have evolved to be enjoyable. Sociability is biologically valuable because it leads to cooperation and mutual help, and this too is enjoyable. Expressing anger is useful in frightening other animals, but why should there be expression of positive emotion? The signals for positive emotion are the same as the signals for sociability; perhaps this is why happiness and extraversion are closely linked, and why social relations are a major source of happiness.

We shall return to this issue again later (Chapter 14), where we examine the *effects* of happiness and joy; this should provide a clue about what happiness is for. One of the main effects is seeking the company of others, playful sociability in leisure, and the sociability of helping others. There are other effects of positive moods—for health, mental health, work (especially being helpful and cooperative), creative thinking, and sociability and altruism. This provides a further explanation for the existence of positive emotions and happiness.

CONCLUSIONS

We have seen that the main positive emotion is joy, though there are some other closely related positive states, such as excitement and deep positive emotions. Emotions vary along the two dimensions of positive to negative and intensity. These dimensions are found both in experience and in facial expression, and less clearly in tone of voice. Facial expressions for emotion are partly innate, partly controlled by display rules. Positive emotions are aroused by social activities, exercise and in other ways, several of them not related to known needs. These positive life events and pleasant activities generate positive moods and, if they are frequent enough, to happiness.

Emotions are generated by activity in the hypothalamus, amygdala and the cortex, and are enhanced by neurotransmitters such as serotonin and dopamine, which can be enhanced by various drugs, such as Prozac, which produce a range of emotional experiences, some of them positive. Some drugs lead to joy because they produce a biochemical short-cut to what is normally generated in the brain by working for it, for example morphine is like endorphins which come from physical exertion.

The reason for the existence of positive emotions is that they lead to certain kinds of sociability that build social bonds; quiet periods of satiation can be used to build other resources; positive experiences reinforce biologically valuable activities; and positive states have substantial effects on health, mental health, work and creativity.

Chapter 4

Satisfaction

INTRODUCTION

We saw in Chapter 2 that satisfaction is one of the main components of happiness. Joy is the emotional part, satisfaction is the cognitive part—a reflective appraisal, a judgement, of how well things are going, and have been going. In surveys we can ask either about satisfaction with "life as a whole", or about specific domains, such as work, marriage and health.

There has been serious doubt of the accuracy of measures of satisfaction, since sometimes they have not correlated very well with objective features of individuals' lives. For example income does not have a very strong effect on satisfaction, even with satisfaction with income, as we shall see in Chapter 9. Does this mean that governments who try to make their populations better off are mistaken, or is there something wrong with the measurement of satisfaction? There is also difficulty with international comparisons, where some countries come out surprisingly low in reported satisfaction; we shall discuss how genuine these differences are in Chapter 12. In the present chapter we will look at how far objective factors influence satisfaction, and shall see that there are some substantial effects here.

We then turn to the other side of the question, the extent to which satisfaction is in the mind, depends on how people think about things. Judgements of satisfaction depend to some extent on comparisons with the past, or with other people; they are also affected by immediate emotional state, and by simply getting used to things—"adaptation", and to different ways of looking at events. Satisfaction could be partly an illusion, due to people deceiving themselves about how satisfied they are. Or does satisfaction depend on the goals people set themselves? Just having a goal could be a source of satisfaction. On the other hand not being able to attain a goal could be a source of dissatisfaction. Some of these effects could be looked at as errors of judgement to be avoided, or as sources of genuine judgements of satisfaction. If this is the case it follows that satisfaction might be enhanced, not only by changing an individual's real situation, but also by changing the way he or she looks at it during therapy for example.

An early measure of satisfaction was the question used by Campbell et al. (1976), illustrated in Table 4.1. It can be seen that most people report themselves to be well above average in satisfaction. Cummins (1998) reviewed many studies of global satisfaction in different parts of the world, and in different domains, and concluded that most studies reported an average level of satisfaction of 70% of the scale maximum. Diener and Diener (1996) also discussed this tendency for people to be above average in reported satisfaction with life, including various groups who might be expected to be dissatisfied. They concluded that people are motivated to have positive experiences.

There is doubt over how adequate single items measures of satisfaction are; in Chapter 12 we suggest that the surprising international differences in satisfaction may be at least partly due to cultural conventions, and that a single abstract question is wide open to such distortions. A longer scale with more specific items would be better. Diener et al. (1985) produced a Satisfaction With Life Scale (SWLS) which has been widely used (Table 4.2). This uses 7-point scales, and the average score obtained is 56%, although it is 67% for students (Cummins, 1998).

There are also scales which measure satisfaction in different domains, and many different lists of domains have been used in different studies. The list used by Headey and Wearing (1992) in their Australian surveys is given in Table 4.3, which also shows the correlations of satisfaction in these domains with overall life satisfaction. Between them these seven domains account for 80% of the variance in global life satisfaction. The *Quality of American Life* study by

Table 4.1 An early life satisfaction measure

How satisfied are you with your life as a whole these days?

COMPLETELY DISSATISFIED			NEUTRAL			COMPLETELY SATISFIED
1	2	3	4	5	6	7
0.9%	2.1%	3.7%	11.3%	20.7%	39.6%	21.7%

Source: Campbell et al. (1976).

Table 4.2 The Satisfaction With Life Scale

Item	Item–total correlations
1. In most ways my life is close to my ideal.	.75
2. The conditions of my life are excellent.	.69
3. I am satisfied with my life.	.75
4. So far I have gotten the important things I want in life.	.67
5. If I could live my life over, I would change almost nothing.	.57

Source: Diener et al. (1985).

Note $n = 176$.

Campbell et al. (1976) referred to above used a similar list and found similar loadings for the domains.

Alfonso et al, (1996) produced an Extended Satisfaction With Life Scale (ESWLS), using five items for each of eight domains. The domains and their correlations with general life satisfaction for an American student sample are shown in Table 4.4.

Another way is to ask people what they think are the most important sources of satisfaction in their lives. Hall (1976) did this with a British national sample, and found that the most often mentioned domains were:

- family and home life
- money and prices
- living standards
- social values and standards
- social relationships
- housing
- health
- work.

Table 4.3 Relationship of domain satisfactions with well-being and psychological distress (Headey and Wearing 1992)

Domain satisfaction	Life satisfaction index	Positive affect	Anxiety	Depression
Leisure	.42	.28	− .29	− .29
Marriage	.39	.17	− .29	− .32
Work	.38	.26	− .27	− .36
Standard of living	.38	.20	− .18	− .26
Friendships	.37	.19	− .15	− .12
Sex life	.34	.17	− .19	− .33
Health	.25	.11	− .23	− .14

Table 4.4 Domains of life satisfaction

Social	.62
Sex	.43
Self	.63
Family	.41
Relationships	.39
Work	.38
Physical	.35
School (i.e., college)	.28

Source: Alfonso et al. (1996).

Fortunately there is a lot in common between this list and the other ones, and the main topics will appear as chapters in this book.

Do people decide on their overall or global satisfaction from taking account of all the different domain satisfactions, which is known as a "bottom-up" process? Or is it the other way round, and global satisfaction influences satisfaction in the domains, a "top-down" process? Or does causation go in both directions? There have been several attempts to answer this question, mostly using statistical modelling. Mallard et al. (1997) used surveys of 11 domains in 32 countries, and found a bi-directional solution in 29 of them and top-down in the other 3. It varied with domain, though not in a consistent way. There was no pure bottom-up effect. However, these studies using statistical modelling do not give very strong evidence of causality, because the data was all correlational, collected at the same time in each study. For more convincing evidence on causation we need longitudinal research. In "quasi-experimental" designs it is possible to see for example whether getting married leads to increased happiness.

Headey and Wearing (1992) have carried out longtudinal analysis, with five waves of repeated surveys of the same sample. What they found was different from the other studies. Marital satisfaction and global satisfaction affected each other. Global satisfaction influenced job satisfaction, material satisfaction and leisure satisfaction (i.e. all were top-down).

Chapter 10 is about personality factors in happiness, and is in effect an analysis of the top-down processes. Some of the other chapters, on work, leisure, etc., are about particular domains, and therefore examine bottom-up processes. An aspect of this issue is about how people make judgements of their satisfaction: are these made by a process of inspection of each domain, or are they decided by some central process, such as emotional state? Schwarz and Strack (1991) suggested that sometimes people use their prevailing emotional state for making judgements of general satisfaction, since this is easier than assessing all the domains individually. For specific domains on the other hand there is detailed evaluation of satisfaction with them and their parts. This may depend on comparisons with others, past life or whatever standards of comparison are readily available. There may be "assimilation" of recent positive events as information about satisfaction.

HOW IMPORTANT ARE OBJECTIVE FACTORS IN SATISFACTION?

A number of researchers on well-being have concluded that objective factors are of little importance, and that individual differences in personality, as well as emotions and cognitive processes are more important (Diener et al. 1999; Schwarz and Strack, 1991). This view has been supported by two findings in particular. One is the apparently very low correlation between income and satisfaction. The other is the reported high level of satisfaction and happiness of those with severe injuries. We will now look at these and some other areas of objective satisfaction.

Money

Diener and Oishi (in press) report the effect on income for 19 nations using the 150,000-subject World Values Survey. The average correlation of income with income satisfaction was .25, and the average correlation with life satisfaction was .13. This is usually found—the correlation of an objective indicator with satisfaction is stronger than the effect on general satisfaction. The effect of income on happiness is much stronger at the lower end of the income scale. Similarly the relation between life satisfaction and income is much stronger in poorer countries, probably because money is primarily for food, housing and other essential needs there.

Correlating average income for each of 28 nations with average life satisfaction produced a correlation of .62 and .59 in different studies. The reason that the international comparisons show a stronger effect on income may be that in within-country studies the effect of individual differences is very strong, but this is eliminated in between-country studies. In addition the effect of money on public goods such as facilities for health and education leads to greater effects on happiness than private goods. I conclude that money really does affect happiness, and that this is much underestimated, by a correlation of .13.

There are other interesting findings about the effect of money, such as the effect of winning the lottery, and the influence of expectations and comparisons; these will be pursued further in Chapter 9.

Health

Okun et al. (1984) carried out a meta-analysis and found that happiness correlated with health at .32; this was higher when subjective measures of health were used—subjective health is almost a part of life satisfaction. And subjective health is not the same as physical health; whereas neurotics exaggerate their subjective ill-health, those with high blood pressure or cholesterol may think they are better than they really are. There is a relation between happiness and having specific illnesses, especially if these restrict activity (Veenhoven, 1994); there are other illnesses where patients feel better than other patients. What is the direction of causation? Headey and Wearing (1992) in their longitudinal study in Australia found that the relation between global satisfaction and health satisfaction turned out to be spurious and to depend on relations between each and neuroticism—happy people are less neurotic, neurotic individuals are less satisfied with their health. However, Feist et al. (1995), in another longitudinal study, found that it was bi-directional. Health is particularly important for the well-being of older individuals, and health always comes out as one the main predictors of their happiness or satisfaction; it looks as if health really is a cause of happiness. One process whereby happiness can affect health is via good moods activating the immune system (see page 81). The effect of happiness on subjective health may also be due to cognitive processes such as looking at life and self differently.

Work and employment

This topic will be discussed more fully in Chapter 7. Unemployment is a major source of unhappiness in the modern world. It produces depression, suicide, ill health, apathy, low self-esteem—every aspect of low satisfaction and unhappiness. The effect is quite strong: Inglehart (1990) found that 61% of European unemployed were satisfied with their lives compared with 78% of manual workers who had jobs. The effect of unemployment is causal, as is shown by the immediate impact of factory closure for example. And the effect holds up when other variables have been controlled, such as income.

Job satisfaction has quite a strong correlation with life satisfaction—.44 in a meta-analysis by Tait et al. (1989). Attempts to tease out the direction of causation have found that both operate, but that the effect of life satisfaction on job satisfaction is stronger than vice versa (Diener et al., 1999). There are big differences in job satisfaction especially between different jobs. In one study, asked if they would choose the same job again, 91% of mathematicians and 82% of lawyers said they would, compared with 16% of unskilled steel workers. Job satisfaction is also strongly affected by relations with co-workers and other social factors. There is no doubt of the effect of objective features of work on job satisfaction, and thus on life satisfaction, as will be described in Chapter 7.

Social relationships

This is one of the greatest sources of happiness, and marriage is the relationship with the most impact. Inglehart (1990) found that in Europe 81% of married women said they were satisfied or very satisfied with their lives, compared with 75% of the single. The effect of being widowed or divorced is more marked—66% of the widowed and 57% of divorced or separated women were satisfied. The effects for men were slightly less. Stroebe and Stroebe (1987) found that 42% of widows were in the mild-to-severe range of the Beck Depression Inventory, compared with 10% of the married. Similar findings have been obtained in many other cultures, though there are cultural variations in the happiness of the divorced, and those cohabiting for example.

These effects hold up after controls for income etc have been applied. And in this case the direction of causation is fairly clear. There have been "high risk" studies, i.e. follow-up studies of individuals in their early 20s who can be supposed to be at risk of getting married. It can be assumed that being widowed is a cause of unhappiness rather than vice versa; for divorce it is not so clear.

There are similar, though smaller, benefits for happiness from other relationships, such as friends, and other family relationships. These will be discussed in Chapter 6.

Leisure

We saw in Table 4.3 that leisure satisfaction has been found to be more highly correlated with total satisfaction than any other domain in some studies, at about .40, though this falls to about .20 if controls for income and the rest are applied. The effects of actual leisure have also been studied, in some cases in experimental or longitudinal designs, which can show causation. For example experiments have been carried out in which people are persuaded to engage in regular exercise. These have found that it reduces anxiety and depression, and increases self-esteem and produces an improved body image (see Argyle, 1996).

Several other kinds of leisure have also been found to have positive effects—social clubs, voluntary work and music for example. However, watching TV is sometimes found to have a negative relation with satisfaction, probably because heavy TV watchers do not have anything better to do. We discuss leisure further in Chapter 8.

Housing

This is not a variable usually studied by psychologists, but it brings up some interesting points. We saw that housing is one of the most often mentioned domains (Hall, 1976). It may also be seen as part of "living standards". Several studies have found how particular aspects of housing contribute to housing satisfaction. In Hall's British survey those who did not have a fixed bath or shower were not very satisfied with their bathrooms, but it had a much smaller effect on their overall housing satisfaction (Table 4.5), and even smaller effect on their life satisfaction. Campbell et al. (1976) in the USA found in a similar way that housing satisfaction depends on variables such as rooms per person, size of rooms and heating.

Housing satisfaction contributes to total satisfaction, typically with a correlation of about .30 (Andrews and Withey, 1976), which is smaller than the other variables we have discussed.

Table 4.5 Satisfaction with bathrooms

	Overall housing satisfaction	Satisfaction with bathroom
No fixed bath or shower	5.5	2.2
Shared	7.3	6.9
Exclusive use	8.0	8.7

Source: Hall (1976).

Education

This is another variable which has a modest effect, but which is of interest this time because of its links with other causes of satisfaction. Many studies have shown the positive effect of education, defined as number of years of education received or the level attained. A typical correlation with well-being in the USA is .13, as found in a meta-analysis by Okun et al. (1984). Education leads to both higher incomes and to jobs of higher occupational status in the USA and Britain.

The effect of education is much stronger in Austria, South Korea, Mexico, Yugoslavia, the Philippines and Nigeria. It is not clear what these countries have in common, but it may be that education in some way does more for people there.

Conclusions on objective sources of satisfaction

I think we have shown that there are substantial effects of money and other conditions of life on satisfaction. On the other hand the relations are not always very strong. Diener and Suh (1997a) found that Austria scored 71 on a combination of objective social indicators (income, health, etc.), and Nigeria 30. However, the life satisfaction scores were only 2 points apart. Adams (1997) found that objective indicators for Black Americans declined between 1980 and 1992, but life satisfaction increased, though there was a fall in happiness. Clearly objective satisfaction is not the only cause of satisfaction, and we now consider some of the others.

THE EFFECTS OF SOCIAL COMPARISON

Social comparison theories say that people evaluate features of themselves or their lives by comparing themselves with others. This was used to explain some otherwise puzzling aspects of satisfaction research. For example the fact that as national income rises there is no increase in satisfaction—perhaps because everyone else has had increased incomes. Wills (1981) assembled a lot of diverse findings to support the hypothesis that people can increase their subjective well-being by comparison with less fortunate others, and the hypothesis that downward comparison is evoked by a decline in subjective well-being. He also concluded that generally people make upward comparisons, but that those with low self-esteem are more likely to make downward ones. Recent experiments have confirmed some of these ideas: Strack et al. (1990) found that being with a handicapped confederate who seemed to be on a kidney dialysis machine increased the well-being of the real subjects. Strack et al. (1985) found that if subjects were asked to think about positive events in the present it enhanced their SWB, but positive events in the past depressed it—supposedly by contrast;

the opposite was found for negative events. Happy and unhappy people make different comparisons. Lyubomirsky and Ross (1997) found that unhappy people were affected in their self-assessments by a confederate who did better or worse at an anagram task than they did, in the expected direction. However, happy people were less affected by a peer who did better—and this produced a more positive mood and greater self-confidence, though not an increased self-assessment. This may because a peer who did well acted as an incentive and increased future prospects. It made them feel happier.

However, attempts to confirm social comparison theory in real-life settings have not always confirmed it. Diener and Fujita (1997) have carried out a number of such studies. In one study if subjects had a room-mate who was more or less attractive or academically successful this had no effect on satisfaction in these domains. Instead they chose their own targets for comparison, based on their own resources. In another it was found that for individuals of the same income living in a richer or poorer area had no effect on subjective well-being. In another the average well-being of countries correlated positively with the economic prosperity of neighbouring countries, not negatively as comparison theory would predict (Diener, Diener and Diener, 1995). Wright (1985) found that there was an effect of self-rated health on satisfaction, but this was not affected by comparison with the health of others.

What is going on is that people choose their own targets for comparison, for example individuals high in well-being make more favourable comparisons with others (Gilbert and Trower, 1990). Different inferences can be made from comparisons. Buunk et al. (1990) found that upward comparison for example can make you feel happier or less happy about your health, feel hope or envy. It appears that comparisons imposed by the external situation do not have consistent effects on satisfaction. "The choice of a comparison target is a flexible process and is not determined solely by the proximity of accessibility of relevant others" (Wood et al., 1985). There may be two exceptions to this. One is academic achievement, for those in a more or less closed community like a school or college, where the evidence of standards for comparison is overwhelming (Diener and Fujita, 1997). The second is industrial wages, when these are the object of intense trade union activity, and where workers know exactly what other workers are being paid; they may go on strike, even when this leads to plant closure, if they think they are being paid less. In fact people often make these comparisons; Ross et al. (1986) found that 89% of people made comparisons with members of their immediate circle for satisfaction at home, 82% for satisfaction at work, but only 61% did this for satisfaction with life as a whole, for which more use was made of unfamiliar others.

Another version of social comparison theory is Multiple Discrepancy Theory (MDT). Michalos (1985) proposed that satisfaction is a product of (small) discrepancies between achievements and aspirations, often defined in terms of comparisons with others. Having high aspirations is a threat to satisfaction according to this theory. The "goal–achievement gap" does indeed correlate with satisfaction. But so does achievement without any consideration of the goal. Several studies have compared the prediction of satisfaction from goal–achievement gaps and compared this with prediction from achievement or "resources" alone. Sometimes MDT does better, sometimes it makes no difference. However the gap could be a product of satisfaction rather than vice versa. This was indeed found by Headey and Veenhoven (1989) with data from the Victorian panel study in Australia: "Life satisfaction causes the gaps and not vice versa". Campbell et al. (1976) used this theory to account for the increasing satisfaction with age— the gap becomes smaller over time.

According to the goal–achievement gap theory, high aspirations lead to low satisfaction. But according to other theorists, having goals at all is beneficial to well-being. But they have to be the right kind of goals, as we shall see in Chapter 10.

ADAPTATION

This is a familiar process in psychology. If someone is asked to judge the weights of a number of objects weighing between 2 and 6 ounces, a 1 pound weight will seem "heavy", whereas if he had been lifting 3–6 pound objects it would seem "light". We get used to a certain range of stimuli; applying this to satisfaction we may get used to a certain level of sources of satisfaction, and come to regard them as normal. The work on quadriplegic and other patients has been thought to support this theory. I mentioned earlier the influential study by Brickman et al. (1978) of 11 paraplegics and 18 quadriplegics. The present happiness of the patients was 2.96, significantly below that of normal controls at 3.82. There was a similar difference in their reported enjoyment of everyday activities. Shulz and Decker (1985) found that 100 similar patients were still less happy than the general population 20 years after their accident (see Table 4.6).

Krause and Sternberg (1997) also studied patients with injuries to the spinal cord, and found that general satisfaction increased with time, with other variables held constant. The disabled are less satisfied than those who acquired their injuries at birth or early in life, and have had longer to adapt (Mehnert et al.,

Table 4.6 Happiness of para- and quadriplegics

	Patients	General population
Subjective well-being	10.76 ($n = 100$)	12–13
Depression	9.74	9.25
Positive feelings	4.04	3.77 (1 is positive)
Present happiness	2.96 ($n = 29$)	3.82 ($n = 88$)
Past happiness	4.41	3.32

Sources: Brickman et al. (1978); Schulz and Decker (1985).

1990). In Chapter 10 we shall show that although the elderly are less well-off, in poorer health, and are likely to be socially isolated, they are not on average less satisfied with life than young people, if anything they are more satisfied. This too may be due to adaptation.

The research on lottery winners has also been used to support adaptation theory, and it does so better, since lottery winners are soon no happier than controls. Some disasters take a long time to get used to; being widowed may take some years. There is a further problem with adaptation theory—most people, including disabled ones, are well above the mid-point of the scale, at about 70% of the maximum, so there are clearly other things going on. However, it is the capacity to adapt to negative events that is most interesting—how do people do it? The answer is that they are engaging in some form of coping, arranging their lives differently or simply looking at things differently, and we turn to this shortly.

Some people are depressed, and continue to be depressed for years; they have not adapted. And the objective events that cause satisfaction and dissatisfaction continue to do so, without much sign of adaptation—eating, sex, social relationships, leisure and work.

It seems that adaptation does occur to some negative changes in life, though not all, but it does not wipe out the enduring benefits of the main causes of satisfaction.

THE EFFECT OF EMOTIONAL STATE ON SATISFACTION

We discussed the Schwarz and Strack (1999) model, according to which judgements of global satisfaction are likely to be based on emotional states, since this is easier than making a lot of detailed comparisons. We saw in Chapter 2 that affect and satisfaction are correlated, at about .50. Schwarz and Strack (1999) and colleagues found that satisfaction and general well-being were said to be greater when the sun was shining than when it was raining, when the German football team had won, and when subjects were tested in a nice room (see Table 4.7).

Why does immediate emotional state influence general satisfaction? The most likely reason is that people use their emotional state as evidence of their well-being. Schwarz and Clore (1983) phoned subjects on sunny and rainy days; they were in a better mood and more satisfied with life as a whole on sunny days. But if their attention was drawn to the weather, this did not affect their mood, but it did remove its effect on their well-being—they no longer used the weather-induced mood as evidence. In other experiments it was found that emotional state influences general well-being, but not satisfaction with particular domains (Keltner et al. 1993), as Schwarz and Strack predicted.

Table 4.7 Life satisfaction and weather, football, and rooms

Pleasant room	9.4
Unpleasant room	8.1
German team won	+ 2.5
German team lost	− 2.8
Sun shining	7.4
Rainy day	5.0

Source: Schwarz and Clore (1983) and Schwarz et al. (1987).

COGNITIVE FACTORS IN SATISFACTION

We shall see later in Chapter 6 that there is a "Pollyanna" type of person who "looks on the bright side". They are happy, optimistic, rate events as pleasanter, have a more positive view of others, recall more positive events and have pleasanter free associations (Matlin and Gawron, 1979). But how do you look on the bright side? If we knew the answer to that perhaps people could be made happier just by thinking differently without the trouble of changing their actual conditions of life. We have seen that making downward comparisons makes people feel better, and this can be done by providing a confederate who seems to be handicapped, or otherwise worse off, or less competent at laboratory tasks. But we have also seen that happy people can have their mood enhanced by a more successful confederate since they can hope to do better themselves.

Just thinking about positive events cheers people up, though the effect depends on the time scale. Strack et al. (1985) found that asking subjects to think about pleasant events in the present or recent past had a positive effect on subjective well-being, but for past events there was more effect on well-being from thinking about negative events (Table 4.8). Past events are used to contrast, while present events are used as evidence of well-being. These authors also found that it depends how you think about these events. The effect on SWB was greater if subjects were asked to give a long and vivid account of events, and to explain how they happened.

The way people attribute the causes of events is also important. It has long been known that depressed individuals have a characteristic way of explaining bad events to themselves—they think these are their own fault, i.e. internally caused, will happen again, and in different ways. It is not established how far attributional style causes depression rather than vice versa. However, Fincham and Bradbury (1993) found that making similar attributions about the behaviour of marital partners was predictive of marital success; blaming things that go wrong on the defective personality of the other is not a success. And attributional therapy is used for depressed patients—persuading them not to blame themselves for everything that goes wrong. We have obtained evidence

Table 4.8 Subjective well-being: The impact of valence of event and time perspective

	Valence of event	
	Positive	Negative
Time perspective		
Present	8.9	7.1
Past	7.5	8.5

Note
Mean score of happiness and satisfaction questions, range is 1 to 11, with higher values indicating reports of higher well-being. Adapted from Strack et al. (1985, Exp. 1).

that happy people do not blame themselves in this way; on the contrary they think themselves responsible for the good things that happen to them (Argyle et al., 1989).

Internal control is a personality variable which is correlated with satisfaction, as we describe in Chapter 6; it is the belief that one can control what happens. This is the main component of "hardiness", the kind of person who is not made ill by stressful events (Kobasa, 1982). Individuals high on internal control interpret stressful events as challenging and think they can cope with them; we have seen that happy people are not upset by being beaten at laboratory tasks by experimental stooges—they see this as an incentive to do better. Higgins et al. (1997) found that individuals who had experienced uncontrollable health problems anticipated recurrences more than for unrelated problems. But subjects who had experienced controllable health problems did not expect recurrences. Oettingen (1992) compared two ways of thinking about weight reduction. Obese women who had optimistic expectations about how much weight they would lose were successful in doing so, but those who had fantasies about weight loss did not.

Another form of positive thinking is humour, or rather a humorous outlook on life. This means seeing the funny side of things, i.e. another side of them, which makes them less important, so that bad events can seem less threatening. We deal with humour in the next chapter.

In Chapter 11 we shall examine the effects of religion on happiness and well-being. Some of these effects are due to looking at things differently. Health is enhanced in religious healing by defining health differently, to include more than just bodily health. Other problems are coped with by various forms of "religious coping", placing events in a religious context, and believing that God will look after us.

POSITIVE ILLUSIONS

Taylor and Brown (1988) put forward the theory that many people have positive illusions about themselves, in particular that they have unrealistically high self-evaluations, exaggerated perceptions of control, and unrealistic optimism—all of which would be expected to enhance subjective well-being. The positive self-evaluations have attracted most research interest. As we have already seen individuals rate themselves above other people or "average people", on positively valued traits. They also rate their friends above average people. And individuals with high self-esteem do all this more (e.g. Brown, 1986; Compton, 1992). Some of these self-assessments are unrealistic, for example when 85% or more think they have better than average jobs, or are better than average drivers. Illusions work well in the field of love too.

In the field of health Harris and Middleton (1994) found that perceived health risks are seen as less for self than for a typical student or an acquaintance. Robinson and Ryff (1999) predicted that self-deception would occur when there is absence of concrete information; they found that future happiness was seen as higher (7.53) than present happiness (6.33) or past happiness (6.21).

The usual theory is that accurate perceptions of things are better, and that it is mental patients who suffer most from distorted perceptions. It has also been argued that on the contrary positive perceptions may be beneficial. Boyd-Wilson et al. (2000) with 209 students found that those with highest subjective well-being also had more positive illusions about their positive traits such as self-actualisation, in that they rated themselves better than other students. Murray and Holmes (1997) found that when members of couples saw their ideal partner and their actual partners as similar, this predicted a successful state of their relationship one year later. This was seen as a leap of faith. The reason for these benefits might be that they enable people to feel good about themselves, or their partners, and give them the commitment and confidence to tackle challenges. There has been a theory of "depressive realism"; Pacini et al. (1998) found that depressed individuals made more realistic choices than controls in a laboratory task but not in real-life decisions; again the happier group were more self-deluded.

Another way of putting together the pressures towards illusions and accurate perception is given by Taylor and Gollwitzer (1995) who found that when planning or deciding about a task people adopted a realistic deliberation set, but when carrying it out they adopted an optimistic and positive attitude. This supports the idea that positive thoughts are beneficial in motivating people, but adds the need to reflect on the true situation sometimes.

Memory research also finds that happy events are remembered better, especially by happy people (Matlin and Gawron, 1979). This may be because we remember things better which happened in the mood we are in, so those often in a happy mood can remember happy things better. However, Seidlitz et al. (1997) found that the better memory for positive life events was really due to the encoding of these events, rather than recall of events in a similar mood.

CONCLUSIONS

Satisfaction with life as a whole, or with separate domains, can be measured by self-report scales, and most people consider themselves to be above average, at 70% of the maximum, not 50%. It is not clear whether domains affect overall satisfaction or vice versa, but both directions of causation have been found for most domains.

Objective factors are important causes of satisfaction—income, health, employment and jobs, social relationships, leisure, housing and education have all been found to have substantial causal effects.

Downward comparisons often increase satisfaction and upward comparisons decrease it. However, comparisons are not usually externally imposed, except in the cases of wages and academic standards. Otherwise individuals choose which comparisons to make, and highly satisfied people can derive satisfaction from upward comparisons.

There is some adaptation to good and bad events, but some people never adapt to bad events, and there is continued satisfaction from the normal sources of satisfaction.

General satisfaction is affected by emotional state, which can be treated as a source of information. Satisfaction is also affected by cognitive factors such as attribution and perceived control, and the way people think about past events.

There are positive illusions in that satisfied people assess themselves and their friends and partners above average, and such optimistic thought motivates behaviour, though periods of realistic reflection may be desirable.

Chapter 5

Humour and laughter

Humour is a positive state of mind produced when someone says or does something incongruous, unexpected or absurd, or this occurs for some other reason, and people laugh. Finding things funny is a special kind of joy, and therefore important for happiness. It is a very common feature of life: it happens about 18 times a day, most often in spontaneous response to situations in the presence of others (Martin and Kuiper, 1999). Humour is important for this book, because it puts people in a good mood, or is the result of a good mood, and it can also have a profound influence on happiness. We shall see in Chapter 13 that humour is one of the standard methods of positive mood induction. A large proportion of TV and radio programmes are devoted to making people laugh; it looks as if there is a widespread desire to be happy, or at any rate to be in a positive mood, and the media are widely used to achieve it—by means of humour. Whatever they are about, TV programmes have to be amusing and entertaining (Argyle, 1996).

There are several aspects of humour—appreciating it, creating it and using it to cope with problems. All three are measured in some tests (Freiheit et al., 1998). And all are parts of having a "good sense of humour"—the "GSOH" often required of lonely hearts partners. And there are different kinds of jokes, but so far no agreed classification of them. There are ethnic jokes, sexual jokes, teasing, nonsense jokes, puns and other verbal jokes and slapstick for example.

Several studies have found a clear relation between humour and happiness—happy people laugh more and have a better sense of humour. Ruch and Carrell (1998), using 263 American and 151 German adults, found very high correlations, .80 or more, between a cheerfulness inventory and Ruch's sense of humour scale. This test measures how far people find things funny. Other humour measures have also been found to correlate with well-being, especially coping humour (Freiheit et al., 1998), and the capacity to initiate humour (see page 60).

Extraverts and others with good social skills laugh a lot and find things funny; we shall see in Chapter 10 that there is quite a strong correlation between extraversion and happiness. It is familiar that extraverts laugh more—reported frequent laughter is part of extraversion scales. Extraverts and others with good

social skills are happy, we conclude, because of their enjoyable social relationships; we have now seen that close relations are greatly helped by humour, and
that extraverts have a better sense of humour.

Humour can be used to induce positive moods. This is often done in the lab,
by the use of clips of funny films—Peter Sellars, John Cleese, etc. There is no
question that such films also induce positive moods, usually strong positive
moods, when watched in the usual way. Houston et al. (1998) found that a
laughter-inducing sing-song in an old people's home led to reduced levels of
anxiety and depression.

THE ORIGINS OF HUMOUR

Humour in animals

The central point of interest here is whether there is an innate basis to humour,
which conveyed some biological advantage. Cats, dogs and many other animals
play, particularly young ones, and this is usually a social activity. It is commonly
believed that the function of such play is to give practice in skills such as fighting
that will be important later. Play is often accompanied by social signals, like the
chimpanzee "play face", which indicate that chasing or attacking are not to be
taken seriously. However, it seems to be only in the apes that have had a lot of
human contact and been taught sign language that something more like
humour can be seen. Washoe used the sign for "funny" for tickling, chasing and
peek-a-boo. She once used a toothbrush as a hairbrush. She thought that urin-
ating on Roger while riding on his shoulders was very funny. Koko also made
jokes: she gave the drinking sign, thumb on mouth, wrongly by putting her
thumb in her ear instead. She liked to tease the experimenter by giving a series
of wrong signs. She watched the humans present, apparently looking for a
positive response (McGhee, 1979). Adolescent chimpanzees also tease each
other (Van Hooff et al., 1972).

Do animals laugh? Van Hooff (1972) studied the facial expressions of different non-human primates, and concluded that there are two possible origins of
smiling and laughing. Smiling he thought was derived from the silent bared-
teeth face, or grimace, laughter from the relaxed open-mouth face, later called
the playface. The open-mouth face is accompanied by quick staccato breathing,
which may have evolved into human laughter.

The social setting of the two faces is quite different. The bared-teeth face is
used as a signal for appeasement, often after aggression by other animals. The
open-mouth face is used to signal play, is directed to partners, and is recipro-
cated. However, the meaning of the bared-teeth face has changed from the
lower to the more evolved primates. In the lower species it is entirely about
appeasement and submission, though it may lead to affiliative behaviour and
bonding. In chimpanzees however there is a more friendly bared-teeth display,

and the same is true of humans; for us smiling and laughter are closely linked and interchangeable (Preuschoft and Van Hooff, 1977; Van Hooff, 1972).

Humour and laughter in children

The points of interest here are how early humour appears in children, what form it takes, how it develops and what influences affect its development.

Children smile very early, in the first weeks, at first to the mother's face or voice, and tickling. They also laugh by 4 months, in response to tickling or other tactile stimulation, peek-a-boo games, and by the end of the first year to incongruous events such as mother drinking from the baby's bottle. Incongruity seems to evoke laughter at this very early age, but only if the situation is safe, and perhaps if play signals are also given, otherwise strange events are found to be threatening.

From about 18 months onwards children engage in fantasy play, where they make up their own exaggerations, absurdities and incongruities. Pretend play is often social and is a source of mirth. Garvey (1977) gives the following example (Table 5.1).

As children get older they find more challenging jokes funny, and after 6–7 they are able to entertain multiple meanings, because they have reached Piaget's stage of "concrete operational thinking". Children find jokes funnier if they have to resolve them themselves, that is work out the second meaning; this is more likely to happen in a humorous context (Rothbart, 1976; Schultz, 1976). Until they are about 7 they are not able to appreciate the following:

"Why did the old man tip-toe past the sleeping cabinet?"
"Because he didn't want to wake up the sleeping pills".

They are also able to appreciate incongruity jokes at this age. For example:

Table 5.1 Pretend play

GIRL (4:9) (writing letter)	GIRL (4:7) (listening)
Dear Uncle Poop, I would like you to give me a roasted meatball, some chicken pox . . . and some tools. Signed . . . Mrs Fingernail. (smiles and looks up at partner)	
	Toop poop. (laughs) Hey, are you Mrs Fingernail?
Yes, I'm Mrs Fingernail. (in grand, dignified voice)	
	Poop, Mrs Fingernail (giggles)

Source: Garvey (1977).

Fat Ethel sat down at the lunch counter and ordered a whole fruit cake.
"Shall I cut it into four or eight pieces?" asked the waitress.
"Four", said Ethel, "I'm on a diet".

(McGhee, 1971)

There is a strong social element in children's humour, from an early age. By age 3 there is a strong desire to tell jokes, share humour with others, to make them laugh. This may be because shared laughter is enjoyable and also establishes in-group membership. Foot and Chapman (1976) found that 7-year-olds laughed more if another child was present, especially if the other child laughed at the same jokes, and if they liked the other. There was more laughter if they sat close together and looked at each other a lot, as if shared laughter is a form of intimacy. Children of 8–10 are preoccupied with riddles and enjoy jokes based on verbal double meanings. For example:

"Order! Order in court"
"Ham and cheese on rye please, your Honour"

(Schultz and Horibe, 1974)

Most of the humour described so far is based on incongruity without any further motivational basis. Most adult humour contains sexual, aggressive or hostile components. The first such humour to appear in children is lavatory jokes, in the Freudian "anal" stage, perhaps because parents indicate that this is a taboo topic; laughter may act as a kind of catharsis. In primary school this is replaced by interest in sex differences, another taboo topic. The main kind of aggressive humour is probably teasing, making jokes at the expense of others, generally regarded as a kind of aggression or bullying. This may be amusing for those who do it but can be very distressing for those who are teased, about their fatness for example. Scambler et al. (1998) found that among 8- to 11-year-olds a humorous response was the most effective and a hostile one the least. However, the nature of teasing changes with age, and playful, benign, teasing has been reported for adolescents (Warm, 1997), and we shall see later that it can be positive, indeed affectionate, in adults.

Where does the social skill of being funny come from? McGhee (1979) reports a longitudinal study which found that humorous children had a close relation with their mothers up to the age of 3 followed by a period when their mothers showed little affection, supporting the idea that humour can help cope with difficult or stressful situations. By age 6 there is a gender difference; boys tell more jokes and fool about more than girls.

Humour and the brain

Humour depends on the functioning of particular parts of the brain. Shammi and Stuss (1999) studied 21 brain-injured patients and some normal controls.

The patients did not appreciate humour if there was damage to a part of the right frontal lobe, the anterior region. It is in this part of the brain that the brain integrates and interprets incoming information, and where self-awareness takes place. Certain drugs also affect humour. Fitzgerald et al. (1999) found that Olanzapine, which contains serotonin as well as dopamine, restrained the excessive laughter of a schizophrenic patient. Laughter, like other facial expressions, depends partly on the frontal lobes and partly on more central areas (Rolls, 1999).

The evolution of humour and laughter

We have seen that apes have a kind of humour and laughter in some ways similar to that of humans, that very young children enjoy humour, and that humour is localised in a certain part of the brain. This all points to the likelihood that humour has an innate basis. If so it must have evolved because it had some biological function, gave some evolutionary advantage—but if so what is it? Humour and laughter seem to be derived from social play in which those concerned enjoy fooling about. McGhee (1979) thought that apes only appreciated humour if they had acquired some language skills, so that they are able to manipulate symbols, and we have seen examples of this. On the other hand apes who have not been so educated engage in play, signalled by the playface, and accompanied by noises that are a possible forerunner of laughing. A central feature of human humour is incongruity, and we have seen that verbal incongruity jokes cannot be appreciated until about age 6–7. On the other hand there is a lot of child humour at much earlier ages, as in absurd fantasy play.

Humour is basically a social phenomenon, and we shall see that it leads to social bonding as a result of the shared positive emotions, and the discharge of negative ones. Perhaps this is the real function of humour. The most important incongruity that is resolved is that due to social differences, between mother and child, between males and females, superiors and subordinates, which can in some sense be "resolved" by seeing them as humorous and therefore a source of enjoyment not conflict. We shall explore these social benefits of humour in the next section.

THE PSYCHOLOGY OF HUMOUR

The basic model

Most psychologists who studied humour have concluded that the central feature of events that makes them funny is incongruity; this is necessary for them to be humorous. The incongruity may be between what is expected or normally happens and what actually happens (Chapters 1–4 Chapman and Foot, 1976). Mother drinking from baby's bottle is found funny by baby. Giving a subject a set of weights to estimate and inserting one that is much lighter or much heavier than the rest is found funny. In a verbal joke a second interpretation of events is suggested. Incongruity can be based on sheer illogicality, as in the joke about the person who wanted her cake cut into 4 not 8 pieces since she was on a diet. Many psychologists have recognised that a second, "motivational" component is necessary too. Wyer and Collins (1992) formulated this as a second, unexpected event or part of the story that in some way diminishes the importance or value of the persons or events described; however, both interpretations are still kept in mind, creating the incongruity.

Several kinds of humour can be seen as examples of incongruity combined with diminished status. Ethnic jokes, based on the supposed stupidity etc. of the target group, as in how many of them are needed to change a light bulb, are perfect examples. Such "superiority" humour may raise the self-esteem of the in-group at the expense of the out-group. Slapstick of the Laurel and Hardy kind can perhaps be seen as a case of incongruity, as the participants are apparently not hurt for example by being hit over the head by blocks of wood (Wyer and Collins, 1992).

A lot of humour is about sex, and this fits the model very well. For example "How was your visit to the nudist camp?" "OK, the first three days were the hardest." And "Did you see her dress?" "No, she wouldn't let me." Both jokes are based on simple verbal double meanings, the classic "double entendre", where the second, less obvious meaning is ruder. Here is a better one:

> An old lady had two pet monkeys. They died, and she took them (in a taxi) to the taxidermist. She said "Please can you stuff my two pet monkeys?" "Certainly Madam; would you like them mounted?" "No thank you, just holding hands".

The Freudian theory of humour (1905/1960) explains sex jokes differently— this kind of humour, he suggested, provides an outlet for repressed sexual and aggressive urges, in a symbolic form. Experiments on motivation show that jokes and other forms of fantasy are found funnier when these drives have been aroused and also when inhibitions have been reduced by alcohol (e.g. Clark and Sensibar, 1955). This is sometimes known as the "catharsis" theory of humour. But note that this too depends on incongruity.

Freud also thought that the expression of aggression in humour worked in the same way, by providing a symbolic outlet for this motivation. This is saying much the same as the vicarious superiority theory, of humour at the expense of others. Slapstick humour can also be interpreted in terms of symbolic aggression, though it may be better classed as nonsense and absurdity. Finally Freud mentioned anal humour, which we saw is very popular with young children. For example "Why do farts smell?" "For the deaf" (Wyer and Collins, 1992).

To make people laugh it seems that two elements are commonly present, incongruity and one of the motivations just described. With incongruity alone they may find a joke amusing and smile, but to make them laugh some motivation is needed too (McGhee, 1979).

The incongruity plus superiority or diminishment theory covers many forms of humour, though not all kinds. Another way of looking at humour is to say that it is playful as opposed to serious behaviour. This fits the childhood origins of humour—tickling, peek-a-boo, chasing games, absurd fantasy play using exaggeration and mimicry. It also fits some kinds of adult humour, such as nonsense humour; this is play with words, as other humour is play with ideas. This also fits the social aspects of humour—play is mainly a social activity.

Individual differences in humour

We may be able to learn more about the psychology of humour from looking at the people who enjoy humour most. Ruch and his co-workers in Germany have been most active here. He developed a measure of sense of humour, the "3WD" test, which assesses how funny and also how aversive people think jokes and cartoons are, of three different kinds—incongruity, nonsense and sexual (Ruch, 1998). In a long series of studies in several European countries they have found a number of personality correlates of appreciating humour. Extraversion has usually, though not always, been found to correlate with the 3WD test, and extraverts like sexual jokes most. In one study it was found that extraverts laughed a lot (Ruch, 1998). In a study with 446 American students Bell et al. (1986) found that reported initiation of humour was predicted by assertiveness and self-monitoring, both of which can be seen as indices of social skills. Sensation seekers find jokes funnier and laugh more, with both German and American students (Deckers and Ruch, 1992). Conservative attitudes and intolerance of ambiguity are related to overall humour scores, and particularly to enjoying incongruity jokes, but those high on this dimension do not like nonsense jokes, perhaps because they can't be resolved. Tough-minded individuals like sexual jokes; liberal-minded ones prefer nonsense jokes.

We see from these findings that there is more than one kind of humour, appealing to different kinds of people. The social side of humour is seen in the correlation with extraversion and with sensation-seeking, and the correlation between humour initiation and social skills. Incongruity is enjoyed most by rigid and intolerant individuals, and can be seen as the way they discharge their tensions.

Kuiper and Martin (1998), using a quite different measure, the Situational Humor Response Questionnaire, have repeatedly found that those with high scores are higher in extraversion and self-esteem, lower in neuroticism and depression. These authors have another scale for Coping Humor, which has similar correlates and is a good predictor of stress buffering (Martin, 1996).

The social side of humour

The classical theories of humour, just described, fail to deal with the social side of it. It is also hard to see from these theories why humour should have massive positive effects, for happiness and stress reduction. And it is hard to see why incongruity, superiority or symbolic expression of sex and aggression should give some evolutionary advantage. However, the social side of humour makes all these things clear.

We have seen that children as young as 2 or 3 want to share their humour, and try to amuse each other or their parents. Chapman and Foot (1976) showed that for 7-year-old children humour is contagious: they laughed more when humour was shared, when they liked their companion and sat close to him or her, and looked at each other a lot. These investigators concluded that laughing acted as a signal for social intimacy, like smiling, looking and proximity. Laughter is rewarding and leads to an individual being liked, and accepted as a member of the group. However, laughing did not act as an alternative signal, as had been expected from Argyle and Dean's intimacy theory (1965); rather all these signals operated together to indicate increased intimacy. Lorenz (1963) thought that laughter "produces a strong fellow-feeling among participants and joint aggression against outsiders" (p. 253). Laughter, like the chimpanzee play face, is a social signal, indicating play and the absence of aggression.

Humour also makes young people more attractive to one another. Lundy et al. (1998) found that self-deprecating humour linked to a photo of the supposed speaker made him or her more desirable when there was an attractive photo; evidence was found that this was because such humour "lightens the dark side" of attractive individuals, as being too competent.

Humour provides strong shared emotion, positive emotion at that, and this is a powerful source of social bonding. So if one person provides humour for a group, the social cohesion of the whole group should be increased. Humour is also able to resolve tensions within the group, both by the shared emotion, and also as a light-hearted and indirect way of dealing with taboo subjects and conflicts within the group (Emerson, 1969). But if the humour is about the failings of an out-group, and the relative superiority of the in-group, this will particularly enhance in-group cohesion. This has been said to be the basis for ethnic humour among members of minority groups like American Jews and Blacks, to enhance their morale (Martineau, 1972).

Joking relationships provide another example of the social side of humour. Radcliffe-Brown (1940, p. 195) described this as a relationship "in which one is by custom permitted, and in some instances required, to tease or make fun of the other, who in turn is required to take no offence". He found that joking relationships were quite common in preliterate societies in Africa and Asia. Joking relationships are usually between certain kin, such as with in-laws, cross-cousins, grandparents, potential marriage partners. The joking is quite strong, usually consisting of insults, teasing, banter, horseplay and obscenities.

Radcliffe-Brown and his followers maintained that the explanation of this relationship is that it allows the harmless expression of aggression and the maintenance of solidarity in relations where there are bonds keeping the pair together but also conflict of interests.

The relationships just described are parts of the social structure of preliterate societies, to which all would conform. There may be another kind of joking relationship, between individuals, which is nevertheless similar. The common forms of humour found in industrial society in some ethnic sub-cultures and in places of work have been described as examples of joking relations, though they are of the individual, voluntary kind. For example in supervisory situations it is common to use humour when making critical comments for disciplining a subordinate, as will be explained later (see page 68).

We saw that teasing is common in children, and is on the whole aggressive. But in adults teasing is usually more positive. Keltner et al. (1998) found a lot of teasing in an American fraternity, as a playful way of dealing with norm-violation, and it led to positive affect and Duchenne smiles (i.e. genuine smiles, with narrowing of the eyes and wrinkling at their corners), especially when teased by equals. Teasing is one of the main ways of flirting; Keltner et al. found that in romantic couples teasing led to increased flirtation and positive affect. Argyle and Henderson (1985) found that it was a widely agreed rule of friendship that people should tease their friends.

Where does incongruity resolution fit into these social functions of humour? It is partly that appreciating humour together is a source of bonding, and the reduction of interpersonal tensions. There is another incongruity to deal with in many social situations—due to differences in status, gender, etc. between people. Humour very often plays on these differences, defuses them, makes them harmless by seeing them in a different way. Mother drinking from baby's bottle accepts and laughs at the differences in status between the two.

HUMOUR AND STRESS

Coping with stress

Humour also plays a role in buffering stress, that is in making it less threatening and harmful. Martin and Lefcourt (1983) developed a Humour Coping Scale, for the reported use of humour in coping. Those with higher scores were less upset by a stressful film, and in a later study blood pressure went up less in response to the stress of immersing a hand in cold water for those with better humour coping scores (Lefcourt et al., 1997). Kuiper et al. (1992) studied the effect of real-life events on positive and negative affect. They found that those who laughed a lot did not show any increase in negative affect, and for males who laughed a lot stressful life events led to *increased* positive affect. The finding that those with a keener sense of humour are in a better mood after negative life events is remarkable. It is assumed that the way humour works here is by enabling people to "look on the bright side", that is have the capacity to see events in alternative ways, especially ways that are humorous and thus less stressful. Lyobirmirsky and Tucker (1998) found that happy people were able to look at the same adverse events in more positive ways than did unhappy people, both for actual and hypothetical events.

Adolescence is a stressful time for many. Plancherel and Bolognini (1995) found that for 276 13-year-olds those who could generate humour were less depressed, anxious and were sleeping better three years later. One of the most stressful events is bereavement, and it is not funny. (The author was bereaved shortly before writing this chapter.) Nevertheless Keltner and Bonanno (1997) studied the effect of bereavement in relation to amount of Duchenne laughter in a standard interview. Those who laughed more were less angry, less distressed, had more positive affect and less negative affect, and had better social relations, including less ambivalence towards the departed. These authors used a measure of dissociation between autonomic and verbal measures of emotion, and found that those who laughed and experienced less distress and who had enhanced relationships had a greater amount of dissociation, which enabled them to experience positive rather than negative emotions.

Humour in working groups reflects the tensions and frustrations of those involved. This boisterous, sometimes obscene, often pointless horseplay and joking can provide substantial benefits. Roy (1959) described the activities of a small group of workers engaged in very boring work. At a certain time each day one man would steal and eat another's banana—this was known as "banana time". At another time one of them would open the window thus creating a draught and a row. Every hour something equally fatuous happened, but one said "If it weren't for the joking and fooling you'd go nuts". The benefits of such humour are (1) increased job satisfaction, (2) improved social relationships, and this in turn can result in (3) more cooperation and productivity (Argyle, 1989).

Sociologists have shown how the contents of humour help cope with social stresses, how they are related to features of the social system. Douglas (1968) thought that jokes are generated by and challenge the social structure and give symbolic expression to the strains within it. We have seen how joking relationships help deal with the hostilities with mothers-in-law in primitive society for example, and we shall see how ethnic jokes help deal with the hostilities between different racial and national groups. Working organisations also generate stresses and produce forms of humour which are related to them. Mulkay (1988) has taken this further and proposed that there are two modes of discourse, the serious and the humorous. The serious mode assumes that there is one point of view, of a hierarchical, ordered social world. The humorous mode supposes that there are different, contradictory points of view, it challenges the serious view of the world and enjoys the contradictions and incongruities in it.

The humorous mode does not however destroy the serious one, but rather sustains it by allowing the tensions in it to be expressed symbolically. This is what jesters and other comedians do, as we will see next.

Mulkay illustrated this idea with his study of "Brady's Bar". The problem here was that while the bartenders were of higher status than the waitresses, they were also at their beck and call, and even worse were forced into a female role of caring for the needs of others. The humour in which they engaged directly expressed these concerns. Shop-floor humour reflects social stresses in a similar way. Collinson (1988) found that the contents of such humour were about resistance to being controlled and to the boring work, sustaining shared values of working-class masculinity, and control of deviates who did not pull their weight. Holdaway (1983) described police humour. This expresses the contradictions between the formal rules of how police are supposed to treat suspects for example, and how they find they actually have to do it, as well as telling stories about car chases, and events that illustrate team solidarity.

Jesters, comedians and wits

Throughout history jesters, clowns, buffoons and other comedians have been found. The earliest were dwarfs or mental defectives, who were seen as a source of entertainment as scapegoats. Jesters were later associated with royal courts and noble families as described by Shakespeare. They had licence to be insulting, poke fun and play practical jokes, though they got into trouble if they went too far. There were joke books with large numbers of their jokes; these jokes were much the same as jokes today: sexual, anal and at the expense of anyone outside the group who could be ridiculed. Their humour was also related to status differences and other sources of tension in the society, and helped to reduce these tensions. Later there were "lords of disrule", who licensed deviance (Welsford, 1961). There had been a decline of such court jesters in the 1500s, as a result of religious pressures, although previously priests and princes had taken part in the fun (Bremmer and Roodenburg, 1997).

In Russia some were poets or prophets, and seen as belonging to the Divine order, like the king. In Greek and Roman society buffoons were professional entertainers who appeared at parties, sometimes in return for food, and competing with acrobats, jugglers and dancing girls.

Pollio and Edgerly (1976) report studies of American comedians. Subjects were asked to provide five adjectives to describe each comedian. One finding was the unexpected frequency of negative words like fat, ugly, clumsy, stupid, weird, skinny and deformed. Apparently the role of the comedian is a very negative one. They were also often described as Jewish, Black, Irish or Italian. In fact many American comedians do come from such ethnic backgrounds, and they make use of this in their humour. They are able to draw upon the rich background of ethnic humour found in these populations, and which we describe later.

We saw earlier that children who initiate a lot of humour have often experienced a period of rejection early in life (see page 57). Interviews with comedians have also found that some of them came from very bad family backgrounds, and had used humour to provide relief from the suffering. Children who were active in producing humour were also found to be assertive and physically and verbally aggressive. This may be an example of the Freudian notion of humour as displaced aggression.

We have seen that those with a good sense of humour tend to be more extraverted, to have better social skills, and be happier than others. Comedians must have the skills of humour to a high degree, yet it is well known that many of them have to visit mental hospitals, with depression or other complaints. The explanation is not known; it may be that comedians have big mood swings, may be manic-depressive, and are able to be so funny only when in a rather high mood. We shall see in Chapter 14 that when strong positive moods are induced people display more creativity, e.g. are able to think of more remote associations—just what is needed to produce humour.

The modern equivalent of jesters may be TV shows, particularly situation comedies, "sit-coms", where the humour is created by the situation and a comic cast of characters. These often deal with topics of social tension, such as race relations ("Till Death Do Us Part"—apparently scandalously racist; "Goodness, Gracious Me"—affectionate Asian in-group humour); social class (part of "The Good Life"); the elderly ("One Foot in the Grave"); low job satisfaction ("The Rise and Fall of Reginald Perrin"); how the TV news is manufactured ("Drop the Dead Donkey"). But some of them play more on absurdity, without much reference to social stresses, as in "Monty Python's Flying Circus".

Ethnic humour

There is the classic "How many Irishmen does it take to change a light bulb?" joke, with its many variations, playing on stereotypes of different groups. "How many psychologists . . . ?" Answer "One, but the bulb has to want to change"—making fun of the simple ideas of psychologists perhaps. There are many ethnic jokes that depend on the beliefs that the Scots are mean, the French amorous, the Irish stupid and so on.

A great deal of humour is at the expense of other social groups, especially other ethnic groups, like blacks and Jews, and other national groups, like the Irish and Poles. A lot of this humour is of the "superiority" pattern, asserting some kind of defect like stupidity to the out-group. The humour depends on the existence of stereotypes, about the stupidity, meanness, etc. of the group in question, and is based on absurd exaggeration of the supposed qualities. Use is also made of the incongruity principle, as for example in the following anti-Irish joke.

O'Riley was on trial for armed robbery. The jury came out and announced

"Not guilty". "Wonderful", said O'Riley, "Does that mean I can keep the money?"

Just saying that another group is stupid and dishonest is not at all funny, but adding the incongruity makes it so.

La Fave et al. (1976) carried out a series of experiments in which the form of jokes was varied to see which was found funniest. In a number of these experiments jokes were found funnier when they esteemed a subject's own group or one with which he identified, and when they disparaged groups to which he did not belong or identify with. Zillman and Cantor (1976) extended this and proposed that there will be more mirth the greater the negative dis-position towards the disparaged agent, and also the more positive the attitude towards the source of humour. These ideas can be incorporated into a later development of inter-group behaviour, "social identity theory", which says that discrimination against out-groups enhances that part of the self-image based on group membership, and hence enhances self-esteem (Brown, 1995). Subjects who were asked to recite jokes that disparaged Newfoundlanders produced more negative attitudes to that group than non-disparaging jokes (Maio et al., 1997).

Some ethnic humour is directed to members of minority groups, such as blacks in the USA. This may involve more than vicarious superiority. The contents of the black stereotype are that blacks are lazy, stupid, dishonest and very highly sexed. Jokes using such ideas may be an indirect way of expressing hostile attitudes. This can be related to the Freudian idea of symbolic expression of aggression.

Some ethnic humour is initiated by members of a minority group, Jews making jokes about Jews for example. It is widely believed that one function of such humour is building social cohesion between members of a minority group. Middleton (1959) found that black Americans found anti-black jokes as funny as whites found them, though they found anti-white jokes funnier than whites did. However, as we saw earlier, jokes at the expense of the in-group are not usually appreciated. Students of black American humour from the period of slavery onwards have concluded that it was a way of "making an unbearable situation somewhat lighter", and was a way of permitting resentment and hostil-ity to be publicly voiced (Goldman, 1960). As well as reducing tensions and allowing the expression of aggression, some of this humour can be seen as criticising society and expressing increasing black pride (Boskin, 1966). How-ever, it is not humour without the ingredients of humour, such as incongruity. Apte (1985) gives the following story.

A Southern officer stationed in England was seated next to a Negro at an official dinner. He completely ignored the Negro until the end of the meal and then commented, "Rastus, Ah reckon you-all miss yo' water-melon". The Negro was then introduced as the guest of honour and renowned

Oxford scholar and gave a brilliant speech. When he returned to his seat he said sarcastically to the officer, "Yes, Rastus sh' do miss his watermelon".

(p. 125)

Bourhis et al. (1977) found that the Welsh did not like anti-Welsh jokes. They did like anti-English jokes, but not if it was too obvious that these expressed blatant hostility to the other group. Jokes at the expense of other groups are indeed expressions of racial or other prejudice, which of course is widespread, but is not politically correct, and one is not supposed to laugh at such jokes.

Jewish humour, that is humour initiated by Jews and about Jews, has some special features. It is based on stereotypes in the usual way—concern with money and social status, and elaborate food rules, for example. It often uses blatant incongruity and logical contradictions. For example:

An elderly Jew had a deathbed conversion to Catholicism. When his friends protested he said "Better for one of them to go than one of us".

Another possible feature of Jewish humour may be "self-hatred". If this is true it may be based on accepting the negative stereotypes held by the outside community, together with ambiguity about the situation of Jews, a partial wish not to be Jewish because of the costs it entails (Rosenberg and Shapiro, 1958). It may be added that there is a great deal of Jewish humour, perhaps resulting from the stresses of being Jewish, and this has led to the large number of Jewish comedians.

During the Gulf War it is reported that Israelis calmed their nerves by enjoying humour that mastered anxiety through looking at things differently, expressed aggression, strengthened social bonds and made humorous sense of it all (Nevo, 1994).

HUMOUR AND SOCIAL SKILLS

We show in Chapter 10 that individuals with better social skills are happier, because they can bring about and sustain better social relationships. In this section we will look at the ways in which humour can contribute to social skills.

Establishing social relationships

All social skills require forming relations with one or more others, and sustaining them. In most cases there will be differences of gender, age, social status, occupation, attitudes, etc., with the result that they have different outlooks and interests. As Mulkay (1988) has argued, the humorous mode is able to recognise that there is more than one point of view, more than one way of looking at things, and entertaining both points of view at once is a basis of humour. Humour can discharge the tensions caused by the conflicting outlooks; Graham (1995) asked pairs of strangers to talk for 30 minutes; a strong sense of humour led to reduction of social distance between them.

We have seen how humour can enhance social cohesion, by the experience of laughing together, and by the expression of shared values, or the rejection of out-groups. Humorous behaviour, such as telling jokes, makes others like the source of jokes more, indeed both like each other (Mettee et al., 1971). It is not surprising then that the rules of friendship include the desirability of joking and teasing (Argyle and Henderson, 1985). However, marriages are less likely to survive if husbands use humour to deal with their wife's stressful life events—this avoids solving the problem (Cohan and Bradbury, 1997).

Humour does more than this, it makes possible the fine-tuning of the relationship in various ways (Kane et al., 1977). Individuals can engage in cautious self-disclosure, in a way that implies that they are not committed to whatever was disclosed. They can probe for information about others, in a light-hearted way. And they can challenge the self-presentations of others, if these are suspected of being bogus (Davis and Farina, 1970).

Sexual interest for example can be communicated by telling sexual jokes, of increasing degrees of sexuality. Davis and Farina (1970) found that young men thought sexual jokes were funnier when they had to tell an attractive female how funny they thought these were. Laughter too can communicate sexual interest. Grammer (1990) found that young men indicated their sexual interest by laughter combined with bodily postures.

Leadership

Leaders need to be able to direct and control the behaviour of subordinates, while staying on good terms with them. This can be achieved by social skills such as consultation and persuasion, but also by the use of humour. Humour can discharge tensions due to the differences of power and status as described above. It is also possible to discipline a subordinate who has been late, slow, untidy, etc., and it is a subtle social skill to be able to do so (Martineau, 1972). Traditional Army sergeant talk is like this—"Stand a bit closer to the razor next time", etc. In this relationship the basic antagonism is expressed but restrained by the positive humorous side to the communication. Decker and Rotondo (1999) found that job satisfaction was greater when supervisors were rated as having a good sense of humour, especially female supervisors.

Psychiatrists and psychotherapists

The benefits from using humour in psychotherapy, including group therapy, have often been written about. Humour has the familiar advantages of reducing tension and enhancing positive affect, as well as increasing the cohesion of groups. It can do more than this. Humour can help to reduce resistance and embarrassment over discussing and revealing information about sensitive topics. And above all it can help the patients see the funny side, see that there is another and less threatening way of looking at their problems. The therapist can encourage this approach by acting as a model (Bloch et al., 1983). It has been suggested that psychiatrists should be trained in the use of humour (Saper, 1990). Humour is used in medicine too, to reduce embarrassment, and other anxiety (du Pre, 1998).

Public speaking

Humour is often used in public speaking, for teaching or persuasion. A number of experiments have been done in which the same speech has been given with and without humour, or with different kinds of humour. The results are clear—the speaker is liked more, the speech is found more interesting, and the audience are in a better mood, when humour has been used. Teachers are liked more if they use humour; Avner et al. (1986) found that the use of a variety of kinds of humour was most popular. Other research has shown that there is more attitude change when recipients of a message like the source and are in a good mood (Petty and Wegener, 1998), as can be produced by humour. Some experiments on persuasion and teaching have found this, but there have been negative results too. The humour has to be right for the job, relevant satire for example, not clowning or sarcasm (Gruner, 1976).

Evidently sense of humour, particularly the capacity to initiate humour, is useful for several social skills. Can it be taught? Nevo et al. (1998) set up a 20-hour course to do so, using modelling, reinforcement and other methods. There were positive though modest effects with 101 Israeli women teachers.

CONCLUSIONS

Humour is an important source of happiness, in a number of ways. Humour is partly innate, there are forerunners in non-human primates, and young children enjoy and initiate humour. It is controlled by a certain part of the brain. If humour gave a biological advantage it may have been its power to enhance social bonding.

Much humour is based on incongruity, usually in combination with vicarious superiority, sex or aggression. The key to most humour is entertaining two versions of events, or stories, where the second and unexpected one is less worthy, e.g. ruder, than the first.

Laughter is an expression of positive affect, but humour can have a causal effect on mood and happiness. Humour is one of the most common and most effective forms of mood induction, and being able to see the funny side reduces the effect of stressful events by making them less threatening. Humour also helps with social stresses, is related to conflicts in society, suggests another way of looking at things and discharges tensions. Joking relationships cope with family conflicts, ethnic humour expresses racial conflicts. Jesters and comedians are sensitive to social stresses, their modern equivalent is some TV sit-coms.

Humour is a social phenomenon, a source of social bonding, it is part of social skills, enabling individuals to discharge tensions, increase cohesion, produce social rewards, and use a subtle way of negotiating relationships and disciplining subordinates which maintains a positive relationship.

Chapter 6

Social relationships

Social relationships have a powerful effect on happiness and other aspects of well-being, and are perhaps its greatest single cause. One way of estimating their effect is from the regression coefficients, which show correlations after other variables have been held constant, and an example from the *Quality of American Life* study by Campbell et al. (1976) is shown in Table 6.1. The first column shows how each domain was rated for importance, 1 being the highest, and the second column shows the independent effect of each domain on overall satisfaction.

We shall look at other studies which confirm that marriage and family life have the strongest overall effect, followed by friendship, though this varies for different age groups. We will look at some of these relationships first and then pull together the overall effect of relationships and consider how they work.

Table 6.1 Sources of satisfaction in everyday life

	Mean importance rating	Regression coefficient
Family life	1.46	.41
Marriage	1.44	.36
Financial situation	2.94	.33
Housing	2.10	.30
Job	2.19	.27
Friendship	2.08	.26
Health	1.37	.22
Leisure activities	2.79	.21

Source: Campbell et al. (1976).

FRIENDSHIP

Positive affect

Being with friends is a major source of joy. We saw in Chapter 3 that this was the most common source mentioned by European students. Larson (1990) carried out a study in which subjects were bleeped on random occasions and asked to report their mood. As Figure 6.1 shows they were in the most positive mood when with friends, followed by family and being alone. Some of these friends may have been of the opposite sex. The benefits of being with friends were greatest not only for those in their 20s but also for older individuals—who are less likely to have been sexually involved.

The benefits of being with friends may be due partly to the enjoyable things they do together: they engage in joint leisure. Argyle and Furnham (1982) found that the things people do with friends more than with others are like dancing, playing tennis, drinking, intimate conversation and going for a walk. These may seem like trivial activities, but nevertheless they can cause a lot of joy and can be part of supportive relationships. Argyle and Lu (1990) studied the enjoyment of 37 leisure activities, and found several factors, as shown in Table 6.2. This was a factor analysis; people who do one activity in a factor are likely to do the others too. Factor 3, belonging to teams and clubs, and factor 4, going to parties and dances, were both associated with happiness, presumably because of the positive affect they produce.

We want to focus on what exactly it is about these social occasions that produces the joy. One is the receipt of non-verbal signals, especially smiles and

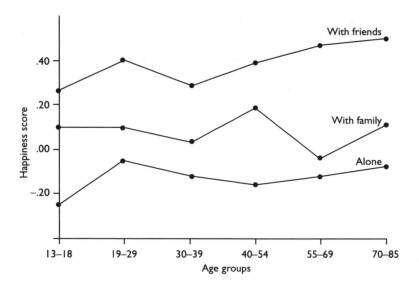

Figure 6.1 Positive affect with different companions (Larson, 1990).

Table 6.2 Factor analysis on "enjoyment" scale

Items	I	2	3	4
22 pottering about the house	0.73			
32 dressmaking/knitting	0.69			
I chat with friend	− 0.68			
27 reading magazines	0.67			
28 gardening	0.62			
7 card games	0.55			
16 reading detective stories	0.54			
31 DIY	0.52			
21 exercise	0.47			
23 writing to friends	0.46			
26 reading newspaper	0.45			
30 driving	− 0.39			
14 TV	0.30			
36 social club		− 0.43		
35 walking by yourself		0.70		
15 reading novel		0.68		
4 country walk		0.66		
18 music (classic jazz)		0.65		
17 reading non-fiction		0.54		
34 sleeping		0.45		
9 quiet family evening		0.44		
37 long bath		0.42		
3 pub			0.66	
2 noisy party			0.65	
29 travelling			0.64	
5 meeting new people			0.59	
20 dancing			0.56	
19 pop music			0.55	
10 debates			0.38	
13 soap opera			0.33	
12 other sports				0.65
11 team sports				0.62
24 film and video				0.54
25 cinema				0.51
8 jokes/funny stories				0.51
33 sunbathing				0.48
6 party games				0.38
Reliability alpha	0.82	0.74	0.70	0.64
Variance explained	15.8	10.7	8.7	5.9

Source: Argyle and Lu (1990).

friendly tones of voice. Kraut and Johnston (1979) found that at the bowling alley, people often smiled at their friends, whether they had hit the skittles or not, but very rarely at the skittles themselves. Babies respond positively to smiling faces and friendly voices at a very early age, and are able to smile back again, and happiness is the first emotion to be recognised (Ekman, 1982). Infant monkeys reared in total isolation start to discriminate friendly and threatening faces at 2 months, so this ability must be largely innate (Sackett, 1966).

Friends are rewarding in other ways. However, if we care deeply for another person we do not just seek rewards for ourselves, but are also concerned for their welfare. Dunn (1988) found that nursery school children often helped or shared; they said that this was simply part of enjoyable social behaviour with friends. Adults in close relationships have been found to attend more to the needs of others than to their own rewards—this has been called a "communal" relationship (Clark and Reis, 1988). Experiments on altruism find that it is a source of positive emotion to do things for others in distress (Batson, 1987). Sociability involves being cooperative, that is taking account of the other's concerns as well as one's own. Extraverts do this more than introverts; we have seen that extraverts are usually happy; Lu and Argyle (1992a) constructed a cooperativeness scale and found that this was a predictor of happiness, and partly explained the happiness of extraverts. In another study Lu and Argyle (1992b) found that extraverts gave more social support to others than introverts did. Females and young people received more support. We also found that there are costs to giving and receiving social support: receiving support correlated with guilt, anxiety and dependence; giving support correlated with feeling burdened and frustrated.

Happiness

Many studies have shown that satisfaction with friends correlates with happiness and life satisfaction, at the level of .30 to .40 or more, after demographic controls. There are similar, though lower, correlations with number of friends, number of close friends, frequency of seeing them, of telephone calls, visits and parties (Veenhoven, 1994). Costa et al. (1985) found a factor of the quality and quantity of friendships, which correlated .29 with happiness. Berry and Willingham (1997) found that individuals high in positive affect had less conflict and more enjoyable relationships, including those with strangers; this was partly due to their different use of non-verbal communication. Happiness may be produced by friends from the frequency of enjoyable contacts with them. Friendship is very important to adolescents, and they spend some hours a day with their friends and more on the telephone if they can.

We will look at the conditions under which friends produce happiness. One of the main sources of friendship is rewardingness, so friends are rewarding, and this produces positive emotion and satisfaction. We have seen that there are three main kinds of satisfaction from relationships—instrumental rewards, emotional support and companionship. We have seen how friends send us positive non-verbal signals. They can also be rewarding verbally, by agreeing, praising, encouraging, being interesting. They can be practically helpful by giving presents, providing food and drink, advice and information. They may be rewarding by their companionship in being amusing and cheerful, making us laugh, a sign of great joy, and joining us in playing tennis together, or other things we cannot do as well or at all alone.

Close friends are a particular source of happiness. Weiss (1973) found that to avoid loneliness people needed a single close relationship and also a network of relationships. To form a close relationship involves an increasing level of self-disclosure, and without it people will still be lonely. Wheeler et al. (1983) found that a number of students who had plenty of friends and spent a lot of time with them, were still lonely because they talked about impersonal topics, such as sport and pop music, rather than about their real concerns. Close friends are likely to be quite similar in attitudes and beliefs, as well as interests. By liking us and sharing our view of ourselves, our self-esteem is raised.

The network of friends is also important. The social network forms an in-group, which is important for maintaining identity and self-esteem, and providing help and social support. We found that friendships were most often lost by individuals breaking such "third party rules" as keeping confidences and standing up for friends in their absence (Argyle and Henderson, 1985).

There are gender differences in friendship and its benefits. Women's friendships are closer, involving more self-disclosure, affection and social support. Men do things together, such as playing sport and drinking. The close friendship is more important to women, the social network to men, and men form clubs very readily, and have a wider range of contacts, from work and leisure. Women are more rewarding to both males and females, and the best predictor of not being lonely is frequency of interaction with women; time spent with men made no difference (Wheeler et al. 1983).

There are personality differences in the enjoyment of friendship. We shall see in Chapter 10 that extraversion is one of the most important sources of happiness. Extraverts have a different style of non-verbal communication—they smile more, look more at others, position themselves nearer and their voices are louder and higher pitched. Part of the reason for the happiness of extraverts is that they do more enjoyable things, and these are of a social nature—they join teams and clubs and they go to parties and dances, shown as factors in Table 6.2 (page 73); it was doing these things that made extraverts happy (Argyle and Lu, 1990).

We also found that extraverts had special social skills, they were more assertive and more cooperative, making them able to manage their relationships better (Argyle and Lu, 1990). Thorne (1987) found that pairs of extraverts placed together tried very hard to get to know each other, by asking questions, agreeing and paying compliments. I have replicated this study and found that pairs of introverts often sit together in total silence. Individuals with extraverted social skills are likely to have more friends and to enjoy their company. Lonely people have been found to be unrewarding, hostile and pessimistic, shy and unassertive, egocentric and to take little interest in others (Jones, 1985).

Mental and physical health

Social support from friends affects health of both kinds. Reis and Franks (1994) studied 846 individuals who were 33 or over and found that anxiety and depression, subjective health and number of doctor visits were associated with both intimacy and social support, but that social support was the key predictor; it consisted here of actual help, group belongingness, positive appraisal and having a special bond.

However, other studies have found that "emotional support" doesn't do any good. Nolen-Hoeksema (1991) asked subjects "What do you do when you feel depressed?" Women often said that they ruminated about the problem or had a good moan with their friends; however, this correlated with a longer duration of depression; shorter periods of depression correlated with activities providing distraction. Men were more likely to engage in some physical activity, which was more successful. Several studies have found that what is needed is social support in the form of actual help, the availability of someone who cares, and companionship rather than intimate discussion of problems. Ross and Mirowsky (1989) found that social support led to less depression, but that intimate conversation about problems made things worse since this meant talking about problems, or complaining, rather than solving them. Help and problem-solving increased perception of being able to control events. The concept of control also explains why women who are married, rich or educated are less likely to become depressed. On the other hand we shall report later studies showing that self-disclosure is good for health, and that emotional support seems to be beneficial in marriage.

These benefits for mental health work partly through the prevention of loneliness, a common source of depression. Social support from the network of friends can also buffer the impact of stress on anxiety, as Bolger and Eckenrode (1992) found for students during a period of exams. Positive appraisal, one of the Reis and Franks social support components, works by enhancing self-esteem. Enjoyable social interaction can have direct positive benefits. Kuiper and Martin (1998) found that frequency of laughter buffered the effect of negative life events on negative affect; seeing the funny side of things makes them less threatening (see page 62).

Friendship has less impact on mortality or other measures of physical health than marriage for example. However, if intimacy or closeness of friendships are taken into account an effect on health is found. Reis et al. (1984) found for female students that their frequency of doctor visits was related to the pleasantness, intimacy, self-disclosure and satisfaction of their friendships. Eder (1990) reports a study of 11- to 15-year-old children in nine European countries. In all of them there was a clear correlation between reported ill-health, feeling lonely and unhappy and feeling that they did not belong to the group. In Austria these lonely children were bullied less. Girls and older children were less happy, less socially integrated and ill more.

LOVE AND MARRIAGE

Positive affect

As we saw in Chapter 3, falling in love is usually rated as the strongest source of positive emotion. Fehr (1988) asked people to list the defining features of love, and these were euphoria, excitement, affection, contentment, laughing, etc. When they marry most people are in love, and 47% in one study were "head over heels" in love (Whyte, 1990). This initial intensity of joy declines over time as we shall see, but there is still a lot of joy in marriage. This depends on the frequency and intensity of rewarding interaction. There is also a lot of conflict in marriage, though curiously the two states seem to be able to go along side by side.

What is the explanation for the intense joy produced by love? The intense experiences due to sex must be part of the reason. These may be part of a broader experience, of great intimacy, which in turn may be due to roots in earlier relations with parents, the forerunners of adult attachments and the desire for union (Hatfield and Rapson, 1996, page 40). In both cases there is experience of great joy from forms of bodily intimacy, which have a certain amount in common, such as interest in the mouth and breasts. And there is the remarkable finding, first made by Hazan and Shaver (1987), that the styles of attachment between adult lovers are similar to the ways in which they had related to their mothers.

There are some more cognitive processes too: being loved and admired enhances self-esteem, it also expands the self, as the other is felt to be part of it. Those in love form an idealised view of the other, and the other moves towards this image so that there is less self–ideal self conflict (Campbell et al., 1994; Murray and Holmes, 1997).

Happiness

Many studies have shown that the married are happier on average than the single, widowed, separated or divorced. The largest such study was Inglehart's (1990) analysis of Eurobarometer surveys, shown in Table 6.3. This study is notable for the very large sample, 163,000, covering all the European Union countries.

It can be seen that there are quite substantial differences in satisfaction with life between the different conditions. It is interesting that the married are on average happier than the cohabiting. Wood et al. (1989) in a meta-analysis of 93 such studies found that marriage gave more benefits for happiness and satisfaction to women. In the Inglehart study the widowed were happier than the separated or divorced—it has often been assumed that being widowed was the worst fate that can befall one, but evidently this is not so. The benefits of marriage for happiness are found in other cultures too: Stack and Eshleman

Table 6.3 Marital status and happiness (percentage saying they are satisfied or very satisfied)

	Men	Women
Married	79	81
Living as married	73	75
Single	74	75
Widowed	72	70
Divorced	65	66
Separated	67	57

Source: Inglehart (1990), Eurobarometer surveys.

Note n = 163,000.

(1998) found that in 17 industrialised countries the effect held in 16 of them, in 14 to much the same extent, that marriage had 3.4 times the effect of cohabiting, and that the effect was partly due to the financial satisfaction and perceived health benefits of marriage.

Some American studies have found a decline over time in the strength of the benefits of marriage for subjective well-being (Haring-Hidore et al., 1985). However, this may be because more of the "unmarried" are actually benefiting from this relationship, while more of the "married" have suffered from divorce, once or more. We shall see later that some European studies have found that the benefits of marriage in preventing depression have actually increased. And the effects of cohabiting depend a lot on cultural attitudes to this relationship.

The quality of marriage is important. Russell and Wells (1994) studied the predictors of happiness in 1207 English couples, and found that the strongest predictor was quality of marriage. Extraversion and neuroticism affected happiness via their effect on quality of marriage. Berry and Willingham (1997) found that happy people had better romantic and other close relations, because they used more positive non-verbal communication and dealt with conflict constructively—they had better social skills.

How does marriage make people so happy? Some of the factors giving positive affect to those in love apply in marriage, especially during the early years. Argyle and Furnham (1983) found three factors of satisfaction in relationships, and marriage scored highest on all three. Our first satisfaction factor was instrumental satisfaction: marriages are most happy when there is financial satisfaction and when the other does some housework (Noor, 1997). Second, there is emotional satisfaction: social support, intimacy and sex are all important predictors of happy marriage. There is an altruistic factor here, and the happiness and health of the other are also predictors of happiness with marriage (Stull, 1988). Third, there is companionship in joint leisure, much the same as with friends, though there is likely to be more of it.

Mental health

The married are on average in much better mental health than the different kinds of unmarried. Cochrane (1988) reports the mental hospital admissions in England for the married and others (Table 6.4). It can be seen that the divorced have 5½ times the admission rate of the married. Gove (1972) found much the same for American males, though the effect for females was weaker. But are these effects caused by marriage, or are the depressed and others less likely to get or stay married? Horwitz et al. (1996) carried out a quasi-experimental study of 829 men and women who were followed up for 7 years, starting when they were 25. Those who got married showed a decline in depression and alcoholism compared with the single. The effect was less for females, probably because women who were initially depressed were less likely to get married.

We said that the effect of marriage on happiness has been declining, in the USA at least. However in the Netherlands and in Scandinavia the benefits of marriage for avoiding depression and suicide, and for longevity, have been increasing during recent years (Mastekaasa, 1993).

Bereavement certainly has an effect on mental health: there is a sharp increase in depression and suicide, as well as loneliness. Depression is common and for some reaches clinical levels. After 2–4 years most have recovered, women more quickly than men. There is more effect for men, probably because they had fewer sources of social support other than their spouse. Depression is more common for those widowed when they were younger, and when the spouse's death was less expected. There is an increased level of psychiatric disturbance, but the main form this takes is depression for women and alcoholism for men. The effects are less if there are alternative sources of social support (Stroebe and Stroebe, 1987).

The benefits of marriage for mental health depend on the quality of the relationship. In a classic study Brown and Harris (1978) found that stressful life events led to depression in women if they did not have a spouse who acted as a confidant, "someone you can talk to about yourself and your problems". But as we saw earlier what seems to be an effect of intimacy may really be an effect of social support of other kinds such as help and companionship. Marital

Table 6.4 Mental hospital admissions and marital status (England, 1981)

Marital status	Mental hospital admissions per 100,000
Single	770
Married	260
Widowed	980
Divorced	1437

Source: Cochrane (1988).

satisfaction and (lack of) depression are closely linked, and there is causation in both directions, as found in longitudinal studies (Fincham et al., 1997).

Paykel et al. (1980) found that the quality of the husband relationship prevented depression during pregnancy, but tangible help had no effect. Umberson et al. (1996) in a large American longitudinal study found that stress, for example from having adolescent children, led to depression, especially for women, but this was buffered by social integration and support from spouses, which led to less depression and alcoholism.

Health

Being in love is good for health. Smith and Hoklund (1988) found that Danish students who were in love had a higher white blood cell count, and had fewer sore throats, colds or after-effects of drinking than those not in love. Table 6.5 shows the death rates for white male American adults for the different marital statuses. These are death rates per 100,000 over the period 1959–61. So 176 married males died compared with 362 divorced. Again the effects are stronger for men than for women.

Table 6.5 Marital status and mortality: Males

Cause of death	Death rates for white men			
	Married	Single	Widowed	Divorced
Coronary disease and other myocardial (heart) degeneraton	176	237	275	362
Motor vehicle accidents	35	54	142	128
Cancer of respiratory system	28	32	43	65
Cancer of digestive organs	27	38	39	48
Vascular lesions (stroke)	24	42	46	58
Suicide	17	32	92	73
Cancer of lymph glands and of blood-making tissues	12	13	11	16
Cirrhosis of liver	11	31	48	79
Rheumatic fever (heart)	10	14	21	19
Hypertensive heart disease	8	16	16	20
Pneumonia	6	31	25	44
Diabetes mellitus	6	13	12	17
Homicide	4	7	16	30
Chronic nephritis (kidney)	4	7	7	7
Accidental falls	4	12	11	23
Tuberculosis, all forms	3	17	18	30
Cancer of prostate gland	3	3	3	4
Accidental fire or explosion	2	6	18	16
Syphilis	1	2	2	4

Source: Carter and Glick (1970, p. 345).

What are the benefits from love and marriage which are lost by bereavement? Reis and Franks (1994) found that health was related to the closeness and other aspects of social support. A series of studies has established that social support, particularly emotional support, has powerful physiological effects. Ushino et al. (1996) carried out a meta-analysis of 81 studies and found three widely confirmed effects of social support: (1) on the cardiovascular system, so that stress has less effect on blood pressure, which explains the reduced risk of heart disease; (2) less effect of stress on the endocrine system, such as the production of epinephrine under stress, arousing the sympathetic nervous system, and producing various bodily stresses; (3) on the immune system. The strongest effects were from emotional support, and support in the family. Ushino et al. (1996, p. 521) observe that "although health-related behaviors, stressful events, and depression clearly influence physiological processes in their own right, they do not appear to be major pathways by which social support influences physiological function". These effects are greater for older people, and social support is even able to reduce biological ageing in these respects.

Bereavement led to marked health deterioration, in the short term, for 28% of cases in one study, and these short-term effects have been found to vanish if depression is controlled for, that is depression is the immediate cause of the illness. There is a sharp increase in mortality, especially for men and in the first 6 months after bereavement. Is this due to a "broken heart" as Lynch (1977) suggested? The most common cause of death in the widowed is indeed heart disease, and there is a large increase in the incidence of deaths from this cause in the first 6 months (Young et al., 1963), and there are also large increases in deaths from homicide, cirrhosis of the liver, suicide and accidents for men. The broken heart remains one of the main theories of bereavement, well describing the hopelessness, depression and loss of will to live (Stroebe and Stroebe, 1987).

Another way in which social support in marriage is good for health is that married people have better "health behaviour", such as smoking and drinking less, having a better diet, doing what the doctor orders, partly because they look after one another. Drinking less reduces the risk of cirrhosis of the liver, smoking less reduces the risk of lung cancer, and better diet, more exercise and less stress reduce the chance of heart attacks. These effects are quite independent of immune system activation (Umberson, 1987), and as we have just seen, Ushino et al. concluded they were a less important cause of ill-health.

Simply talking about things is good, and spouses do a lot of it. Pennebaker (1989) found that individuals who had experienced traumatic events, and then disclosed them, even to a tape recorder, made fewer visits to the doctor in the next 6 months. This also worked for those who had been widowed by the suicide or accidental death of their spouses.

FAMILY

Positive affect

There is a lot of joy in the family. Most parents give "stimulation and fun" as an advantage of children, even more mention "affection" (Hoffman and Manis, 1982). Children and their parents laugh a lot. Of course there is also negative affect in families, and a lot of the time there is neither positive or negative emotion. The early mother–child relation is particularly close, biologically, and in Freudian theory, where it is seen as a kind of primal bliss.

Happiness

The overall effect of having children on the happiness of their parents is zero (Veenhoven, 1994). However, the effect varies with the stage in the family life cycle. Marital satisfaction has been found to decline over time and then rise again, in American and British studies, as shown in Figure 6.2. Note that there are two bad periods for marital happiness—when there are very young children, and when they are adolescents. The time of the "empty nest" is a good time, provided there is good contact with those who have left the nest. In an Australian study, Feeney et al. (1994) found that this pattern only held for women, not for men.

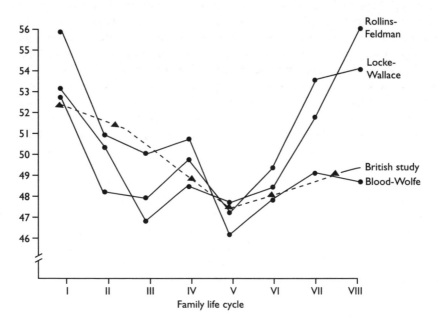

Figure 6.2 Mean scores on marital satisfaction by stage of family life cycle (Walker, 1977).

Children are a source of several benefits and Table 6.6 shows these. The author found that parents value most the affection, fun, help, and later economic help in emergencies from children. When there are benefits, it is the mother–daughter link that gives the greatest satisfaction. When they are attuned to each other there is a high level of happiness for both (Gavin and Furman, 1996). However, satisfaction with parenting and marital satisfaction both cause each other, and this is true for fathers as well as mothers (Rogers and White, 1998).

Love and intimacy in the family is to some extent a recent phenomenon. In England between 1400 and 1600 there was little domestic privacy, the emphasis was on survival, most children died young, were neglected and received harsh discipline. Women were subordinated to their husbands and there was no time for companionship (Stone, 1977). For working-class families things were little better up to the end of the nineteenth century.

Grown-up kin are not seen as often as friends, but they are a greater source of serious help, for example with money, accommodation, sickness, trouble with the law; this is especially the case with working-class families in Britain, probably because they tend to live near one another, and maintain more frequent contact than the geographically more mobile middle class (Willmott, 1987). This may be because of the "selfish gene" process of recognising one's own genes in kin because they look similar, and wanting to look after the welfare of those genes. It may be due to early bonding in childhood, and this is supported

Table 6.6 The value of children (percentage of sample)

	Women		Men	
	Parents	Non-parents	Parents	Non-parents
Advantages of children				
Primary group ties and affection	66	64	60	52
Stimulation and fun	61	41	55	35
Expansion of the self	36	34	32	32
Adult status and social identity	23	14	20	7
Achievement, competence, and creativity	11	14	9	21
Morality	7	6	6	2
Economic utility	5	8	8	10
Help expected from sons/daughters				
Give part of their salary when they begin working	28/28	18/18		
Contribute money in family emergencies	72/72	65/63		
Support you financially when you grow old	11/10	9/9		
Help around the house	86/92	88/91		

Source: Hoffman and Manis (1982).

by the finding that favourite cousins in later life are those who were childhood playmates (Adams, 1968). The relations between siblings is complex, and there can be strong positive feelings, as well as a lot of rivalry, over achievement and success (Ross and Milgram, 1982). Women are much more involved with kin, and it is the female–female bonds that hold kinship together, especially by the sister–sister and mother–daughter links. It is women who provide most social support in the home not only for children but also for their husbands (Vanfossen, 1981). This is the classic female role; how far it is genetic, and how far due to the way women are socialised is not known.

Children are happier when their parents get on well. When they do not, and even more if they split up, the children are likely to become delinquent, aggressive and disobedient, depressed and anxious, and enuretic (Emery, 1982).

Mental health

We saw in Figure 6.2 how children are a source of stress to their parents at two stages, when they are babies and when they are adolescents. Umberson (1997) found that having adolescent children was normally a source of stress to their mothers, which was partly offset by spouse support. On the other hand couples with children live longer, so it looks as if having children may be good for health (Kobrin and Hendershot, 1977). And when we come to look at the effects of overall social support on health and mental health, the effect is greatest for women who have children, husbands and jobs (Kandel et al., 1985). Lu (1997) studied 191 adults in Taiwan. She found that perceived reciprocity in the family was related to lower levels of negative affect, with other variables held constant. Fathers are more depressed when divorced, particularly when they are separated from their children (Shapiro and Lambert, 1999).

Recent studies have found that the divorce and separation of parents are less traumatic to children now. Morrison and Cherlin (1995) followed up 1123 children over a 2-year period. They found no effect of marital dissolution for girls, and the effects for boys were partly due to economic difficulties and downward social mobility. This was an American study, and recent British research has found the usual effects of divorce for girls.

Pets are part of the family in a way. Controlled studies of those with and without pets find that those with pets have a lower level of anxiety, though not of depression, and are less at risk for heart disease, e.g. lower cholesterol and blood pressure. This is partly due to the exercise of taking dogs for a walk but there may be an intimacy effect too (Garrity and Stallones, 1998). The benefits for health are striking: Headey (1999) in an Australian survey found that only 11% of those who had dogs were on some medication compared with 19% of those with no pets; the pet owners went to the doctor less too.

THE GENERAL EFFECTS OF RELATIONSHIPS

In this section we will look at the common effects of different relationships, and also see which ones are most important, and why they are.

Positive affect

We have seen that in studies of students and other young people, joy is most commonly due to being in love, or to spending time with friends. For a different age group there is a lot of joy from interaction with children, for both parents and children. The setting for all this joy seems to be situations of play or leisure, and where pursuing and enjoying the relationship is the main activity. The explanation is partly the enjoyable nature of these leisure activities, but also the exchange of non-verbal signals, which we recognise and respond to positively without need to learn to do so. It also seems likely that the experience of closely synchronised and coordinated interaction, which is experienced as intimacy, is very rewarding. Mothers and babies do it, so do lovers, and in both cases there is bodily closeness too. Experiments have been done in which a stooge increases the level of bodily synchrony, and this has been found to increase both positive mood and attraction. At a more cognitive level, it is nice to be loved, self-esteem is enhanced.

Happiness

Argyle and Furnham (1983) studied the sources of satisfaction in different relationships, and found three clear factors—instrumental help, emotional support and companionship, as shown in Figure 6.3. It can be seen that the spouse was reported to be the greatest source of satisfaction for the first two factors, but was only just ahead of friends on companionship. Work relations and neighbours were said to be very weak as sources of satisfaction. These three factors offer an explanation of why relationships are sources of satisfaction, why they make people happy.

These benefits could be explained in terms of the satisfaction of social needs. McClelland (1987) assessed need for affiliation by means of a projection test, and found that those strong in this need had higher levels of dopamine, a neurotransmitter that we have seen is central to the reward system in the brian. They also have a more active immune system, and they spend time with friends, join clubs, avoid competition and conflict. Another social need is for intimacy, and those strong in this are found to be cooperative and loving, high in self-disclosure, sensitive to faces (McAdams, 1988). A strong correlation, .6 to .7, has been found between the satisfaction of such needs and life satisfaction (Prager and Buhrmester, 1998). Another way of looking at relationships is to see them as "resources", like money and good looks, properties which can help us to achieve our goals, and which must be conserved (Hobfoll, 1989).

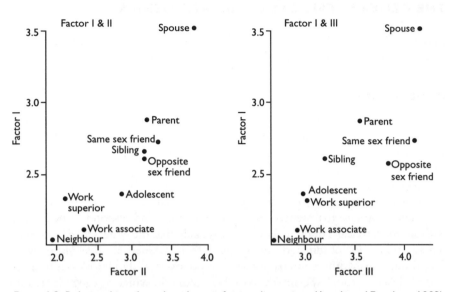

Figure 6.3 Relationships plotted on the satisfaction dimensions (Argyle and Furnham, 1983).

The importance of different relationships varies with stage in life. For young children parents are the most important, then friends, then there is love and marriage. Later in life friends become important again. For students friends of both sexes are the main source of social support and happiness (Cooper et al., 1992). The causes of happiness at different stages of adult life were studied by Lu and Lin (1998) in Taiwan. For newly-weds the marital relationship was the most important; at later stages the worker and filial (parental) roles became more important. At each stage women are important, as mothers, as rewarding and intimate friends and as wives. Hall and Nelson (1996) found that the well-being of a sample of patients depended on the percentage of women in their networks, providing social support.

There is a negative side to relationships; Argyle and Furnham (1983) found that the spouse was the greatest source of conflict as well as of satisfaction. However, the clear overall benefits of marriage for happiness (as well as health) show that the satisfaction outweighs the conflict for most. This does not work for all, since so many break up.

Mental health

How do relationships produce better mental health? There seem to be several processes. Material help doesn't have much effect, though fall in income is a factor for divorced women and their children. Social support is much more important, but what exactly is it? It can be defined as "the perception that one feels cared for, esteemed or otherwise closely involved with other people"

(Reis, 1984, p. 29), or it can be looked at in terms of social integration into a social network. Both explanations have been confirmed, and Henderson et al. (1980) found that the effect of stress on health was reduced more for women by affectional bonds, and for men by social integration. We saw that there are two kinds of loneliness, a major source of depression. People need a close attachment and also a network of friends.

Many studies have found a "buffering" effect of social support, that is it helps people when they are under stress. This can work by the provision of tangible help, and this can make them feel they can cope with their problems, and by restoring self-esteem. It can produce a more positive mood through enjoyable companionship. There can also be help through social integration or attachment, and Williams et al. (1981) found that the total set of attachments and ties is associated with better mental health, at all stress levels. Those who have a concern for other people and concerns that go beyond the self are less affected by stress; they make more active attempts to cope with their problems (Crandall, 1984). We described similar effects of the benefits of concern for others when discussing happiness due to friends.

Health

Social relations have a powerful effect on health and mortality. Berkman and Syme (1979) followed up 7000 individuals in California for 9 years. The strength of their supportive social networks, from various sources, had been assessed: this predicted mortality, so for example for men originally in their 50s 30.8% of those with the weak networks had died, compared with only 9.6% of those with the strong networks (Figure 6.4). There have been many replications of this study. A meta-analysis of 55 of them by Schwarzer and Leppin (1989) found that the effect of social support on health was greatest:

- for women
- for those supported by family and friends
- for those with emotional support
- for those under stress.

It has been found that such support affects cancer, arthritis, complications during pregnancy, and as we saw earlier heart attacks. How do social relations affect health? We saw earlier how close relations lead to better health behaviour, partly due to family members looking after one another. We also saw how close relationships produce activation of the cardiovascular, endocrine and immune systems. This particularly applies to the effects of marriage, but merely being in a good mood energises the immune system (Stone et al., 1987).

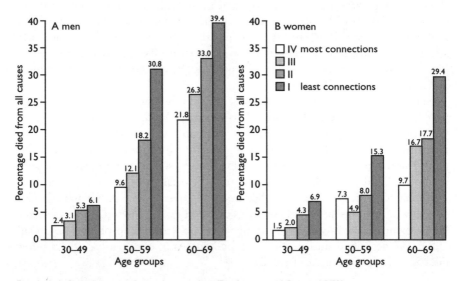

Figure 6.4 Social networks and mortality (Berkman and Syme, 1979).

CONCLUSIONS

Social relations affect all aspects of well-being. Friendship produces strong positive moods, happiness, health and mental health, and prevents loneliness. Falling in love leads to great joy and self-esteem. Marriage has strong effects on happiness, health and mental health, but bereavement is very distressing. Family life is a source of happiness, but stressful at certain periods.

The general explanation of these effects is that positive affect is caused by companionship in pleasant activities, and the exchange of positive non-verbal signals, mental health by close relationships buffering stress, and health by the emotional activation of biological systems and by better health behaviour. Extraverts and those with good social skills benefit most from social relationships. Social support is central to some of these effects, but it can incur costs for both giver and receiver, and it should take the form of emotional support, companionship or problem-solving rather than ruminating.

Chapter 7

Work and employment

JOB SATISFACTION

Extent and measurement

Most men in the modern world work, if they can get jobs, and so do an increasing proportion of women. In Britain 70% of women do paid work, making up 48% of the labour force; in Europe and the USA rather fewer women work (Warr, 1999). So work is an important part of life; how much do people enjoy it? First, how do we measure job satisfaction?

Many studies have done this by using a single question, such as Hoppock's famous one (1935) "Choose one of the following statements which best tells us how well you like your job." There were seven alternatives from "I hate it" to "I love it". There are longer and more elaborate measures, but Wanous et al. (1997) carried out a meta-analysis of how these compare and found an average correlation of .63 between single-item measures and the longer scales. We shall see in Chapter 12 that single-item measures have not worked well for international comparisons.

In a survey of 7000 workers from nine European countries, Clark (1998a) found that 42% reported having "high job satisfaction". On the other hand 37% thought that their incomes were low and that they also had poor jobs, in terms of being boring, not interesting, not helpful to society etc. I will refer to this extensive survey again in this chapter.

In the *Inner American* study of 2264 participants Veroff et al. (1981) offered several alternative responses to the question "Taking into consideration all things about your job, how satisfied or dissatisfied are you with it?", and found the following distribution of replies:

	Males	Females
Very satisfied	27	29
Satisfied	47	42
Neutral	5	4
Ambivalent (like some aspects of it, dislike others)	12	14
Dissatisfied	1	1

Another way of getting at the extent of job satisfaction is to ask people if they would work if this were financially unnecessary. The replies in Britain are shown in Table 7.1.

It looks as if 30–40% really like their jobs, a similar group is satisfied but less enthusiastic and would like to change jobs and 25–30% don't really enjoy their work. People can be asked if they would do the same job again; this shows which jobs give high satisfaction and which do not.

For serious research, psychologists prefer more than one item in order to sample different areas of job satisfaction. There are several longer scales, of which the most widely used is the Job Descriptive Index devised by Smith et al. (1969). This scale has 72 items that assess satisfaction in the following areas:

- the work itself
- pay
- opportunities for promotion
- quality of supervision on present job
- relations with co-workers.

For each of the items respondents are asked to choose which of three words or phrases best describes their feelings, for example "Work on present job"— "Routine, Satisfying or Good". The first sub-scale is about satisfaction with the actual work, sometimes known as "intrinsic" job satisfaction; two are about pay and promotion, two aspects of "extrinsic "satisfaction; and two are about the social aspects of work, that is supervisors and co-workers.

Is job satisfaction a cause of life satisfaction?

Since the majority of people work for 7–8 hours or more a day, it is very likely that satisfaction with work and with life as a whole will be related. Indeed they are, with an average correlation of .44 according to a meta-analysis by Tait et al. (1989). The strength of this correlation varies, is greater for men, older workers, those more involved in their work, with higher incomes, more education and self-employed (Warr, 1999). These are all people for whom work is important.

Table 7.1 People who would work if it were financially unnecessary

	Men	Women
	%	%
Would work, stay in present job	31	34
Would work, try to change job	35	29
Would stop work, might work later	10	12
Would never work	15	18
Don't know	9	7

Source: Warr (1982).

If there is a relation between job satisfaction and satisfaction in general or in other areas, which causes which? Longitudinal studies, using statistical modelling, have found that job satisfaction and life satisfaction both influence each other, but that the stronger effect is from life satisfaction to job satisfaction rather than vice versa (Headey and Wearing, 1992; Judge and Watanabe, 1993).

One theory about the relation between satisfaction with work and with other areas of life is the "spillover hypothesis". And it has sometimes been found that satisfaction with family affects job satisfaction and vice versa. The spillover theory does better than the other alternatives, for example that there is no relation between the two or that there is compensation, predicting that family life would be better when job satisfaction is low. Another possibility is that work and non-work have much in common, such as friendship, status and personality, so that both are closely linked to satisfaction with life as a whole (Near et al., 1980). This is the top-down part of the relation, but there is also a bottom–up bit, in which satisfaction with work has some effect on overall satisfaction.

The causes of job satisfaction

Pay

The effect of pay on job satisfaction reflects the wider issue of the effect of income on happiness, which will be discussed in Chapter 9. The overall correlation between pay and job satisfaction is low, typically .15 to .17, so pay is not an important cause of job satisfaction. For European workers pay is a much weaker predictor of job satisfaction than good relationships at work and job content (Clark, 1998a). However, members of working organisations often compare their pay with that of other members, and are very pleased if they earn more than they think others are getting. They are very concerned about fairness, that is being paid less than similar workers. In one American study it was found that supervisors earning over $12,000 were more satisfied than company presidents earning under $49,000 (Lawler and Porter, 1963). We shall see in the Chapter 9 that pay satisfaction and job satisfaction are low for workers who are paid less than similar workers, or who think that their wages are not fair (see page 141).

Money is quite a minor factor in occupational choice, which depends much more on abilities, interests and values. And there are some who do not need to work for money, such as those doing voluntary work. These individuals are sometimes found to enjoy their work as much or more than paid workers (Furnham and Argyle, 1998).

Although pay is quite a minor factor in job satisfaction and occupational choice, it is widely believed to be very important; workers, trades unions, governments and politicians think about it a lot. It looks as if they are mistaken in exaggerating the importance of levels of pay. However, differences of pay, and changes in pay, are very important matters.

Nature of the job

There are large differences between jobs in how much people enjoy them. One index is the number who say they would do the same job again. Blauner (1960) found that this varied from 91% for mathematicians to 16% for unskilled steel workers (see Table 7.2).

What exactly is it about different jobs which makes them so desirable or undesirable? An obvious feature is job status, and this includes a number of factors, such as pay, conditions of work and the actual skills used. A meta-analysis of job status however found a rather modest overall correlation of .18 with job satisfaction (Haring et al., 1984). Noor (1995) found that job overload led to less happiness and more stress, for secretaries but not for professional women; job status buffered this source of stress.

Hackman and Oldham (1976) thought it depended on the experienced meaningfulness of the task, which was measured by the combination of skill variety, task identity and task significance, combined with autonomy and feedback, especially for workers with high "growth need strength", that is the desire for challenging and interesting work. Two hundred studies have found that job satisfaction does correlate with these job characteristics (each at about $r = .30$)—if these are rated by the same workers, especially if they are high on growth need strength. However, the relation is much weaker if someone else rates the job characteristics, and objective manipulations of these characteristics have rather modest effects too (Spector, 1997).

Another well-known theory about jobs is Karasek's (1979) model that satisfaction depends on the combination of job demands and control. Job satisfaction was predicted to be lowest with high demand and low control. Van der Doef and Maes (1999) report a meta-analysis of 63 studies of this issue. They concluded that the combination of high demands and low control is associated as predicted with low job satisfaction, low subjective well-being and distress. However, control acted as a buffer to reduce the effects of demands only in some studies, and not in longitudinal ones, and not for women. High social

Table 7.2 Percentage of workers who would choose the same work again

Mathematicians	91
Lawyers	83
Journalists	82
Skilled printers	52
Skilled car workers	41
Skilled steel workers	41
Textile workers	31
Unskilled car workers	21
Unskilled steel workers	16

Source: Blauner (1960).

support was correlated with reduced strain, but again not in most longitudinal studies.

Warr (1999) listed ten features of jobs which he believes produce well-being, including those mentioned above. The distinctive part of his theory is that some of the relationships with well-being are thought to be curvilinear. Some are like vitamins C and E, which increase health up to a point, after which further amounts do no good: pay and physical conditions of work may be like this. Others are like vitamins A and D, where there is an optimum dose and too much of them is bad for us: it is believed that six job features are like this—opportunity for control, skill use, job demands, variety, environmental clarity and opportunities for interpersonal contact. De Jonge and Schaufeli (1998) have found support for some of these patterns of influence on well-being.

These variables go some way to explaining why people objected so much to early assembly-line and mass production methods. There was little personal control, or skill variety. In addition the work was very monotonous, with repetition of very short work units, 3 seconds in some cases (Argyle, 1989). Other industrial work is physically stressful in several ways. Miners, steel workers, those on oil-rigs, divers and others do work that is dangerous, dirty, noisy, hot, physically demanding, or unhealthy. These affect all aspects of well-being. Many of these boring or dangerous jobs have disappeared and are done by machines; the nature of work is changing fast.

Gallie et al. (1998) studied changes in the nature of work in Britain, and concluded that there had been a considerable increase in skills used, at all levels, connected to more use of advanced technology, and a lot more workers needed social skills. Jobs had also become more insecure, especially for men. Many workers are temporary, 25% in the USA, and this is growing rapidly. Their job satisfaction is considerably less than that of permanent employees, or of those who are doing temporary work voluntarily (Krause et al., 1995).

New technology can have negative effects on job satisfaction. Korunka et al. (1995) found that the introduction of computers led to reduced job satisfaction for those at lower levels of skill who now did boring work, but more satisfaction for those at higher levels, especially if they had participated in the change.

Many office workers have been moved from local branches of organisations such as banks into "call centres", where they look at computer screens. This is made possible by computerisation, saves money but creates work that is boring, has little autonomy and much reduced social contacts (Gallie et al., 1998).

Social aspects of work

For European workers, having "good relations" at work, with management and colleagues, was the strongest predictor of job satisfaction; these relations were reported to be good by 69% of them.

Workers on assembly lines or in very noisy factories can scarcely speak to each other, while members of small teams who can, such as the crews of ships or planes, form close groups. Job satisfaction is greater when workers belong to cohesive groups, produced for example by cooperation and close proximity. Job satisfaction is much greater for those who are popular ($r = .82$ in one study), when the working group is small, and when there are opportunities to interact. We have found that there are often a great deal of games, jokes and gossip between friends at work. Table 7.3 shows that activities which were engaged in more often by closer work-mates.

A number of studies have found that this sort of thing leads to increased job satisfaction, and also to more cooperation, mutual help and productivity as well. Positive effects on job satisfaction and productivity have been found when workers engaged in time-wasting jokes and games. This may be encouraged by the sociotechnical system, if it creates cooperation in small groups of workers (Argyle, 1989). Well-being is greater for those who work in teams, especially when levels of cooperation are high, and in autonomous work-groups that can arrange their own work (West, et al., 1998). We shall see later that social support from such groups relieves work stress. Too much social support may be unnecessary, and the effect on job satisfaction levels is curvilinear.

Herzberg et al. (1959) found that supervisors are often a source of dissatisfaction, and we found that there is more conflict in this relationship than in most others (Argyle and Furnham, 1983). Supervisors may demand more work, or be seen as unfair, and they enjoy better pay, status and conditions of work. On the

Table 7.3 Social interaction with four kinds of workmates

Activities	Rating in which highest percentage of each work category accrues*			
	Person A	Person B	Person C	Person D
1. Helping each other with work	4.5	3	2	1
2. Discussing work	5	4	2	1
3. Chatting casually	5	4	3	1
4. Having an argument or disagreement	1	1	1	1
5. Teaching or showing the other person something about work	2	2	1	1
6. Joking with the other person	5	4	2	1
7. Teasing him/her	5	3	2	1
8. Discussing your personal life	4.5	1	1	1
9. Discussing your feelings or emotions	2	1	1	1
10. Asking or giving personal advice	4.5	1	1	1
11. Having coffee, drinks, or meals together	5	3	3	1
12. Committee work, or similar discussion at work	1	1	1	1

Source: Argyle and Henderson (1985).

* Note: 1 = never or very rarely, 5 = nearly all the time, 4.5 = collapsed rating of 4 + 5.

other hand they can also provide great benefits. They have the power to solve problems at work, they can provide rewards, praise and a pleasant social atmosphere, and can relieve the effects of work stress. One of the main dimensions of supervisory skills is "consideration", and this is a powerful source of job satisfaction for workers (Fleishman and Harris, 1962).

Conflict between roles

Role-conflict occurs when an individual is under different pressures from others. For example there may be different demands from subordinates and work superiors, from other sales staff and customers, or from patients and research colleagues in the case of doctors. Role ambiguity is where it is unclear what the role requires. A meta-analysis of 200 studies found that job satisfaction was less when there was role conflict ($r = -.30$) or ambiguity ($r = -.31$) (Jackson and Schuler, 1985). We do not know whether this effect is causal, but it seems likely.

Another kind of role-conflict is between the demands of work and of family. A meta-analysis found that overall there was a correlation of $-.27$ with job satisfaction; this was greatest for those in dual-career families, and was somewhat greater for women—the conflict between work and family (Kossek and Ozeki, 1998). Haw (1995) found that there was most distress for young women, with children, who were working over 25 hours a week.

Individual differences in job satisfaction

Age

It has often been found that job satisfaction increases with age. It has recently been found that there is a U-shaped pattern here, as younger workers are also satisfied; with 80 variables controlled, the age of lowest satisfaction was 36 (Clark et al., 1996). The reason for the age increase is partly that older workers have better jobs, are paid more, have more intrinsic rewards, and have more employment commitment. They may also expect less, or have become more adjusted to their work situation (Birdi et al., 1995).

Gender

Many American studies have found no difference in job satisfaction between men and women. However, a large-scale British study found that women were more satisfied than men (Clark, 1996). It would be expected that male workers would have greater job satisfaction since on average they have better jobs than women, with more pay and higher occupational status. The explanation may also be that women have different expectations of work, for example may accept being paid less. They may be satisfied by different aspects of work; Mottaz

(1986) found that personal control was more important for men but support from supervisors was more important for women.

Personality

Staw and Ross (1985) found that when people changed jobs their job satisfaction changed little. Arvey et al. (1994) studied 2200 pairs of twins and found that 30% of the variability in job satisfaction could be explained by genetic factors. We shall see that positive affect in general is related to extraversion and negative affect to neuroticism (Chapter 10); job satisfaction is less for those scoring high on neuroticism or psychoticism, especially for stressful jobs. Level of extraversion needs to fit the nature of the job (Furnham, 1997).

We have seen that personal control is a desirable feature of jobs. Individuals who are high in internal control as a personality trait have higher job satisfaction, and the relation is stronger for the Work Locus of Control Scale devised by Spector (1997). The effect of negative affect (NA) on job satisfaction has been found to be mediated by the effect of NA on control (Moyle, 1995). We saw earlier that "growth need strength" affected whether people found challenging jobs satisfying (Loher et al., 1985). This can be looked as a matter of fit between job and person. Furnham and Schaeffer (1984) found there was more satisfaction if an individual's profile of needs matched the profile of rewards offered by the job. Another example is that people will enjoy their job more if their abilities match those needed, and if their need for sociability matches that available.

The effects of job satisfaction

Performance

Do happy workers work harder? It was widely assumed that they would, and many have investigated this. However, a meta-analysis of 217 studies found an average correlation of only .17 (Iaffaldano and Muchinsky, 1985). It is possible this is an underestimate since the measures of performance often have reduced range and there may be rater biases (Spector, 1997). Some studies have found a stronger correlation for workers at higher levels of skill such as managers and professionals ($r = .31$, versus .15 for others (Petty et al., 1984). There is some evidence of a stronger relation if the unit of comparison is an organisational unit, since the effects of job satisfaction on citizenship behaviour will be shown (Cheung, 1997). And if there is a correlation, which is the direction of causation? One direction that has been found is from performance to satisfaction, as a result of the rewards received for good performance.

"Organisational Citizenship Behaviour" (OCB)

Perhaps job satisfaction has another effect, on how helpful and useful people make themselves at work. This can be divided into "altruism", that is helping other people and making suggestions, and "compliance", doing what is required without having to be monitored, like being punctual and not wasting time. Studies of job satisfaction have found much the same correlation with both aspects of OCB as with measures of performance, i.e. .25 (Spector, 1997). As for direction of causation—it goes both ways, it is reciprocal (Bateman and Organ, 1983).

Absenteeism

Many studies have been done, and have found small correlations with job satisfaction, for example Scott and Taylor (1985) report a meta-analysis of 114 such studies with an average correlation of only −.15. This weak relationship may be partly because absenteeism is very skewed—it is mainly due to a small minority, and because there are other causes more important than job satisfaction such as child care. When someone is "absent" it is because they are "present" somewhere more important to them. Rate of absence also depends very much on the norms, the extent to which group or organisation accept it (Spector, 1997).

Labour turnover

Job satisfaction affects whether workers will leave, as has been shown in predictive studies, where job satisfaction is found to predict quitting or intention to quit by a year later. The average correlation with turnover is about .33, but is greater when there is low unemployment (.51) and there are plenty of other jobs, than when unemployment is high (.23) (Carsten and Spector, 1987). The causal chain is from low job satisfaction to forming the intention to quit, with a search for other jobs, and finally leaving. Job satisfaction is as strong as wages as a predictor of workers leaving.

THE EFFECT OF WORK ON DISTRESS AND MENTAL HEALTH

Overall, work is good for mental health, which is improved when people start work and gets worse when they stop. Murphy and Athanasou (1999) reanalysed 16 longitudinal studies and found that the overall effect size for mental health, assessed by the GHQ or similar measures, was .54 for starting work and .36 for stopping it. But for some individuals work is stressful, and it can be a source of mental ill-health. A measure that has commonly been used is the General

Health Questionnaire, the GHQ (Goldberg, 1978), which was described earlier (see page 16). Different aspects of work affect different parts of it: for example paced work affects anxiety but not depression. Stress at work can also cause physical ill-health, and this will be discussed later.

It has often been found that job satisfaction correlates with and is predictive of scores on the GHQ and similar measures (e.g. French et al., 1982). Jobs differ greatly in their stressfulness. Cooper (1985) obtained ratings of stressfulness from 1 to 10 of a number of jobs in Britain, with the results shown in Table 7.4.

Many studies have investigated the features of jobs that make them stressful. Some of the main ones are as follows.

- *Level of skill.* Kornhauser (1965) found that among car workers 65% of white-collar workers had good mental health, compared with 18% of those doing repetitive and semi-skilled work. Many other studies have found the same.
- *Job overload.* Manual workers doing paced work on assembly lines, professionals with deadlines or too many visitors and demands on their time, are under greater stress and their mental health suffers. Haw (1995) found that British female factory workers were under stress when they had preschool children and worked more than 25 hours a week; when they had school-age children work had positive effects. Hours of work in Britain have been falling continuously since 1800, but they started a sudden upturn in 1980, either as a result of anxiety about losing jobs or the desire to make more money (Gershuny, 1992). Recent British and European surveys have found evidence of "work intensification" during the 1990s, in the form of fewer work breaks, understaffing, or pressure to work fast or to tight deadlines a lot of the time. This leads to higher GHQ scores, and to headaches and heart problems (Burchell, 2000).
- *Repetitive work.* This is a source of stress as well as of low job satisfaction, because of boredom, lack of autonomy, little use of skills, and difficulty of social interaction.

Table 7.4 Survey of occupations rated on a nine-point scale for stressfulness (Cooper, 1985, Feb 24).

	High		Low
Miner	8.3	Museum worker	2.8
Police	7.7	Nursery nurse	3.3
Construction worker	7.5	Astronomer	3.4
Journalist	7.5	Vicar	3.5
Pilot (civil)	7.5	Beauty therapist	3.5
Advertising	7.3	Librarian	2.0
Dentist	7.2		
Actor	7.2		
Politician	7.0		
Doctor	6.8		

- *Danger.* Those in the armed forces, police, mining, and test pilots are certainly exposed to danger, but often say they like the work and find the most difficult part of it is the administrative side (Kasl, 1978).
- *Environmental stress.* Heat and dust, noise and pollution, shiftwork and loss of sleep, and other aspects of the physical side of work are all sources of stress.
- *Role conflict.* This is a source of anxiety, depression and irritation, as well as of reduced job satisfaction (Caplan et al., 1975), as described above.

Personality and stress

Work is more stressful for those whose talents or personality do not match their job. Figure 7.1 shows how work can be a source of depression if it is too difficult or too easy.

Social support at work

Social support from co-workers or supervisors can do a lot to relieve work stress, and more than support from friends or family outside. This was shown in a study of factory workers by House (1981) (Figure 7.2). We found that feelings of job stress were less for those who had at least one friend at work. What such friends did for them was provide tangible help, informational help, integration into a social group, acceptance and confidence, and be a confidant (Henderson

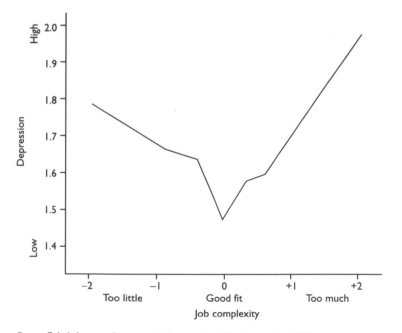

Figure 7.1 Job complexity and depression (Caplan et al., 1975).

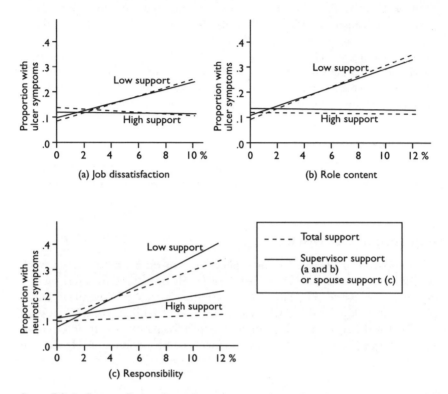

Figure 7.2 Buffering effects of social support on relationships between stress and health among factory workers (House, 1981).

and Argyle, 1985). Dormann and Zapf (1999) found that supervisor support had more effect than co-worker support in reducing the effect of stress on depression, but only in the long term, 8 months here.

Burn out

This is a special form of stress experienced particularly by medical and social workers, who have had long exposure to disgusting, aggressive, abusive, or otherwise unrewarding clients. Burn out leads to emotional exhaustion and feeling callous towards clients. Those in this condition may withdraw from contact with the clients and seek more social support from colleagues. These occupations also have high rates of suicide and alcoholism (Maslach and Jackson, 1982).

Reducing work stress

This can be done by changing the people, changing the jobs or matching workers to jobs better. Follow-up studies of stress management training courses show they have sometimes been found to increase job satisfaction, but there are clearer effects on absenteeism, turnover and visits to the clinic (Murphy, 1994). Some American companies have introduced fitness programmes, and these have been found to reduce anxiety, depression and other measures of stress, as well as less absenteeism and labour turnover (Falkenburg, 1987; Melhuish, 1981). A few follow-up studies have been made of redesigning jobs, usually by increasing control and autonomy, and participation in decision making, as in some Swedish car factories. This has been found to reduce distress (Murphy, 1994). Selection procedures can be improved to match individuals better to jobs. Social support can be increased by including it in supervisor training and keeping work groups intact.

EFFECT OF WORK ON HEALTH

The health of those at work is better than the health of those not at work. Ross and Mirowsky (1995) followed up 2500 individuals for a year, and found that those in full-time work showed almost no decline in health, whereas all the other groups did, including housewives. Being paid explained some of this, but full-time college (unpaid) was as good as work. There was some reverse causation, in that for women poor health made them less likely to be employed.

Job satisfaction correlates with health, for example fewer psychosomatic symptoms such as headaches and upset stomachs, and also with fewer illnesses such as heart attacks and arthritis and a shorter length of life. Sales and House (1971) found a correlation of −.83 with heart attacks, and in the next section we shall see the massive effects of unemployment on health.

There are large differences in health between different jobs. One of the main source of difference is job status. Marmot et al. (1978) found that those in the lowest grades of the British Civil Service had 3½ times the rate of fatal heart attacks as those in the top administrative grade (Figure 7.3). This was partly due to differences in health behaviour such as smoking, obesity and physical inactivity. Further factors may be the high level of constraint in low-skilled jobs: less "control", less "autonomy" and the low level of support in some (Fletcher, 1988). We have seen that there are some stressful professional jobs too, such as that of doctors. Cholesterol and blood pressure levels have been found to increase in air traffic controllers at busy times, and similarly in accountants and managers. Responsibility for others has been found to have the same effect (French and Caplan, 1970). Another job factor that affects the health of manual workers is dust (in coal miners), noise (in weaving sheds), and other sources of environmental stress and pollution.

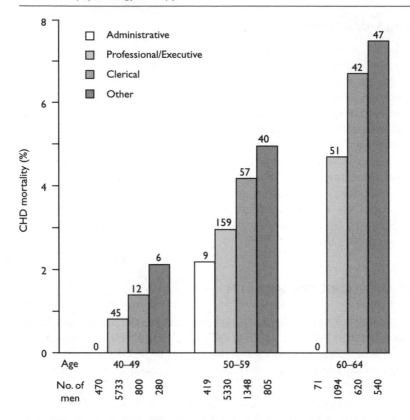

Figure 7.3 Coronary heart disease mortality (and number of deaths) in seven and a half
    years by civil service grade and age (Marmot et al., 1978).

Social support may reduce the level of stress experienced, or it may activate
the immune system. Wickrama et al. (1997) found that health was better for
those workers in high quality jobs, and this includes the features we have been
discussing, occupational status, social integration, autonomy, use of skills and
low demands.

Personality

This affects health at work. Type A personalities are interesting, because they
work hard and are very ambitious. However, their high level of arousal, and the
stresses they create for themselves, lead to high cholesterol levels and blood
pressure, and they have over twice as many heart attacks as the more relaxed type
Bs. Later research has found that the particular feature of Type As that has these
effects is their hostility (Matthews, 1988).

Another aspect of personality which affects health is "hardiness", the term given to those who are not made ill by stress. Several aspects of personality have been found to contribute to hardiness. One is internal control, with the belief that health can be controlled. Another is happiness and the associated properties of optimism, assertiveness and self-confidence. This may be due to optimism making stressful events seem controllable or unimportant, or to the effect of mood on the immune system (Salovey et al., 1991).

Occupational health can be improved in a number of ways. The physical conditions of work are under constant scrutiny in Britain by the Health and Safety Executive, but this only covers one area of health causation. Job satisfaction affects health as well as mental health, as does social support.

THE EFFECTS OF UNEMPLOYMENT

This is an important topic since unemployment and the fear of losing jobs is one of the greatest sources of unhappiness in the modern world. The level of unemployment in Europe has been between 6% and 9% during the last decade; in Britain it reached a peak of 13.1% in 1986, and is still high in some areas, though overall it is 4.2% (in 2000). Many social scientists think that the long-term outlook is not good, as the nature of work is changing fast with the introduction of more computers and other machines. This topic is very interesting for the study of happiness since research here can tell us what it is about work that people enjoy or need and are upset about when they lose it.

Effect on happiness

One of the main effects of unemployment is that most of those who lose their jobs become less happy. American surveys have found that 10–12% of the unemployed described themselves as "very happy" compared with 30% of the general population. This effect is causal as shown by the effects on workers when their works closed and they did not find other jobs (Warr, 1978). Unemployment affects every aspect of happiness, including positive affect, life satisfaction, and negative affect. The unemployed feel bored, have low self-esteem, are sometimes angry, sometimes apathetic. Self-esteem is lower both for unemployed young people and for people who don't want to work, more for those who have been out of work for some time (Goldsmith et al., 1997). There is more psychological distress for those who had rewarding, complex jobs (Reynolds, 1997).

A recent analysis of British data found that the leisure of the unemployed was different from that of others in that there was less membership of leisure groups, less sport, less sociability and hence less social support. There was a lot more passive leisure (TV, radio, sitting around), nearly 5 hours a day for unemployed men compared with 2½ for those with full-time jobs (Gershuny, 1994). A study of 150 unemployed in Belfast found that they did a lot of domestic jobs, and structured their time like housewives; however, they had little social life, sport or other active leisure (Trew and Kilpatrick, 1984).

Mental health

The unemployed have often been found to be more depressed, anxious, or to show other signs of poor mental health. But is this because of unemployment or are they unemployed because they were mentally disturbed? A number of studies have been designed to investigate this issue, such as the one by Banks and Jackson (1982), who studied 2000 school leavers in Leeds. As Table 7.5 shows the GHQ scores of those who got jobs declined, that is their mental health improved, while the mental health of the unemployed became worse during the next 2 years. However, there was also evidence of reverse causation, in that those who did not find jobs had higher GHQ scores in the first place.

Particular aspects of mental health are affected. Depression is higher on average, 11 on the Beck Depression Inventory for unemployed Australians versus 5.5 for those at work (Feather, 1982). Clark et al. (1996) conclude that the effect of job loss on general mental health as measured by the GHQ is worse than that of divorce. The total level of alcohol consumed is no greater but there are more "heavy drinkers" among the unemployed, i.e. those who drink seven or more glasses once a week or more (44% versus 28%). Suicide has sometimes been found to be higher; there are eight times more suicide attempts than average in Edinburgh (Platt, 1986), but this has not always been found.

The study shown in Table 7.5 illustrates that work is actually good for mental health. Murphy and Athanasou (1999) carried out a meta-analysis and found that starting work led to increased mental health with an effect size of .54, while losing a job led to deterioration with an effect size of .36.

Table 7.5 The effects of unemployment on the GHQ (Banks and Jackson, 1982)

	Before leaving school	6–15 months after leaving school	16–23 months after leaving school
Unemployed	11.4	13.6	
	11.2		13.4
Employed	10.6	8.4	
	10.5		7.7

Health

The unemployed are on average in worse physical health. This is partly because some gave up work because of ill-health, such as work-induced heart and lung diseases. Warr (1984) studied 954 British unemployed and found that 27% said their health had become worse since giving up work but 11% said it was better—because of less stress, more relaxation and exercise. The mortality rate was 36% higher in Britain in the 10 years after 1971 (Moser et al., 1984), and there are long-term effects of unemployment by age 33 (Wadsworth et al., 1999). There are several reasons for this poor health—poverty and its effect on diet, heating, etc., poor health behaviour, such as more drinking and smoking, and increased stress, affecting the immune system and increasing heart disease.

When is unemployment distressing?

Money

This factor certainly makes a difference. The unemployed are happier if they are in a good financial situation, as is the case in Holland and Sweden for example (Winefield, 1995). Even in these countries however there are still negative effects of job loss. In Britain it has been found that income explains less than a quarter of the reduction of GHQ scores for the unemployed (Clark, 1998b). On the other hand Gallie and Russell (1998) found that unemployment led to more distress in those European countries, like Britain and Ireland, where unemployment benefits are low, compared with those in Spain, Belgium and Denmark where they are high.

Social support from the family

This is a major factor in coping with job loss. Some studies have found large effects here; for example Cobb and Kasl (1977) found that for men who lost their jobs through factory closure, 4% of those with good support from their spouses became arthritic, compared with 41% for those with low support. Similar results have been obtained for depression and other aspects of subjective well-being. This is usually found to be a "buffering" effect, i.e. the effect of social support is only found in those who are under stress (Winefield, 1995).

Personality

Unemployment creates more distress for those high in neuroticism (Payne, 1988). Other studies have found more distress for introverts and type A personalities. Those who are neither young nor old do worse, probably because of their family responsibilities.

Perception of the causes of unemployment

Job loss is less distressing if everyone in the place of work has lost their job, or if the general level of unemployment is high. Warr (1984) found greater self-esteem among the unemployed in Britain under such conditions, and Turner (1995) found more ill-health and more depression among the unemployed if there was low unemployment, due to the loss of self-esteem and financial stress. We shall see shortly that the retired are much happier than the unemployed, and this may well be because of the different ways they see their situation: the unemployed may feel that they have failed and been rejected while the retired (who are also unemployed) may feel that they are enjoying a well-deserved rest. Self-esteem and social comparisons are important here: Clark (1998b) found that there was more distress when other members of the family had jobs—an effect of comparison, which goes against rational or common sense expectations.

What can be done to relieve the unhappiness of the unemployed?

It is not inevitable that those without work should be unhappy, distressed and ill. After all housewives are in this position, and so are the retired, and both of these groups are in good mental and physical health.

However, research on unemployment has drawn attention to some of the less obvious benefits of work. These benefits will need to replaced, and they include:

- structuring time
- providing social contacts outside the family
- linking the individual to broader goals and purposes
- giving status and sense of identity
- providing a raised level of activity.

(Jahoda, 1982; Warr, 1984)

Full employment may no longer be possible, so what can psychologists do to help with this major source of unhappiness? The key is to persuade people to use their increased free time well. Winefield et al. (1992) found that those who did nothing much of the time, or watched a lot of TV, had low self-esteem, more depression, hopelessness and *anomie*. This may take the form of "unstructured time", when nothing in particular needs to be done, and it is found that the unemployed organise their time less (Feather and Bond, 1983), and that this is a cause of lower psychological health (Wanberg et al., 1997). The unemployed often get up late and do nothing, watch TV, and hang around. Few take up any new leisure activities. Some do, and Fryer and Payne (1984) describe a group of individuals who were happier after they lost their jobs—

they had found better things to do, such as running a community centre or a nature reserve, where they could use their skills, had autonomy and were useful. A large-scale experiment was carried out in Britain in which unemployed youth were offered facilities and training in sports; this increased their interest in sport but also led to other purposeful activities, such as voluntary work, study and politics (Kay, 1987, cited in Glyptis, 1989).

The National Centre for Volunteering in London has been studying and encouraging the benefits of volunteering for the unemployed. At least 20% of unemployed young people do some voluntary work. In addition to the immediate effect on morale, they also receive training in some new skills, and gain self-confidence, some of them are later employed in related work (Gay, 1998). When voluntary workers are compared with paid workers doing the same work, the voluntary workers have been found to have higher job satisfaction (Pearce, 1993).

One answer to the problems of the unemployed then is the right kind of "leisure", involving constructive activities with others, such as sports and voluntary work. These activities help with another problem, the loss of social contacts, which is very damaging, not only contacts with workmates, but also through withdrawing from the company of employed people, and normal society.

There are other ways of tackling unemployment, but these are outside the scope of psychology. These include:

- banning overtime, which would save a quarter of a million jobs in Britain
- shorter working week
- shorter working life
- more part-time jobs.

RETIREMENT

Here is another group of people who have stopped work, but for very different reasons from the unemployed. We shall see that the effects are also very different. This is central to our interests in work and happiness. Do people need work? What do they do when they are free to do what they like?

Happiness

On average the retired are happier than those at work; Warr and Payne (1982) found that in Britain 36% of retired men and 35% of women "felt very pleased with things yesterday all of the time", compared with 23% of men and 17% of women in full time work. Campbell et al. (1976) in the USA found that those over the retiring age were a quarter of a standard deviation above the population mean in subjective well-being. This is not true for all. Those with stressful or boring jobs are happy to stop work, but those with very interesting, rewarding and well-paid ones are less pleased. Parker (1982) found that in Britain 31% of the retired missed the people at work, 31% the money, 11% the work itself and 10% the feeling of being useful. These are some of the crucial benefits of work, the causes of job satisfaction.

Mental health

Retirement has often been classed as a "stressful life event", though it is found to be less stressful than getting married (Holmes and Rahe, 1967). And it does take most people a few months to get used to it. American studies find no difference in mental health before and after retirement (Kasl, 1980), and the retired are certainly in better mental health than the unemployed.

Health

This raises difficult research issues, since many people retire *because* of ill-health, 50% of those who take early retirement. But does retirement cause ill-health? Some longitudinal studies have found very little effect, though there is a small improvement in life expectancy for those in heavy, unskilled jobs producing a lot of stress and fatigue, and a small decrease for those in better jobs (Kasl, 1980). A recent analysis by Ross and Mirowsky (1995) however found that stopping work, for whatever reason, led to a decline in health over the next year. Length of life seems to depend on when people stop work; the longer they go on working the longer they live (Beehr, 1986); this may now be less true.

When do people enjoy retirement?

Money

This is a cause of concern we have seen, though less important than loss of social contacts. The retired are mostly less well off, although the difference is not great. In Britain in 1985 per head expenditure in families where the head was retired was £58 per week, compared with £68 when they were working.

Activities

We saw that the unemployed tend to do nothing. A Canadian study of the retired found that they spent an *extra* 65 minutes per day watching TV, 57 minutes reading, 40 minutes on conversation with family or friends (Elliot and Elliot, 1990). They are found to have less feeling of control, since they solve problems less and have less enjoyable social interaction (Ross and Drentea, 1998). This does not always happen; McGoldrick (1982) reported a study of 1800 men who had retired early though in good health and who were quite well off. They engaged in a lot of active leisure, including serious hobbies (37%), voluntary work (19%), easier or part-time jobs (33%), committees and clubs (24%), and further education (9%). It has been found that the main predictors of life satisfaction in retirement are the amount of social interaction and the variety of skills used (O'Brien, 1986).

Education and social class

Although middle-class people are giving up more interesting jobs they have more resources and interests with which to replace work. Some professionals can keep up their work in some capacity.

CONCLUSIONS

Most people are happier and in better mental and physical health when they have jobs. Work is good for us. Job satisfaction has several components, and itself is a cause of life satisfaction, though the reverse effect is stronger. Job satisfaction is increased by pay though not much, and more by work that has features such as the use of skills, autonomy and skill variety. The nature of work is changing and it is becoming less satisfying for example for those on temporary employment or who work in call centres. Social aspects of work lead to satisfaction and cooperation, but role conflict is bad. Job satisfaction also varies with age and personality.

Job satisfaction has a small effect on rate of work, it also enhances cooperation and helpfulness, and reduces absenteeism and labour turnover.

Work can be stressful and affect mental health, if there is job overload, boring work, danger or other undesirable features. Stress is less for some kinds of personality and is less if there is social support at work. Physical health is also affected, for example those with low job status and those in stressful jobs suffer many more heart attacks.

Unemployment is a major source of unhappiness, and of poor mental and physical health. This can be mitigated by doing voluntary work, or taking up sport or some other serious leisure. The retired however are happier than those at work on average, but length of life is greater for those who carry on working.

Chapter 8

Leisure

WHAT IS LEISURE AND HOW MUCH DO WE HAVE?

Leisure can be defined as those activities which people do in their free time, because they want to, for their own sake, for fun, entertainment, self-improvement, or for goals of their own choosing, but not for material gain. It is not the same as free time; for example some people have a lot of this, but don't know what to do with it and don't regard it as leisure. However, free time is necessary to have leisure at all.

Time budget studies show that we have quite lot of free time. In 1992–93 in Britain, free time was as follows, after allowing for work and travel, sleep, essential housework, child care and shopping.

	Weekdays	*Weekend days*
Employed males	5.0	10.3 (hours per day)
Employed females	3.0	8.2
Housewives	6.6	9.0
Retired	11.25	12.65

(Henley Centre, 1995)

Several American surveys have asked about overall leisure satisfaction. On the "delighted–terrible scale":

11% were delighted with their leisure
32.3% pleased
36.5% mostly satisfied
11.5% mixed
8.5% dissatisfied (only 1% said "terrible").

(Andrews and Withey, 1976)

In another survey leisure was reported to be more satisfying than work by 19% of those with jobs, and 34% of housewives. Leisure was said to be equally satisfying as work by another 32% of men with jobs, 36% of women with jobs and 32% of housewives (Veroff et al. 1981).

However, there are several groups for whom leisure, or lack of it, is a problem. Women have less free time than men, especially those with full-time jobs and those with children. This is because women, even when working, do most of the housework, and there is a sense in which their work is never done.

Working-class people have about the same amount of free time as middle class, but do less of nearly every kind of leisure activity, apart from watching TV, which they do a lot more. This is because their work is more tiring, they have less spare money, and they have had less opportunity to acquire leisure interests, at college for example. The unemployed have much more spare time than those at work, but take part in less of nearly every kind of leisure, apart from TV watching, as we showed in the last chapter. The reasons for this are only partly economic, since many rewarding kinds of leisure are free.

Retired people also have a lot of free time. Some of them take up new interests, such as voluntary work, reading and study, hobbies and church. However, most of them do not, and there is a continuing decline with age in active sport and exercise, despite the benefits of active leisure for happiness and health in this age group (Argyle, 1996).

There have been major historical changes in the amount and nature of leisure, from the Stone Age (when there was a lot) to the present. There was a continuous reduction in average working hours, from the 1830s, when men worked 72 hours a week, to the early 1980s, when they worked 36–38 hours a week (Gershuny, 1992). Since then the average hours of work have increased. Since World War II the number of women at work has also greatly increased. The greatest recent change in the nature of leisure has been the introduction of TV; it now takes up 3–4 hours a day, more than any other form of leisure.

THE EFFECTS OF LEISURE ON HAPPINESS AND OTHER ASPECTS OF WELL-BEING

Positive affect

We will take this first since there are lots of studies showing a clear causal effect of some kind of leisure on good moods. We saw earlier that leisure satisfaction can be caused by happiness as well as vice versa, but mood-induction experiments are a clear example of the effects of leisure on well-being. The experimental design is to administer self-report mood scales to people before and at various times after some event. Cheerful music, succeeding on a test, finding a coin, asking subjects to say how happy they are several times, all these cheers them up, for 10–15 minutes at least. We shall see shortly that a 10-minute brisk walk can cheer people up for 2 hours, and more serious exercise until the next day. There have been many studies of the effects of sport and exercise, which we shall report later.

Lewinsohn and Graf's "pleasant activities therapy" (1973) discovered which pleasant activities affect subjects' mood at the end of the day; all are leisure activities. This and similar forms of therapy are discussed in Chapter 13. In a survey of students in five European countries, Scherer et al. (1986) asked for the causes of joyful experiences. These were most commonly said to be relationships with friends, food, drink, sex and success experiences. Other studies have found that sport and games, and cultural activities like music and reading were also common causes of joy.

Another method is "experience sampling" in which subjects are paged at random times and asked to report the activity and the mood they are in. This has been used to study the effects of social activities. From all this work there is no doubt of the powerful effects of a number of leisure activities on positive affect.

Happiness

If leisure can make people happy this is very important, since leisure is largely under our own control, and easily changed—unlike relationships, jobs and our personalities. We saw in the last chapter that the unemployed spend a lot of time doing nothing in particular, and that this is associated with unhappiness. Several studies have found a negative relation between TV watching and happiness. Mishra (1992) studied 720 retired men in India and found that life satisfaction was greater for those who were involved with activities connected with their former occupation, voluntary groups and friends. Lu and Argyle (1994) found that British adults who had a serious and committing leisure activity were happier than those who had not, although they found it more stressful and challenging.

These studies do not demonstrate a causal relation however. Some studies have used another method, modelling by multiple regression and found that leisure activities were the strongest source of life satisfaction (e.g. Balatsky and Diener, 1993) There have also been one or two experiments, for example Reich and Zautra (1981) who asked students to engage in either two or twelve pleasant activities for a month; both groups reported an increased quality of life and pleasant experience compared with a control group. Active participation in leisure is very good for the unemployed, and field experiments in providing sports training and facilities for unemployed young people have had very positive outcomes (Kay, 1987, cited in Glyptis, 1989). There seems little doubt that leisure, especially of some kinds, can have a positive effect on happiness.

Mental health

Riddick and Stewart (1994) studied 600 black and white retired American women and found that mental health was greater for those with more leisure activity, but only for the whites. Iso-Ahola and Park (1996) found that in members of American Taekwondo groups leisure companionship buffered life stress, particularly on depression, while leisure-generated friendships buffered the effect of stress on physical illness. It seems that actually engaging in the leisure together was the crucial factor for depression. We come to the same conclusion for belonging to churches (Chapter 11).

We shall look shortly at the particular effects of sport and social forms of leisure on mental health, and will conclude that these two aspects of leisure have the greatest effect.

Health

Sport and exercise of course have massive effects on health and longevity, as will be documented shortly. Social support, as may be obtained from leisure groups, also affects health, as we saw in Chapter 6. Both exercise and social support have a buffering effect in reducing the effect of stress on health.

BENEFITS FROM PARTICULAR FORMS OF LEISURE

In another book (Argyle, 1996) I distinguished between 10 common forms of leisure. These were—watching TV, music and radio, reading and study, hobbies, social life, active sport and exercise, spectator sports, religion, voluntary work, holidays and tourism. There may be some more; shopping and sex have been suggested to me. Since leisure is what people do when they are free to choose, and presumably they choose things they enjoy, it is likely that all of these activities have some benefits. In this section we shall see exactly what they are, and how they are beneficial. Two leisure activities are dealt with in other chapters—social life and religion; both are found to have strong positive effects. Social life is very pervasive and is part of the benefits of leisure, including religion. Some, like sport and exercise, have been extensively studied and have been found to have strong effects on well-being. Others have scarcely been studied at all, and some are unlikely to have much effect, for example it is doubtful whether listening to music affects health.

Sport and exercise

Positive affect

Thayer (1989) found that a 10-minute brisk walk resulted in less tiredness, more energy and less tension 2 hours later. Other studies found that after an hour's exercise, such as aerobics, those involved felt less tense, depressed, angry, tired or confused, and had more vigour, for the rest of the day and, in some, for the next day (Maroulakis and Zervas, 1993). Regular exercise, such as four times a week for 10 weeks, has produced more enduring positive states of the same kind. These effects are partly due to the social interaction with others, although

Steptoe (1998) found an effect for solitary exercise. Hsiao and Thayer (1998) found that while beginners at exercise said that they did it primarily for health or aesthetic reasons, experienced exercisers did it more because they enjoyed it and it improved their mood.

The main reason for the positive effects of strenuous physical exercise on mood is probably the release of endorphins by sustained exertion, which produce a kind of euphoria, "runner's high". The morphine-like properties of endorphins also explain why those concerned do not feel pain from cuts and bruises at the time, and why they may become addicted to exercise—they are strongly rewarded by a drug-induced state (see page 35). There are other reasons for these positive moods—the enjoyable social interaction, and the feeling of self-mastery in performing successfully.

Happiness and satisfaction

We have just seen that regular exercise produces an enduring state of positive mood, though we do not know how long this lasts or how often it needs to be topped up. Hills and Argyle (1998b) found that those who were members of sports clubs had higher scores on the Oxford Happiness Inventory than those who did not; belonging to churches or choirs had no such effect in this study (Table 8.1).

Exercise and sport lead to greater self-esteem and a more positive body-image. Sonstroem and Potts (1996) found that perception of sport competence, physical condition, attractive body, strength and general physical self-worth all predicted self-esteem, as well as positive affect and (lack of) negative affect.

The main reason for the effect of exercise on happiness is probably the undoubted effect on mood, the positive mood produced by endorphins, sociability and success, and the reduced depression and tension.

Mental health

Tucker (1990) studied 4032 adults and found that the fitter ones were also in better mental health, but what caused what? There have been some interesting

Table 8.1 Mean OHI scores for leisure activities

Activity	Mean OHI values		
	Participants	Non-participants	t
Sports	44.0	40.0	−3.58***
TV	41.9	41.4	−1.54
Church	41.8	41.5	−0.23
Music	40.9	41.9	0.79

Source: Hills and Argyle (1998b); ***$p < .001$.

experimental comparisons of exercise with more familiar forms of treatment for mental illness. Klein et al. (1985) allocated 74 depressed patients to 12 weeks of either running, group therapy or meditation. Nine months later all had improved the same amount. In another study they found that counselling plus running had more effect that counselling alone. A number of such studies have shown clearly that exercise is good for depression, that the results last for at least a year, and that this is as good as counselling or psychotherapy, for the less severe cases at least (Biddle and Mutrie, 1991). There have also been some successful attempts to treat anxiety states with exercise, but here the evidence is less clear.

The result is that many doctors and psychiatrists are now prescribing exercise, especially for their depressed patients, though there may be a problem in persuading them to do it. Some employers are also introducing exercise programmes for their staff. It is reported that as a result employees are less anxious, depressed and tense, especially on exercise days, that there has been improved work performance, and that they are more easy-going and lower in type A personality (Falkenburg, 1987).

Does exercise have to be exhausting and aerobic for these benefits? Possibly not; Moses et al. (1989) persuaded 94 volunteers to do high intensity (70–75% maximum heart rate) or moderate intensity exercise, or strengthening exercises, three times a week for 10 weeks. Only the moderate aerobics exercise was successful in improving perceived coping ability and well-being. Other studies have found the same (Biddle and Mutrie, 1991).

What is the explanation for these mental health benefits? Several studies have found that exercise produces a reduced response to stress; Crews and Landers (1987) report a meta-analysis of 34 such studies. This may be because greater fitness gives a greater physiological capacity to deal with stress, or because the greater sense of mastery makes people believe they can cope with it.

Health

It is no surprise that exercise is good for health. The effects are quite strong. Paffenbarger et al. (1991) followed up 17,000 Harvard alumni over a period of 16 years and found fewer heart attacks for those who did more exercise. Thirty minutes a day was enough to give maximum benefits. There were 31% fewer deaths (Figure 8.1).

Former athletes have been found to live longer than non-athletes (Shepherd, 1997). The effects of exercise on heart attacks are the most striking but there are others, including less risk of cancer, high blood pressure, obesity, diabetes, osteoporosis, and back pain. There have been a number of follow-up studies of the effects on the cardiovascular system of taking courses of aerobics, swimming or jogging. Occupational exercise programmes have been found to lead to better health, reduced weight, reduced tension, less absenteeism and greater productivity (Feist and Brannon, 1988). A correlational survey of 3000 adults

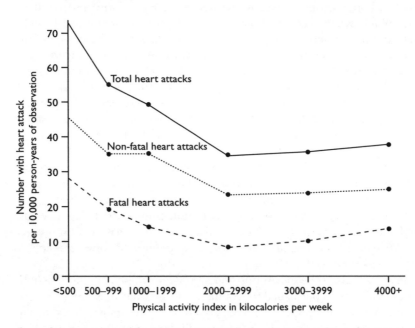

Figure 8.1 Age-adjusted first heart-attack rates by physical activity index in a six- to ten-year follow-up of male Harvard alumni (Paffenbarger, et al., 1978).

found the regression weights predicting subjective health for different kinds of exercise were:

- swimming .24
- dancing   .19
- jogging   .13
- walking   .11

(Ransford and Palisi, 1996)

This relationship was much stronger for older people: swimming correlated .41 for older and .16 for younger individuals.

One way that exercise improves health is by buffering the effects of stress. Kobasa (1982) found that stress had no effect on illness for individuals who took a lot of exercise and who were also "hardy", that is high in internal control and similar personality factors. A high level of exercise leads to more immune system activity (Wannamethee et al., 1993).

Social clubs and leisure groups

Joy

In a survey of several hundred members of leisure groups in the Oxford area members were asked to rate their mood at the end of a typical meeting. The results are shown in Figure 8.2. The greatest joy was reported for dancing, charity work, music, and church. The explanation is not hard to find. In each case they are very enjoyable activities, some include music, and in all cases interaction with friends. Each component alone would produce joy, and combinations of them magnify the effect.

Happiness and satisfaction

We carried out a study of 39 leisure activities. Factor analysis produced four groups of leisure activities, as shown in Table 6.2 (see page 73). Those who engaged in social leisure activities were happier and also more extraverted than those who did not; their extraversion explained their happiness. We show in Chapter 10 that extraversion is a cause of happiness.

Hills, Argyle, and Reeves (2000) carried out a study of the leisure motivations of 183 young people, for 36 kinds of leisure. Reported frequency of participation and enjoyment of these activities was correlated with social satisfaction for four of the six clusters of activities found, as will be described shortly. We reported earlier how companionship in leisure activities reduces the effects of stress on depression (see page 76).

Membership of leisure groups often enhances social skills—leadership, making speeches, dealing with the public, committee work. This has been seen by

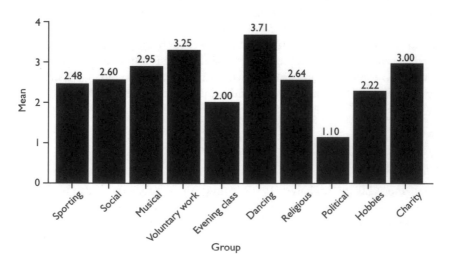

Figure 8.2 Joy by group (Argyle, 1996).

some sociologists as one of the main "functions" of leisure groups. From a psychological point of view social skills are valuable since they are a source of good social relationships and happiness (Lu and Argyle, 1992a).

Leisure groups with a strong shared interest create "leisure worlds" for their members. Some are complete mini-cultures, with their own values, traditions, skills, costumes, skill and expertise, weekly and annual events, and a complete set of social relationships. This applies to Scottish country dancing, church membership, bell-ringing, sailing, pigeon fancying, field archeology, gliding and others. It also applies to some of our main kinds of leisure, such as religion and sport. They are all great sources of happiness.

Mental health

Palinkas et al. (1990) found for a large sample of over-65s, that depression was less for those with friends or who belonged to organisations, while marriage had no effect. We saw that Iso-Ahola and Park (1996) found that leisure companionship buffered the effect of stress on depression. This probably explains some of the apparent benefits of sport. Companionship in joint leisure may be more important than "social support". Thoits (1985) thought that the crucial factor is "regular and sustained contacts with others, a sense of purpose and behavioural guidance, and perhaps a global sense that support is available". There are many support groups like Alcoholics Anonymous where those with similar problems meet and talk about these problems.

Health

Social support and companionship are good for physical health too. For example House et al. (1982) with 2754 adults found that men lived longer if they attended leisure groups, engaged in other active forms of leisure, and were married. Women lived longer if they went to church and did not watch much TV. As we explained in Chapter 6 this is due to basic physiological responses whereby close relationships stimulate the immune system, and cause stress to have less effect on heart rate, anxiety and other aspects of arousal.

Watching TV

Positive affect

Kubey and Csikszentmihalyi (1990) paged their subjects electronically to find their mood while watching TV. They felt less active and alert, with less challenge and concentration than before or after. There was a slight fall in positive affect, they were much more relaxed and they were said to be a state of consciousness "somewhere between being awake and being asleep". However, TV programmes can produce positive and other moods, and are often used to do so in laboratory experiments. TV can be used to control one's own mood: Bryant and Zillman (1984) found that experimentally bored subjects chose to watch exciting films whereas experimentally stressed ones preferred comedies. The most popular programmes are soap operas, sit-coms, game shows, etc., all forms of pleasant light entertainment, which would be expected to produce a low key but positive mood.

Happiness and satisfaction

Since in the modern world TV watching is now the third greatest use of time after sleeping and working, it must be generally rewarding. Curiously it is hard to find evidence that this is so. Robinson (1977) found that only 17% of an American national sample said that TV gave them "great satisfaction", compared with 25% for housework, 26% for sports and games, 34% for religion and 79% for children. It is commonly found that those who watch a lot of TV are less happy than others (e.g. Lu and Argyle, 1993), but this is probably because only those who are isolated or have nothing better to do watch a lot of TV. Indeed the housebound or isolated may benefit a lot from TV and might be even less happy without it. Lu and Argyle found that those who watch a lot of soap opera were happier than those who watched little of it (Figure 8.3). This may be because regular watchers think they enjoy the company of "imaginary friends". Livingstone (1988, p. 70) found that 62% of regular soap opera viewers agreed that "after a while the characters become real people and we are concerned for their well-being just as we are for our friends and colleagues". There are other social gains from TV, if the family watch it together, as they used to do before families acquired multiple sets. TV gives friends something in common to talk about. However, Robinson (1990) compared large numbers of individuals from different countries with and without TV and found that one of the main activities which is sacrificed is time spent with real friends.

Mental and physical health

We have already seen several studies that found an apparently negative effect of TV watching. This is almost certainly because those who watch a lot do not belong to leisure groups and engage less in the kinds of active leisure that are beneficial.

Music

Positive affect

Music can certainly generate positive moods, and has been found to be one of the most effective methods of mood induction in the lab, Haydn trumpet concertos or Bach Brandenburg concertos for example (Clark, 1983). Barschak

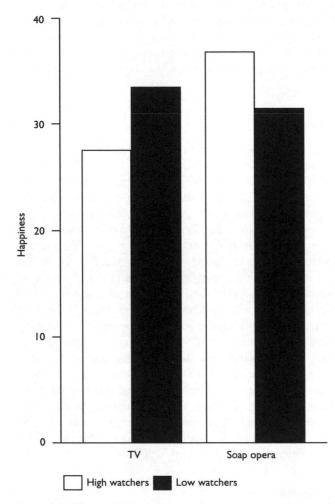

Figure 8.3 Effects of TV watching and soap opera watching on happiness (Lu and Argyle, 1993)

(1951) found that music was mentioned frequently by girls as a source of happiness. We have seen that dancing produces a very high level of joy, and this is partly due to the music. Different kinds of music produce different moods. It can produce a high level of arousal or excitement, as at pop concerts, partly by the sheer volume, aggression as in revolutionary or warlike music, deep joy as in religious music, and indeed any number of subtle variations of mood. The emotions generated by music can be very strong. Hills and Argyle (1998b) found that the moods experienced by members of choirs were similar to those for religion, but the musical ones were stronger, even on dimensions usually associated with religion, like "glimpses of another world"—see Table 8.2.

Table 8.2 Differences in means for common items of musical and religious experience scales (members of both musical groups and churches)

Item	Music scale		Religious scale		
	Mean	SD	Mean	SD	t
Being bathed in warmth and light	2.65	1.43	2.61	1.56	0.23
Bodily well-being	2.89	1.41	2.57	1.46	1.76
Enjoying company of others' present	3.43	1.16	3.48	1.11	−0.32
Excitement	3.52	1.27	2.57	1.41	4.80***
Feeling uplifted	4.30	0.86	3.91	1.00	2.54*
Glimpsing another world	3.13	1.53	3.00	1.57	0.60
Joy/elation	3.79	1.04	3.30	1.29	2.79**
Loss of sense of self	3.02	1.39	2.41	1.47	3.62***
Positive feelings about life	3.62	1.10	3.91	0.95	−2.09*
Taking part in a shared performance	4.02	1.00	3.20	1.35	3.88***
Timelessness	2.63	1.50	2.59	1.53	0.20

Source: Hills and Argyle (1998a).

Note $*p < 0.05$; $**p < 0.01$; $***p > 0.001$

Music can be calming; Konecni (1982) found that playing simple melodies at a low volume led to insulted subjects being less aggressive.

Many people collect recordings of music, presumably of pieces they like or that generate moods they like. They are then in a position to use music to control their own moods, and this can be done very precisely.

How does music generate emotions so effectively? The main process is by music imitating emotional features of the human voice in emotion. Scherer and Oshinsky (1977) generated 188 sounds from a Moog synthesizer and asked subjects to rate the emotions expressed. Sounds were said to be happy when they were high pitched, with gentle upward pitch changes, pure tones and regular rhythm; others have found flowing melody and major key are also sounds of joy. Sounds were thought to be sad when they were slow, with a low and falling pitch, and low volume.

Happiness and satisfaction

People listen to music quite lot, about 1¼ hours per day on average, though they may be doing something else as well. Teenagers listen more than this. While it is clear that music can produce positive moods, there is no evidence of its effect on enduring happiness or satisfaction. Hills and Argyle (1998b) found no effect of belonging to musical groups, as there was for belonging to sports clubs.

Mental health

Music is a recognised form of treatment for patients. It works partly through the calming effect of certain kinds of music (Thaut, 1989). This is a kind of therapy that people give themselves quite a lot.

Holidays and tourism

Positive affect

While people are on holiday they are certainly in a good mood. Rubenstein (1980) surveyed 10,000 readers of *Psychology Today*, and found how they felt (Table 8.3). They were much less tired and irritable. The only exceptions were the workaholics, who were itching to get back to the office.

Studies of what people want from their holidays find that the most common desire is for relaxation. Sitting in the sun, beside the sea, is relaxing. The countryside and natural scenery are found very relaxing, and in American studies the "wilderness". Even watching videos of the wilderness has been found to lower blood pressure. Holidays can produce other kinds of positive mood: adventure holidays, remote places, exciting rides and dangerous sports provide excitement, while visiting religious and historical sites can be "sacred journeys" (Pearce, 1982).

Happiness and satisfaction

The benefits of holidays can last for some time; they can also be anticipated, so the relaxation and good moods generated can be a regular part of life. One of the motivations found for tourism is "self-actualisation" and self-fulfilment, finding inner peace and harmony, and there may be gains of self-esteem from the prestige and glamour of the travels made (Pearce, 1982). There can be educational benefits; a friend of mine returning from China said "Nothing will ever look the same again".

Table 8.3 Percentages reporting symptoms while on vacation, and during the past year

	Vacation	During past year
Tired	12	34
Irritable	8	30
Constipation, worry, anxiety	7	27
Loss of interest in sex	6	12
Digestive problems	6	16
Insomnia	4	11
Headaches	3	21

Source: Rubenstein (1980).

Mental health

Relaxation is good for mental health, and getting away from a stressful or boring life is a common motivation for holidays. A study of people on holiday on Brampton Island, near the Australian Barrier Reef, found that by the fourth or fifth day there was a marked drop in the symptoms listed in Table 8.3. (Pearce, 1982).

Health

We have seen that individuals are less constipated, and have fewer digestive problems and headaches while on holiday. On the other hand, tropical diseases, too much sunshine and dangerous sports can have a bad effect.

Religion

Chapter 11 deals with this in detail; here are the main points. There is strong *positive affect* of a special quality produced by church services, similar to that from classical music. The effects on *happiness* are fairly weak, though stronger for the elderly, and are due to the close support of church communities, a relationship with God and an optimistic outlook. *Mental health* is better, mainly due to religious methods of coping and to social support. *Health* is much better, partly because of the better health behaviour of members.

Voluntary work

Positive affect

Figure 8.2 showed that voluntary work and charity work were sources of joy only a little behind dancing, and ahead of most other kinds of leisure activity.

Happiness

Wheeler et al. (1998) analysed 37 studies of voluntary work done by the elderly, and concluded that this enhanced their sense of well-being. In addition 85% of the people they were looking after felt better than clients of younger workers. Surveys of the satisfactions reported by British voluntary workers have found that these are considerable (see Table 8.4). Respondents said it was very import-ant to them to see the results of their good works, and they enjoyed making friends while doing it. It is a familiar finding in social psychology that helping others is a source of joy.

However, nothing is known about the possible effects of voluntary work on *mental or physical health*.

Table 8.4 The benefits of volunteering

	Very important %	Fairly important %	Not very important %	Not important at all %
I meet people and make friends through it	48	37	11	4
It's the satisfaction of seeing the results	67	26	5	2
It gives me the chance to do things that I'm good at	33	36	24	7
It makes me feel less selfish as a person	29	33	24	13
I really enjoy it	72	21	6	2
It's part of my religious belief or philosophy of life to give help	44	22	9	23
It broadens my experience of life	39	36	15	9
It gives me a sense of personal achievement	47	31	16	6
It gives me the chance to learn new skills	25	22	29	23
It gives me a position in the community	12	16	33	38
It gets me "out of myself"	35	30	19	15
It gives me the chance to get a recognised qualification	3	7	15	74

Source: Lynn and Smith (1991).

OVERALL BENEFITS OF LEISURE

A major benefit of leisure is the immediate effect on *positive affect*. In the cases of TV and music this may be the only benefit, in the case of holidays the main one. Church services have this effect too. The effect of leisure on *happiness* is smaller, strongest for social clubs, and most of the effects on happiness of other kinds of leisure depend on social relations. Sport is good for *mental health*, especially depression, not entirely due to the social content, and social clubs and religion are good too. *Health* benefits are found from sport and exercise, from social clubs and from religion, due partly to their social content, partly to the better health behaviour.

What is the explanation of the benefits of leisure?

I will deal with positive affect, and mental and physical health first, and then with happiness at greater length.

Positive affect

Some of the main benefits are immediate and temporary, though they are often very strong. In the cases of music and TV this is the main and possibly the only benefit of these kinds of leisure. Enhanced positive affect is produced by immediate physiological effects on emotion, mostly based on innate responses. Strenuous exercise and sport stimulate the endorphins, which activate certain brain cells that give positive emotional experiences. Music consists of sounds, many of which are similar to the human voice in emotional states, which we can recognise and respond to innately. Social interaction is a basic source of joy, and is mediated by smiling faces, friendly voices and other social signals. Often these different signals are combined, as in dancing, which includes music, exercise and in some cases intimate social interaction; dancing was the greatest source of joy in the study of leisure groups reported in Figure 8.2.

Mental health

Some kinds of leisure have a considerable effect on mental health, particularly depression. We have seen that exercise may be a good treatment for some kinds of depression, and it is also good for anxiety and reducing tension. This may be due to the positive moods and the relaxation generated by exercise. Music is used as a form of therapy, by calming patients. Other forms of relaxing exercise may be beneficial for those under stress—TV, reading novels, etc. Social support, especially companionship in shared leisure, is good for mental health, by buffering the effects of stress. This may be through positive emotions or by a more cognitive process of creating a feeling of competence in coping. Religion is beneficial, by causing beliefs that one will be cared for, giving meaning to negative events, and the use of methods of religious coping.

Health

Some forms of leisure have a strong effect on physical health. Sport and exercise have the greatest effect, adding years of life by exercising the heart and other organs. Church can add some years of life, mainly by the improved health behaviour demanded. The social aspects of church and other leisure groups are good for health too, partly by people looking after one another, but also by activating the immune system. Health is better while people are on holiday, mainly due to the relaxation; it is possible that other kinds of relaxing leisure are good for health too—such as music and TV.

Explaining the effects of leisure on happiness

Social motivation

Leisure may affect happiness because many forms of leisure allow the satisfaction of social needs of different kinds. There are a number of such social needs, including needs for affiliation, close relationships, dominance and power, status and fame, altruism, competition and cooperation. Depending on individuals' pattern of social needs they will choose those forms of leisure which might meet them. Drama, politics, tennis or squash, team games, church house groups, would all meet different social needs (Argyle, 1996).

Hills et al. (2000) asked 183 students to report their enjoyment of 36 leisure activities, and how much these satisfied social and other motivations. A cluster analysis reduced the 36 activities to 6 clusters, those inside each having similar motivational patterns. Four of the clusters showed correlations between enjoyment of activities and reported satisfaction of social needs. These were:

1   active sports, dangerous sports, fishing, musical performance ($r = .27$)
2   dancing, eating out, family activities, parties, pubs, holidays/travel, leisure groups, social life with friends, theatre/cinema, watching sport ($r = .45$)
3   DIY, evening classes, gardening, meditation, exercise, serious reading, sewing ($r = .46$)
4   political activities, raising money for charity, religious activities, voluntary work ($r = .55$).

These correlations were reasonably high for three of the six clusters, even when other sources of motivation had been accounted for, some more than others—as shown in brackets. It is also interesting that a number of leisure activities were thought to satisfy social needs that are not obviously social, such as serious reading and meditation; the explanation may be that they involve imaginary social activity.

When we looked at the other components of subjective well-being we saw that positive affect was generated by social interaction, especially smiling faces, friendly voices, and other positive signals, verbal and non-verbal. Mental and physical health are strongly affected by social support, from family and friends and from groups such as church. This is further support for the social motivation theory.

Enjoying the use of skills and other abilities

Bandura (1977) proposed that motivation, such as for putting effort into sport, depends on "self-efficacy", the belief that one is good at it, based for example on past success. It has been found that self-efficacy will predict whether patients will take up and continue to engage in exercise programmes that have been prescribed.

In the Hills et al. (2000) study subjects were asked to rate their ability at each of the 36 activities ("How good do you think you are at this activity?"). Do you need to be good at leisure to enjoy it? For many leisure activities this seems unlikely, such as watching TV, reading a book, going for a walk. In fact we found that reported enjoyment correlated with reported ability for all activities. There was a good correlation and this remained after other motivations had been partialled out in the cases of cluster 3 (hobbies), and 4 (DIY etc.). The correlation for cluster 6 (voluntary work etc.) disappeared when social motivation was taken into account. However, there was a higher correlation for more passive activities, so for active sport it was .27 but for watching sport it was .42, which is odd. Either the theory is wrong or we have failed to measure self-efficacy. However, in most of the Bandura research rather high levels of skill were often involved, such as in back-diving, and it may be that the theory only works for such activities.

This theory could explain the findings about self-efficacy and self-esteem mentioned earlier. However, leisure can contribute to identity and self-esteem in another way. Sociologists have argued that although paid work is the main source of identity for many, it is not for the unemployed, retired, housewives, or those for whom work gives little satisfaction, or when it is not admired or approved of. Mass forms of leisure do not give much of a sense of identity, apart from supporting sports teams, which certainly does. It is the more engrossing and less common forms of leisure that may do most for identity—amateur archaeology, drama, Scottish country dancing, and amateur but high-level sport or arts (Stebbins, 1979). A study of backpackers, kayakers, guitarists and others found that these groups had distinctive images, and that members wanted to possess these characteristics (Haggard and Williams, 1992).

It is possible that skilled performance in leisure pursuits can provide satisfaction through adding to self-esteem. This could be done by successful performance, or by merely taking part—by dressing up in the costume or kit, being a member of a special group, acquiring special skills, putting on public performances, and being involved in leisure worlds with their mini-cultures (Kelly, 1983): "A potter finds meaning not only in the product and in the experience of creating something, but in *being* a potter whose skills are exercised" (p. 119).

Much leisure is enjoyed without being good at it, as with most exercise, though having skill seems to add to the enjoyment. We saw earlier that exercise and sport are very good for both mental and physical health; this may be due to the exercise rather than the self-efficacy—but people may not persist if they think they are not doing well.

Intrinsic motivation

People work, partly at least, because they are paid for it, but they engage in leisure for nothing, children play for hours without being paid, so this is said to be "intrinsically motivated", it provides its own rewards, but what are they?

The operation of intrinsic motivation has been assessed by asking subjects how strongly they want to do what they are doing and how much they would rather be doing something else. A strong correlation is found between intrinsic motivation and positive affect (e.g. Graef et al., 1983); it is stronger for leisure than for work. Markland and Hardy (1993) asked 400 English students why they engaged in sport or exercise, with the answers as shown in Table 8.5. The second most common answer "enjoy physical activity" was endorsed by 51.3%; this is a form of intrinsic motivation.

A number of leisure activities produce what might be called "bodily pleasures"—swimming, dancing, running and whatever you have come to enjoy. Other bodily pleasures are of course, eating, drinking and sex, intrinsic motivations that need no other explanation.

Intrinsic motivation has been found to possess certain general features. One of these is perceived freedom from restraints (Neulinger, 1981); we saw earlier that autonomy is important for job satisfaction. A lot of free time is not free in this way, because of obligations to other people.

Then there is challenge. Csikszentmihalyi (1975) tried to find how leisure is motivated by interviewing 173 individuals engaged in serious leisure activities—such as rock climbers, dancers, composers, basket-ball players. He found that they experienced deep satisfaction when they were confronted by challenges, for which they also had the skills to cope. He theorised that if the challenge is too high there is anxiety; when it is too low there is boredom.

In our study of 183 students we tried to test this theory Subjects were asked to estimate the amount of challenge they faced in the 36 activities and the amount of skill they possessed. When the challenge was too high or too low, enjoyment was less; when it was a little less than skill enjoyment was higher, almost as the theory predicted. We also found that, if the 36 activities were compared, challenge and skill were always in balance, suggesting that people choose the leisure activities for which they have the skill, which is also consistent with the theory. Some of our findings did not fit the theory: the most enjoyable activities were not the most challenging, but the most social; the social theory can explain this. And dangerous sports were most enjoyable although challenge greatly exceeded skill; the excitement-seeking theory can explain

Table 8.5 Reasons for engaging in sport or exercise

	%
Fitness	56.6
Enjoy physical activity	51.3
Social and affiliative	35.3
Health related	30.3
Stress management or relaxation	29.0
Weight control	22.4
Develop personal skills	17.1
Competition	7.9

Source: Markland and Hardy (1993).

this. Another anomaly is TV watching—no challenge or skill, but very popular.

Seeking relaxation and seeking excitement

Sometimes people seem to be seeking goals, and when these are attained they relax, at other times they seem to be seeking excitement. So which is the most fundamental motivation. Apter (1982) proposed that we seek both, at different times. When we are in a "telic" state we seek goals; when we are in a "paratelic" state we seek excitement, and there are switches from one state to the other.

We explored the application of this theory to the explanation of the benefits of leisure in the study of 183 students. They were asked to rate the 36 activities for how purposeful they were. For some of them enjoyment correlated positively with purposefulness, and for others negatively. The most paratelic (least purposeful) were computer games, theatre and cinema, parties, pubs, listening to music, social life with friends, fishing, eating out, holidays and travel. These seem to be the purest kinds of leisure, and are mostly social. The most telic, i.e. purposeful, were serious reading and study, collecting for charity, political activities, religious activities, voluntary work, DIY, gardening, evening classes. These are more like work. Comparing the 10 most telic and the 10 most paratelic we found that the paratelic leisure activities were thought to involve less skill or challenge; they were also judged to satisfy social needs more, and to be more enjoyable. Are we to conclude that serious leisure is not enjoyable? Perhaps not; these subjects were quite young, first- or second-year students, and may not yet have found satisfaction in work-like activities. In another study reported earlier we found that high levels of joy were reported for voluntary work and collecting for charity, and that people with committed leisure pursuits were happier than those who had none (see page 117). The conclusion is rather that there are two kinds of leisure satisfaction.

Some paratelic activities include seeking excitement or arousal. Dangerous sports are an interesting example; they are dangerous and people often get injured or even killed, so why do people do them? Part of the answer may be that these are paratelic activities, people seek fun and excitement. Since only certain people like dangerous sports we can look at the personality traits involved. Zuckerman (1979) found that those who engage in dangerous sports are high on his "sensation-seeking" scale. Sensation seeking correlates with extraversion and psychoticism. Those high on this trait seek high arousal, by activities involving risk, high speed and sex, and take part in white-water rafting, biking, parachute jumping and the rest.

Eysenck et al. (1982) found that successful sportsmen have a special kind of personality, they are high on extraversion and psychoticism. They do particularly well at, and presumably enjoy, team sports and rough sports such as ice hockey, partly because they don't mind injuring other people.

CONCLUSIONS

Leisure has a strong effect on all aspects of well-being, particularly on positive affect, on mental and physical health, and to a lesser extent on happiness itself.

The strongest benefits are from sport and exercise and from social leisure groups. Chapter 11 will discuss the similar benefits from church.

Positive affect is due to direct physiological effects, for example of strenuous sport on endorphins. Mental health is improved by the effects of leisure on positive moods and relaxation, and health by better health behaviour, relaxation, and the effects of social support on the immune system.

The benefits of leisure for happiness can be explained partly through the social satisfaction provided by much leisure, satisfaction at successful performance, meeting challenge with skill, and the different benefits of serious leisure or which is pursued for its own sake.

Chapter 9

Money, class and education

INTRODUCTION

Economists are concerned with human welfare, and have often assumed that human happiness can be measured by how much money people have. But does money make people happy, and if so, how much, which people and why? Others apart from economists seem to assume that money will make them happy: there is widespread participation in the British National Lottery, and in the Football Pools, while advertisers commonly offer large prizes as an incentive to buy. Governments and political parties appear to have increasing individual and national prosperity as their main aims. Wage bargaining is often very intense, so much so that workers sometimes lose their jobs through driving too hard a bargain. Workers will work longer and faster if offered a wage incentive (Furnham and Argyle, 1998).

However, research does not entirely confirm this public preoccupation with money. Campbell et al. (1976) in their *Quality of American Life* study found that "financial situation" was rated 11th out of 12 possible sources of life satisfaction. King and Napa (1998) found that their subjects estimated money as worth one-fifth of the effect of happiness and one-sixth of meaning as components of the good life.

The effect of money is a very important issue, and one that has been in doubt. Some early studies reported small correlations between income and happiness, in some cases no relation at all. There has been virtually no increase in subjective well-being during a period of greatly increased prosperity for many countries. It is known that there are some unhappy millionaires, that the lottery doesn't always make people happy, and some have heard that there are "satisfied poor". If money really has no effect on subjective well-being then many people, including governments, have been seriously mistaken. Perhaps the answer is more complicated than that. We will examine how far money makes people happy, before looking for an explanation.

INCOME AND HAPPINESS

Positive affect

One of the earliest studies was the one by Bradburn (1969) of positive and negative affect. Positive affect had a clear relation with income, from a score of .32 for the poorest group to .57 for the richest; the relation with negative affect was much weaker. Diener and Biswas–Diener (2000) report a number of later studies from different lands, and found that affect balance and happiness are more closely related than satisfaction to income, but still only a correlation of .15 to .18. Another way of expressing it is that 80% of the top half in incomes were above the mid-point in affect balance compared to 56% of the bottom half.

Happiness and satisfaction

Diener and Oishi (in press) report correlations with income for 40 nations, and the average correlations are shown in Table 9.1.

These are modest correlations, which can also be expressed as a difference of 11% on the satisfaction scale between top and bottom income groups. Not surprisingly financial satisfaction has a closer connection with income than life satisfaction does.

The relation with income is stronger at the lower end of the income distribution, as shown by the results from American surveys carried out between 1981 and 1984 (Figure 9.1). The very poor are definitely unhappy. These effects of income are very robust, they are obtained in other countries, and are still found when controls for education or other variables have been applied.

The effect of money does not entirely stop at the top end, however, and studies by Diener and co-workers have found that for those in the top income category in the World Value Survey there was almost no difference in satisfaction from those in the next, 7.69 versus 7.63, though the first definitely had more financial satisfaction. Diener et al. (1985) also carried out a study of 49 rich Americans, all earning over $10 million per annum, compared with 62 chosen at random who lived in the same areas. They would have been quite well off to live there, but were not millionaires. The very rich claimed be happy 77% of the time, compared with 62% for the controls. A possible criticism of this study is that it involved a rather rare group of exceptionally rich individuals,

Table 9.1 Correlations between satisfaction and income across nations

Life satisfaction	.13
Life satisfaction (students)	.10
Financial satisfaction	.25
Financial satisfaction (students)	.18

Source: Diener and Oishi, in press.

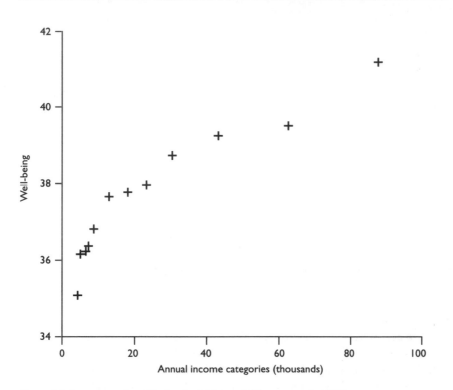

Figure 9.1 Income and well-being for US time 2 (Diener, et al., 1993).

who would differ from other people in many ways apart from being rich; it would be very hard to find a convincing control group.

There are also happy people at the lower end of the scale, the "happy poor". They have been explained as being in a state of adaptation and learned helplessness produced by a long period of experience of being able to do nothing about it (Olson and Schober, 1993).

In the survey used for Table 9.1 the correlations between income and satisfaction were much higher in some countries, e.g. Slovenia .52, South Africa .50, Turkey .39 and Estonia .34, all of them countries with a lot of poor people in them. Veenhoven (1994) reports the same for some other poor countries— Tanzania (.68) and Jordan (.51). Figure 9.2 shows a comparison of the effect of income on life satisfaction for the nine poorest and the nine richest countries in the study. This is like the stronger correlation with income found for poorer people in the USA and Britain. In poorer countries it could be because money is spent more on the satisfaction of basic needs, or because of the greater social inequality.

The relation with satisfaction is greater if other financial measures are used. Mullis (1992) found a correlation of .23 for the USA using an economic index

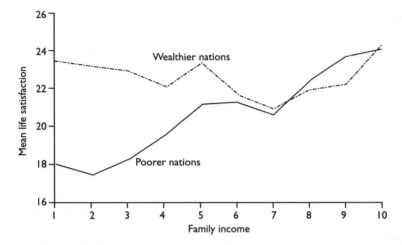

Figure 9.2 Family income and financial and life satisfaction in poorer and wealthier societies (Diener and Oishi, in press).

that took account of economic assets and total family income. The correlation was stronger, but not much stronger. And the relation with happiness and satisfaction is stronger if additional social indicators such as health and education are included, as we showed in Chapter 2. These considerations take us beyond the effects of money, although some social indicators, such as health and education, are affected by national and individual prosperity.

If there is a relation between income and happiness are we sure that it is causal? One line of evidence here is from the effects of winning lotteries. This is discussed later and we conclude that winning them is not a reliable source of happiness, but mainly because of the disruption of life that is produced. Perhaps happiness affects income. However, longitudinal data shows that happiness has only a very small effect on later income (Diener and Biswas-Diener, 2000). So the relation between income and happiness is mainly due to income being the causal agent.

Negative affect, mental disorder

Bradburn (1969) found a rather weak relation between income and negative affect. However, studies of depression or other aspects of mental disorder find a stronger relation. Kessler (1982) analysed data from eight American surveys, with 16,000 subjects. He found that for men income, especially earned income, was the strongest predictor of depression; occupational status was much weaker. For women education was a stronger predictor. West, Reed, and Gildengorin (1998) carried out a large community study and found that the frequency of depression was much lower for those with larger incomes; the effect could be explained by differences in health, disability and social isolation. For men the benefits of income levelled off at $75,000, but for women the richest were more depressed than those in the next lowest income band. In three large surveys Lachman and Weaver (1998) found that those with lower incomes reported more depression as well as more ill-health and less life satisfaction. These results are shown in Figure 9.3.

Most research in the area of mental health has taken social class as the variable of study, and this will be discussed later. However, part of the explanation for the effects of class on mental health is in terms of economic differences. Working-class people are under more stress through being short of money, having money problems, and they have smaller financial resources to deal with other difficulties (Argyle, 1994). These effects could partly be explained by the lower feelings of mastery, of control.

Health

The Lachman and Weaver study (1998) found that poorer people reported worse health. A British study by Blaxter (1990) obtained objective measures of health; she found that the poor were in much worse health than the better off, but there was an upturn in bad health for the very rich, which she concluded was mainly due to drinking too much (Figure 9.4).

As with mental health most of the research on physical health has been on the effect of social class, and again part of the explanation of the class differences is economic. Poorer people have poorer nutrition, heating, air, surroundings. However, there are other factors in class differences in health that have little to do with money, such as health behaviour (Argyle, 1994).

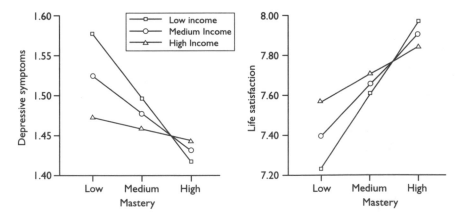

Figure 9.3 Predicted regression lines for psychological well-being in study 3 (Lachman and Weaver, 1998).

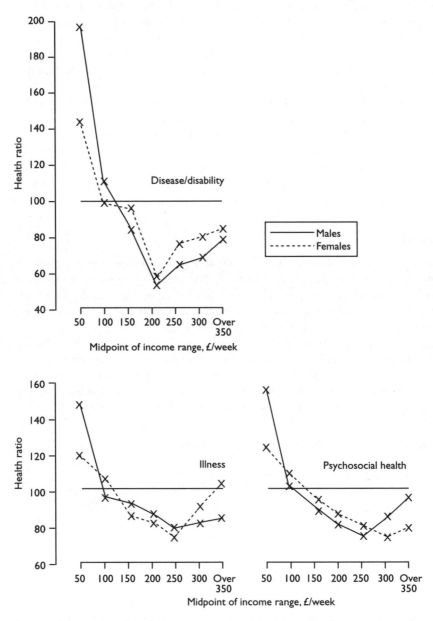

Figure 9.4 Income and health: age-standardised health ratios, illness and psychosocial health, in relation to weekly income, demonstrating the effect of £50/week increments in household income, males and females age 40–59 (all of a given age and gender = 100) (Blaxter, 1990).

International comparisons

Another way of studying the effects of income on happiness is to study the relation between average incomes and average happiness for whole countries. There have been a number of studies like this, using up to 55 countries. All have found a strong correlation of about .60 (Diener and Biswas–Diener, 2000). Comparing the richest and poorest nations there is a difference of about 7 out of 30 units of the Satisfaction With Life Scale, a quarter of the whole scale. Some studies found a levelling off part of the way up the income scale, but other studies did not. Diener et al. (1995) did not find any levelling off, and they found that per capita GDP and average purchasing power correlated with satisfaction at .33 and .37 with basic need fulfilment held constant.

There are real problems of validity in comparing happiness in different countries, as we show in Chapter 12; in some cultures people exaggerate their happiness and in others they conceal it. This could explain some of the differences of satisfaction as a function of wealth, since Americans (we shall argue) tend to exaggerate their happiness, while in Asia and Eastern Europe (all poor areas) they conceal it. On the other hand Veenhoven (1993) found that use of different languages and formats did not have much effect on scores, and in some of these studies there was good convergence of different measures (Diener et al., 1995). And despite a number of anomalies, such as the low subjective well-being in Europe, differences between the main areas make sense (Table 9.2). It is unlikely that cultural differences in response style could explain all or much of the correlation of .60.

Why is there such a large correlation for between-nations studies and such a small one for surveys of individuals within nations? This is partly a statistical artefact. A major source of variation in happiness is differences in personality, such as in extraversion and neuroticism. This is averaged out in international comparisons, a major source of "error" is removed, so the correlation obtained with income increases.

Table 9.2 Percentages "very happy" in different parts of the world

	Very happy	Highly satisfied with		
		Standard of living	Housing	Family life
N. America	40	46	55	73
Australia	37	—	—	—
Europe	20	35	49	64
Latin America	32	36	37	60
Africa	18	5	14	18
Far East	7	8	14	18

Source: Gallup (1976).

This is not the whole explanation, and a further part of it must be that there are benefits for happiness from living in rich countries, over and above benefits from individual prosperity. This could be such public goods as health facilities, education, safety, parks, leisure facilities and so on. It could also be due to the greater income equality, democracy and political freedom, and individualism, found in wealthier countries. We will look at the separate effects of these variables in Chapter 12.

Effect of pay rises for individuals

Another way of finding out if income causes happiness and satisfaction is to look at the effects of changes in income. Inglehart (1990) found that 85% of Europeans who said that their financial situation was now "a lot better" were satisfied compared with 57% of those who said it was "a lot worse". Clark (1996) studied data from 9000 British adults and found that job satisfaction was greater for those who had the largest pay rises during the past year (61.3% of those with the largest pay rises said they were satisfied). However, their data suggested that the gains in satisfaction were in the short term only, and some kind of habituation sets in. The effect of pay rises was most for those with low pay, less education and who were young; pay falls had little effect.

Another kind of economic benefit is from winning lotteries. Brickman et al. (1978) found that 22 lottery winners averaged 4.0 on a happiness scale compared with 3.82 for controls. Smith and Razzell (1975) studied 191 large winners on the British football pools; many claimed to be a little happier than before but there were a lot of serious problems too, due to the disruption of their lives; 70% gave up their jobs, many moved house, thus losing both workmates and neighbours, some were not accepted by their new neighbours, some quarrelled with their families. One of many press interviews with British National Lottery winners was of a 24-year-old woman who bought a car but couldn't drive, bought a lot of clothes but had to put them into storage, and went to an expensive restaurant but decided she preferred fish fingers. She was still unemployed, single and unhappy. It looks as if suddenly acquiring large sums of money does not make people very happy.

Several studies have found that income increases can be a cause of stress. A group of Americans who received higher welfare payments were under more stress (Thoits and Hannan, 1979); another group with increased incomes had a raised divorce rate. This could be due to disagreement over how to spend it leading to increased conflicts in the family. There may also be increased material expectations, so that those involved are less satisfied than before.

Effects of national economic changes

In many countries there have been great increases in prosperity and average incomes since World War II. In the USA there has been an increase of average incomes by a factor of four since before the war, and in Japan the increase has been greater than this (Figure 9.5). In neither country has there been any increase in satisfaction. Blanchflower and Oswald (1997), using different survey data, found that there has been a small increase in happiness in the USA, especially for those under 30. In 1972 16% of young Americans said they were "not too happy", but in 1990 this was only 9%. And in 1972 30% were "very happy", which rose to 33% in 1990. Similar results were obtained in Europe from the Eurobarometer surveys; there was a small increase in happiness for 12 of the 13 countries, especially for the young; the exception was Britain.

It is agreed however that the increases in happiness are very small, as are their correlations with changes in income. The average correlation with changes in income for the 15 countries for which repeated survey data is available was .007 (Diener and Oishi, in press). There were no very poor countries among the 15, and there is limited evidence suggesting that the relation with increasing prosperity is higher for some of them—India .09, Portugal .09, Mexico .06 and perhaps Brazil and Korea, though these are still very low.

What about falls in national incomes? There is a striking European example, Belgium: between 1978 and 1983 the percentage who said they were "very satisfied" with their lives in general fell from about 45% to 20% (see Figure 12.1, page 182). This was a period of economic depression in that country. We shall discuss the large and inexplicable differences in reported satisfaction

Figure 9.5 Satisfaction in European countries (Myers, 1992).

between different European countries in Chapter 12. There was a smaller fall in general European happiness between 1980 and 1982 and there have been similar effects of economic depression in Brazil, Ireland and Japan (Veenhoven, 1989). The explanation may be that people do not adjust very fast to falling income by reducing their material expectations.

Oswald (1997) has looked at the effect of economic changes on other possible indices of happiness. He used the General Health Questionnaire (GHQ), a measure of mental distress and negative affect. He did not find any effect of income on the GHQ in Britain among the employed, but there was a strong effect on distress caused by unemployment—itself a consequence of low economic prosperity. We have discussed unemployment in Chapter 7. Another index he used was job satisfaction. In Britain there was a slight fall between 1973 and 1983, from 42.7% very satisfied with their job to 39%. Taussig and Fenwick (1999) found the same in the USA; this was mainly due to work re-organisation, with increased job demands and less pay.

Finally Oswald looked at suicide rates. In Britain the suicide rate is low compared with other industrialised countries, and has been falling over the century. "Over the long run, as Britain has got richer, the suicide rate has declined" (Oswald, 1997, p. 13). The rate is much greater for the unemployed.

Some of these findings require explanation. Why have really large average income increases had so little effect on satisfaction? It may be because of adaptation, that is simply getting accustomed to a pattern of life and expenditure, or it could be due to rising expectations, which can indeed rise faster than actual incomes. Esterlin (2000) found a correlation between income and material aspirations, the things people wanted to have, which rise as income rises. People also have insatiable income aspirations: in 1987 Americans wanted $50,000 per annum to fulfil their dreams, in 1994 they wanted $102,000 (Schor, 1998). Another explanation could be in terms of income comparisons, the theory that people are satisfied if they have more than others, so if all become richer happiness is unaffected. This will be discussed below.

However, there has been some correlation, of up to .09, between rising incomes and increasing satisfaction, but only in poorer countries. As we saw in connection with income differences within countries, income does affect happiness at the lower end of the income scale, probably because of the satisfaction of basic needs.

Why, in Europe and the USA, have the young become happier? (see page 139). Blanchflower and Oswald (1997) tested various explanations and found that it was the unmarried young who had become happier, perhaps because of the increased freedom for love outside marriage.

The effect of income comparisons

We saw in Chapter 4 that social comparisons have variable effects on happiness. However, in the field of incomes the effects are much clearer. Clark and Oswald

(1996) studied the wages of 10,000 British workers, and calculated the average pay of individuals with the same occupation, age, education, location, etc. A regression analysis with many controls found that job satisfaction was not affected by actual income, but it was affected by expected income, that is with income held constant those with the lowest expectations had the highest job satisfaction ($r = -.26$). In another study Clark (1996) found that job satisfaction was lower if a spouse or other members of the household earned more (Clark, 1996).

In the case of wages people know what some other groups are paid. Runciman (1966) found that among British skilled manual workers 39% of those in the better manual jobs could not think of any other group that was doing better, 56% thought their pay was about right or within 10% of the right level, and only 15% of manual workers disapproved of non-manual pay levels. The manual workers evidently were not aware of the pay being given to lawyers and managing directors. He found that manual workers in the top third of all salaries were more pleased with their salaries than non-manual workers earning the same; he suggested that this was because the well-paid manual workers were comparing themselves with other manual workers, while the non-manual ones had in mind more prosperous non-manual workers.

People do like to have wages that are felt to be "fair". Berkowitz, and his colleagues (1987), in a survey in Wisconsin, found that inequity was the strongest predictor of (low) pay satisfaction. Nevertheless people like to be paid more than their just reward as well. Leicht and Shepelak (1994) studied 4567 employees in American firms and found that pay satisfaction depended on when there were procedures for ensuring fair pay, but was also enhanced by over-reward. A British study by Sloane and Williams (1996) found much the same, job satisfaction was greater for those who were paid "somewhat more than I deserve", though this only worked for males. In both studies being underpaid was a major source of dissatisfaction. The strength of wage comparisons was shown in a study by Brown (1978) who found that industrial workers preferred a wage situation where they were paid £1 per week more than members of another department to one where they were paid £2 a week more than this, but less than the other department. There have been cases when a factory has closed or moved to a region of cheaper labour, because of such comparisons.

Do people compare their present situation with the past, are they happier if their financial situation has improved? There are immediate effects, but these do not last very long, and there seem to be no reliable effects of comparisons with the past.

Explanations of the effects of money on happiness

Meeting basic needs

Veenhoven (1995) among others put forward the view that money enhances happiness when it can contribute to the satisfaction of basic and universal needs for food, shelter and clothes. This is consistent with the finding that within societies there is a relation between income and satisfaction at the lower end of the scale only (apart from a possible small rise for the very rich), and that the relation is stronger in poorer countries, indeed is very weak in rich ones.

Maslow's theory (1954) has been used to explain this. His idea was that as lower needs, first physiological and then for safety, are satisfied, then higher needs become important, for social acceptance, self-esteem and finally self-actualisation. This theory has not received much confirmation, but can interpret the findings here—money meets lower needs for those individuals and societies which have not advanced to higher needs. It does not fit the finding that inter-country incomes and satisfaction are related to some extent over the whole income scale. This might be explained by noting the very broad effects of national income on facilities, not only better food and housing, but also leisure, education, medicine, transport and environment.

What needs explaining even more is why the effect of money on subjective well-being is so very small, when we look at within-country data or the historical effects of rising incomes. Part of the reason is that there are other causes of happiness that are more important than money, and these will not change historically. People spend money on things or activities that they want, and that they assume will give them satisfaction or pleasure. And some of them do—food and meeting other basic needs, and also some kinds of leisure. However, other and more important sources of happiness are less obvious. Work for example is a major source of happiness but it *makes* money. Love and other social relationships are free, more or less. Some kinds of leisure are expensive—foreign travel, sailing, horse riding, but other forms of leisure are virtually free—most kinds of exercise, church, voluntary work, reading and study, and watching TV, and some make a profit, as with gardening. Having a positive and optimistic attitude, and choosing goals, are free.

Meeting non-biological needs

The Maslow theory predicts that in rich countries, where money is a less important source of satisfaction, other (higher) needs will be stronger predictors. Oishi et al. (1999) found that satisfaction with self-esteem and with freedom were stronger correlates of life satisfaction in richer nations. However some non-biological needs, including self-actualisation, can be fulfilled with the help of money, as for example in the case of leisure, which may involve expensive material possessions and other expenses, as with sailing and horse riding for example. Some material possessions and activities, for which money is needed, may enhance life, whereas others, such as drink and drugs, diminish it and cause unhappiness.

However, individuals who think possessions are important and judge their success by them are found to be less happy, and often disappointed when they have bought them. This may be because they are really seeking self-fulfilment or happiness, and find that material things fail to provide this (Dittmar, 1992). Kasser and Ryan (1993) similarly found that those who thought financial success important or who estimated their chances of achieving it were high, were lower on self-actualisation, vitality, and higher on depression and anxiety. The reverse was found for those who valued self-acceptance and contributions to the community. Chan and Joseph (2000) found that happiness, measured by the Oxford Happiness Inventory, was predictable from extraversion and neuroticism as usual, and was also greater for those concerned with the community and less for those who rated financial success highly. This may be because concern with material things draws attention away from more important matters, which would give greater satisfaction. Inglehart (1971) thought that many in affluent societies now value non-material goals, such as freedom, participation, quality of life, the environment. These "post-materialist" values are found to be stronger in the middle-class young in rich societies.

The symbolic value of money

Money is also valued because it symbolises success and social status. These are symbolised by clothes, cars, houses and other possessions, all part of "self-presentation", influencing the perceptions and reactions of other people. Veblen's "Theory of the Leisure Class" (1899) was that rich people display their wealth by for example wearing clothes obviously unsuitable for work, and engaging in expensive and time-consuming forms of leisure, showing that they have time and money to burn. Simmel (1904) said that the upper class start new fashions, which others imitate, and Hurlock (1929) found that 40% of American women and 20% of men said they would follow a clothes fashion to appear equal to those of higher social status, and about half would change their styles when their social inferiors adopted them. It doesn't work quite like this for clothes any more since new fashions are mass produced at all levels, but the trickle-down process may well play an important part in the economy, by helping to persuade people that they need new things all the time, because their social status will fall if they don't have them. Advertising plays an important part in launching new products, and appealing to their symbolic value is a central part of this process (Furnham and Argyle, 1998).

The very rich are interesting. Why do they want to be so rich, what possible needs could they want to meet? What they do is to take up a superior way of life with more servants, more and bigger houses, more elaborate holidays, bigger parties. And the real gain from all this may be to enable them to join a superior social group, which in Britain consists of those who live in large country houses, own land, engage in country sports, send their children to certain schools and colleges, and are titled. Indeed they have to join another social group since they no longer fit in the previous one. There is a lot of symbolic impact here: if you become a member of a higher social group you can see yourself as a different, and superior, kind of person, and be treated by others as such. This is all due to the symbolic power of money. Does it make them any happier? As we have seen, not much.

People may want more money because they think it will make them happier, or they believe that what money can buy will make them happier, or because spending it produces short-term positive feelings, or because it will increase their control over events (Diener and Biswas-Diener, 2000).

Controlling events

In other parts of the book we discuss the advantages of feeling that you have "control" of events. This is particularly found at work, also as an aspect of personality, and as a way of coping with stressful life events. Control is increased by "resources", and one of the most important resources is money—when you can afford to pay for something that might solve the problem (Campbell et al., 1976). Lachman and Weaver (1998) found that individuals with higher incomes had greater perceived mastery, and that in all income groups those with more mastery had more life satisfaction, better health and less depression. Class differences, defined here in terms of income, in well-being, could be partly explained by class differences in control. We return to this topic shortly when discussing class.

SOCIAL CLASS AND WELL-BEING

Social class is sometimes assessed in terms of income, but usually it is seen as rather different. In British studies a hierarchy of occupations is used, mainly based on skill; in American research it is the combination of income, education and occupation; for Marxists occupations are classified in terms of the amount of control exercised. Several studies in Britain and the USA using different measures of class have found clear curvilinear effects of class on happiness. Table 9.3 gives one of them, from a British national survey, using occupation as the measure of class. Again there is a curvilinear pattern: occupational class has a greater effect at the bottom end of the scale.

Haring et al. (1984) did a meta-analysis of American studies, and found that class correlated .20 with satisfaction, more than the effect of income or job status. The greatest effects in both countries are for measures of positive affect.

The correlation of class and well-being is much greater in some other countries, such as Israel .55, Nigeria .52, Philippines .44, India .42, and Brazil .38

Table 9.3 Social class and happiness in Great Britain

	Very happy	Positive affect	Negative affect
Income			
High	44	3.2	1.2
Middle	42	2.7	1.1
Low	30	2.3	1.5
Occupation			
Professional and management	43	3.3	1.1
Non-manual	34	2.8	1.0
Skilled manual	40	2.8	0.9
Unskilled manual	42	2.7	1.3
Unemployed	27	2.1	1.6
Retired	28	2.2	1.2
Education ended			
Before 15	35	2.4	1.3
15	40	2.5	1.2
16	40	2.7	1.3
17–18	40	3.0	1.2
19+	36	3.0	1.1

Source: Harding (1985).

(Cantril, 1965). What these countries have in common is large class differences: they are more unequal, apparently in happiness as well as in other ways.

The effect of class on health is very marked. Marmot et al. (1984) found that rate of fatal heart attacks was 3.6 times greater in the lowest rank of the British civil service compared with the highest (see Figure 7.3, page 102). They found that this could only be partly explained in terms of differences in smoking, blood pressure, blood sugar and cholesterol, reflecting class differences in life style. The rest of the effect could be due to differences in social status, and their emotional consequences. Health depends not only on individual circumstances, but on those of the geographical area. Poorer areas are more unhealthy and have poorer health facilities (Robert, 1998).

Mental health is much worse in lower social classes. This is partly due to differences in income, discussed above. We have just seen that there are occupational differences due to the nature of work. Working-class people have a lower sense of internal control, partly reflecting the nature of the work they do, long experience of not being able to control things, and socialisation in the working-class culture of powerlessness (Kohn and Schooler, 1982). This makes working class individuals less able to cope with stress, and they are also under more stress, part of it financial, from poverty and unemployment, and ill-health (McLeod and Kessler, 1990).

Some of the major causes of happiness are weaker in working-class life. Working-class marriages often get off to a bad start, hurriedly decided when the girl is pregnant, and having to share a house at first with parents (Argyle, 1994). Working-class people engage in less leisure of every kind, except watching TV, one of the least satisfying leisure pursuits. This seems to be mainly due to less opportunity to acquire leisure interests, often dicovered at college (Argyle, 1996).

THE EFFECTS OF EDUCATION

Many surveys carried out in the USA have found that there is some correlation between happiness and education, assessed by number of years of education received or the level of the highest qualification acquired. The effect in the USA has declined over time. So in 1957 44% of university graduates said they were very happy compared with 23% of those who did not finish high school, but in 1978 the corresponding figures were 33% and 28% (Campbell, 1981). However, Kessler (1982) using data from 16,000 people in eight surveys, found that for American women education was a stronger predictor of good mental health than income or occupation were; for men earned income was a better predictor. The effect of education is also weak in Europe and Japan. However, the effect is much stronger in some other countries—such as South Korea, Mexico, former Yugoslavia, the Philippines and Nigeria (Veenhoven, 1994). This suggests that the key variable is national wealth—the effect of education is greater in poorer countries.

When there is an effect of education, how does it work? A meta-analysis by Witter et al. (1984) found that education affected subjective well-being primarily by affecting occupation, not income, and had little effect apart from this, although occupation in turn affects income. Ross and Van Willigen (1997) in an American national sample found that education benefited subjective well-being, mental health and health, and did so via its effect on getting satisfying work, increased control and better access to marriage and other forms of social support.

Does education have any effect on satisfaction apart from its effect on jobs and income? Bradburn (1969) found they had separate effects, as shown in

Table 9.4 The effects of income and education on happiness

Education	Income		
	Less than $5000	$5000–7999	$8000 or more
Less than high school graduate	.35	.44	.52
High school graduate	.47	.47	.56
Some college	.51	.53	.55

Source: Bradburn (1969).

Table 9.4. In more recent American studies the residual effect of education is small or zero, but in a British study Clark and Oswald (1996) found that education had a clear negative effect, when income and occupation had been held constant, which they put down to the effect of raised expectations, i.e. comparison level. In the Bradburn study shown in Table 9.4 the effect of education was greater, as Campbell (1981) also found; he put this down to the effect of education on leisure and the "inner life".

CONCLUSIONS

Money has several effects on happiness. Within prosperous countries there is a small correlation between them, though income has more effect at the bottom end of the income scale; in poorer countries the relation is much stronger. There is a much stronger correlation between the happiness and average incomes of countries, partly because the provision of public goods and facilities is important. There is a very small increase in happiness with increasing incomes, mainly for the young unmarried, probably through habituation and rising expectations, but there is much more effect of economic depression.

Money meets basic needs, but does more than this, and must meet a wider range of needs. It also has symbolic value, and acts as a resource, giving control of events. Further explanation of the weak effect of money within countries is that satisfaction depends on comparison with others, particularly for industrial workers. Social class affects happiness too, independently of money, especially in socially stratified countries, and has a strong effect on health through lifestyle differences, and on mental health through better coping methods. Education has weak effects on well-being, mainly through affecting occupation and income, but has more effect in poorer countries.

Money is certainly not a measure of happiness, and for those social groups and those nations that are prosperous it has very little relation with it. Because we spend money on things we want, and that we assume will cause us pleasure, there is an illusion that money is the root of happiness. But other more important causes cost little or nothing (love, most leisure, positive attitudes, choice of goals), and some make a profit (work). Money can certainly satisfy basic needs, but in many countries most individuals have met these already. Making individuals or countries richer has very little effect on their subjective well-being. Nevertheless very poor individuals and those in very poor countries are definitely less happy than those that are better off.

Chapter 10

Personality, age and gender

The other chapters in this book are about external, environmental causes of happiness. This chapter is about the effect of enduring features of the person, which affect happiness from the inside rather than the outside. It does not imply that this aspect of happiness is unchangeable, since personality can be changed, for example by psychotherapy or by serious life events, good or bad.

ARE THERE HAPPY PEOPLE?

It seems to be generally agreed, by psychologists and others, that there are depressed, i.e. unhappy, people, though they may not be depressed all the time. Are there also happy people, and if so, who are they? If there are, is this because they experience a lot of pleasant activities or situations, or is it due to something more fundamental about their personalities? We have seen that joy and other aspects of well-being depend on a number of factors in the environment, such as social relationships, work and leisure. We now want to know how far happiness is due to the person as well as to situations and events. Popular books on happiness are all about what people can do to make themselves happier, and fail to mention that there is another major factor that may be more difficult to change—their own personalities.

We have already seen some of the evidence on whether there are happy people, when we discussed well-being in Chapter 2. We showed that different measures of well-being, satisfaction, happiness and positive affect all correlate quite strongly together, and produce a clear general factor. So happiness, or well-being, is like a personality trait, in that it consists of a number of related elements, and is stable across situations and over time.

We saw in Chapter 3 how states of joy are aroused in different situations, and in Chapter 13 we shall describe methods of inducing positive and negative moods in the lab. This means that the same individuals can experience different degrees of joy depending on the situation. Individuals also report different levels of overall life satisfaction. It is a general finding in social psychology that the sources of emotional states can be divided up between persons and situations. In one of these studies Diener and Larson (1984) found that positive and negative affect in various work and leisure situations was more due to persons (52%) than to situations (23%). Individuals were more consistent for negative emotions and for life satisfaction, less for positive emotions.

There is also *interaction* between the effects of person and situations. Larsen and Ketelaar (1991) found that extraverts react more strongly to positive stimuli than do introverts, so that the combination of extraversion and pleasant situations produces positive affect. There is a second kind of interaction between persons and situations, since persons can *choose* or *avoid situations*. They choose certain kinds of situations, which suit them, and which are congruent with their personalities. For example extraverts spend more time in social activities and physical pursuits. Those who are anxious or otherwise neurotic, or low in social skills, avoid social situations, as was found by Headey and Wearing (1992), in their longitudinal study. Argyle and Lu (1990) found that the happiness of extraverts could be partly explained by their choice of enjoyable social situations. In earlier research Argyle (1994) found that the socially unskilled avoid many social situations that others enjoy.

We showed in Chapter 2 that happiness measures are very stable over time. I and my co-workers have found that scores on the Oxford Happiness Inventory are more stable than scores on the rather similar Beck Depression Inventory (Argyle et al., 1995). Other studies have found test–retest reliabilities of over .50 after an interval of 6 years or longer, and that this works for ratings by others as well as self-reported well-being. However, this apparent consistency could be because the subjects' circumstances were very similar at time 2. It has been found that the test–retest reliability of other measures of well-being is only slightly reduced if there have been major changes of income or other life conditions (Diener and Lucas, 1999). Nevertheless there can be long-term changes in happiness over time. We saw in Chapter 6 that being in love, or experiencing other favourable social relationships, can alter the level of well-being. But the same is true of the personality trait of extraversion: Headey et al. (1985) found that good social relations over a period of time produced an increased level of extraversion, and this in turn led to increased well-being.

Extraversion and some other personality traits correlated with happiness are known to be partly inherited. The same is true of happiness itself. The largest study of this issue was by Lykken and Tellegen (1996) who studied the happiness of 1400 pairs of twins, and calculated the correlations between the happiness of pairs of twins of different kinds, with the results shown in Table 10.1.

The importance of inheritance is shown here mainly by the greater similarity of identical compared with fraternal twins, but also by the strong similarity of identical twins who had been reared in different families. The authors estimated that genetics accounted for more variance for negative emotionality (55%), compared with 48% for well-being and 40% for positive emotionality. Positive and negative emotionality had a different genetic basis, negative emotions being

Table 10.1 Correlations between the happiness of different kinds of twin pairs

	Identical	Fraternal
Reared together	.44	.08
Reared apart	.52	−.02

Source: Lykken and Tellegen (1996).

more innate, and positive emotionality owing more to shared family environment. Other twin studies have obtained different estimates of the degree to which happiness is inherited—it varies with the measure used as we have seen, and inheritance will appear stronger if there is less environmental variability, but they all agree that a substantial amount of variance is due to this cause. This agrees with the high level of consistency found over time. And we shall see later that happiness is quite strongly correlated with both extraversion and the absence of neuroticism, two traits known to have a strong genetic component, about 50%, which suggests that happiness may have a similar basis.

Socialisation experiences in early childhood may also affect whether people become happy personalities or not. Maletasta et al. (1986) found that mothers trained infants as young as 2½ months how to express their feelings in a socially desirable way; expression of feelings affects the experience of feelings.

EXTRAVERSION

Extraversion has often been found to be correlated with well-being, but particularly with positive affect (Costa and McCrae, 1980). The relation is so robust that Costa et al. (1981) found that extraversion could predict happiness 17 years later. When extraversion is divided into sociability and impulsiveness, it is sociability which correlates more highly. The extraversion scale on the Eysenck Personality Questionnaire is nearly all sociability, and we find that it correlates at .50 or above with happiness, measured by the OHI. Herringer (1998) used that part of the "Big Five" scale (see later, page 154) that measures extraversion, which has six facets. He found that the facet with the strongest correlation with life satisfaction was assertiveness, especially for males, and warmth and gregariousness, especially for females. Looking at the other side of the relationship, Francis (1999) with 356 subjects found that most of the items on the Oxford Happiness Inventory correlated with extraversion, as they also did with neuroticism.

Why are extraverts happier than introverts? Gray (1982) proposed that because of differences in brain structure extraverts are more responsive to rewards, and hence are happier; neurotics are more responsive to punishment, and hence are unhappier. We have just seen that Larsen and Ketelaar (1991) found that extraverts were more influenced by positive mood induction than introverts; there was no difference for negative mood induction.

We have carried out a series of studies which have shown that the happiness of extraverts is partly due to the joys of social interaction with friends, which extraverts are able to enjoy more, because they have superior social skills that enable them to do so. Argyle and Lu (1990) asked subjects for their frequency of enjoyment and participation in 37 leisure activities, and factor analysed this list of items. Several factors were found, as shown in Table 6.2, page 73. Frequency of participation in the activities in factor 4, belonging to teams and clubs, and in factor 5, going to parties and dances, correlated with happiness and with extraversion. Some introverts are happy, and this can be partly explained by their taking part in these activities. Headey et al. (1985) found in a longitudinal panel study that extraversion predisposed people, especially young people, to have favourable life events, especially in the domains of work and leisure. This can be done by choosing to enter such events, or by being able to change events once they are in them. This led to higher well-being, and also to raised extraversion.

Why do introverts not do these things too? Perhaps because they do not have the social skills needed. Argyle and Lu (1990) carried out a longitudinal study; it was found that extraversion predicted happiness 5 months later, but this was mediated by assertiveness, extraverts were happy because of their assertiveness, as shown in Figure 10.1. It should be noted that assertiveness is quite different from aggressiveness, it is the skill of influencing others while keeping on good terms with them.

Studies of depressed individuals, one variety of unhappy individuals, find that they tend to be lonely, isolated, unrewarding, that is generally lacking in social skills (Argyle, 1994).

In a series of studies with adult samples Hills and Argyle have regularly found strong correlations between happiness and extraversion (e.g. Hills and Argyle, 2001). However, even if the correlation is as high as .60 there is still a substantial minority of happy introverts. We thought that this might be because they have a more intense inner life or fewer and deeper social relations than happy extraverts or unhappy introverts. This was not the case, indeed it was expected that introverts would watch more TV but we found that extraverts watch more TV soap operas for example. But there is no real mystery here: when two variables have even a quite high correlation, as there is between happiness and extraversion, there is still going to be a minority who do not fit the overall pattern.

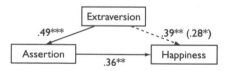

Figure 10.1 A longitudinal study of the effect of extraversion on happiness (Argyle and Lu, 1990).

Notes: *p < .05, **p < .01, ***p < .001.

Happy introverts simply scored high on other personality variables. We now turn to some of these other personality traits, starting with neuroticism.

NEUROTICISM

This too has a regular and strong association with happiness, in this case a negative one. DeNeve and Cooper (1998) report a meta-analysis of 74 studies using various measures of neuroticism in relation to well-being and happiness measures, and neuroticism was found to have an overall correlation with happiness of −.22, the strongest of the Big Five groupings in this analysis. However, these studies included a variety of measures of happiness. Of the different components of well-being, neuroticism has the strongest correlation with negative affect (Costa and McCrae, 1980). Watson and Clark (1984) concluded that the relation between neuroticism and negative affect is so strong that the two variables can be regarded as equivalent. We also found a correlation of −.67 with happiness as a whole, as shown in Table 10.2.

In Chapter 12 we shall use extraversion as a possible measure of happiness in international comparisons, since the single item measures often used have been unsatisfactory. We showed in Chapter 2 that the absence of negative affect such as anxiety and depression is one of the main components of happiness or well-being. Individuals high in neuroticism are likely to be anxious, and the depressed are of course depressed. The happiness of real psychotics is probably unmeasurable, but the Psychoticism scale on the Eysenck Personality Questionnaire (EPQ), which really measures tough-mindedness, has a modest negative correlation with happiness (see Table 10.2). But what about manics, who often seem happy, if not too happy? In fact their mood is primarily one of

Table 10.2 Partial correlations of happiness with the component scales (controlling for gender and age)

	OHI	OHI[a]
Extraversion	.61 ***	—
Neuroticism	−.67***	−.63 ***
Psychoticism	−.27***	−.28 ***
Lie-scale	.21 ***	.23 ***
Preference for solitude	−.18**	.09
Life orientation	.75 ***	.69 ***
Affiliative tendency	.51 ***	.06
Life regard index	.85 ***	.82 ***
Empathetic tendency	−.02	−.14*
Self-esteem	.78 ***	.71 ***

Notes *p<.05, **p < .01, ***p < .001.
[a] controlling for gender, age, and extraversion.

Source: Hills and Argyle (2001).

excitement, of high arousal, rather than happiness, and they are often irritable. They can be characterised as follows:

> Manics are euphoric, self-confident and full of energy . . . They wear smart, striking but rather loud clothes, look extremely well and very pleased with themselves, are smiling and alert, and have a loud confident voice of robust, resonant quality. They talk incessantly, and tend to monopolize the conversation with their hilarious jokes and outrageous stories, but are easily distractible and move from topic to topic. Their excitement and jollity are infectious, and they are good at being the life and soul of the party. [but] Their delusional self-importance, their constant talking, and a tendency to bizarre behaviour may lead to their becoming a public nuisance.
>
> (Argyle, 1994, pp. 218–219)

THE BIG FIVE

British and European personality research has most often used the EPQ, with the three dimensions of extraversion, neuroticism and psychoticism. American personality research has used the "Big Five" scales of extraversion, agreeableness, conscientiousness, neuroticism and openness to experience. There have been many studies of how these relate to well-being, and DeNeve and Cooper (1998) in the study as described above carried out a meta-analysis of 148 of them. The overall correlations with life satisfaction, and other happiness measures are shown in Table 10.3. These correlations are smaller than those for the EPQ, both for neuroticism and extraversion. This may because the Big Five scales are very broad, and fail to tap the more specific aspects of personality which relate to happiness. The third area of most relevance to happiness is probably conscientiousness, which came out just below neuroticism and above extraversion in the meta-analysis above. Furnham and Cheng (1997) used the OHI and the Big Five, and found that neuroticism had the highest correlation with happiness (−.44), extraversion .39 and conscientiousness .31. The latter is a less familiar and less understood personality trait, but may be similar to internal

Table 10.3 Happiness and the "Big Five"

	Overall r	Number of studies
Extraversion	.17	82
Agreeableness	.17	59
Conscientiousness	.21	115
Neuroticism	− .22	74
Openness to experience	.11	41

Source: DeNeve and Cooper (1998).

control, which we discuss soon. The Big Five list fails to include some personality dimensions that have been found to have a strong relationship with happiness, and we now turn to these. These are cognitive aspects of personality, probably with less linkage to biological factors.

"COGNITIVE" ASPECTS OF PERSONALITY

Hills and Argyle (2001), while studying the problems of happy introverts, ran correlations with some of these cognitive dimensions. Table 10.3 showed their partial correlations with the Oxford Happiness Inventory, before and after controlling for extraversion. The cognitive dimensions of personality we are thinking of here are self-esteem, optimism and purpose in life. There is a fourth dimension, not included in the study above, control or internal control, and this also correlates with happiness. The correlations between happiness and these four variables are often so high that some investigators have treated them as parts of happiness. This was done by Ryff (1989) who made self-acceptance, purpose in life and autonomy three of the six aspects of well-being that she located. We are using different measures of well-being and so will regard these cognitive variables as separate aspects of personality, which may be found to act as causes of happiness, which may have independent origins, and which it might be possible to manipulate in happiness enhancement. They have been called "cognitive" aspects of personality, since they are primarily styles of thinking, although they also contain emotional reactions.

Self-esteem

Self-esteem has been found to correlate with well-being in many studies, with a correlation of .50 or more (Veenhoven, 1994). It is often measured by Rosenberg's scale (1965), with items like "On the whole I am satisfied with myself". Grob et al. (1996) found a correlation of .82 between self-esteem and positive attitude to life. In an American national survey satisfaction with self has a higher correlation (.55) with overall satisfaction than any other domain examined (Campbell, 1981). Hills and Argyle (1998b) obtained a correlation of .78 with a British sample as shown in Table 10.2, again one of the highest. More than the other cognitive variable self-esteem has been regarded as part of well-being. Notably it correlates with well-being measures more strongly than extraversion, as Hills and Argyle found. In a job satisfaction study of 1775 workers, Arrindell et al. (1997) found self-esteem correlated with life satisfaction .45, neuroticism .30 and extraversion at only .10.

Rosenberg et al. (1995) compared the effects of global and academic self-esteem for 2213 10th-grade school children. Global self-esteem was much more strongly correlated with happiness (.50) and with negative affect (−.43), but academic self-esteem was more closely related to school marks. Statistical modelling found that academic self-esteem and school marks both influenced each other, but the effect of self-esteem on marks was greater than the reverse.

While this strong relation with self-esteem is widely found in the USA, Britain and other Western cultures, it is much weaker in collectivist cultures (Diener and Diener, 1995). The self-image in collectivist cultures like China is not based much on individual characteristics such as intelligence or attractiveness, but more on properties of the family and other social groups; self-esteem likewise depends more on the success of such groups (Markus and Kitayama, 1991).

Control

This was originally called "internal control" by Rotter (1966), who thought that individuals have "generalised expectancies" to believe either that events are under their own control, or that they are due to other people or fate or luck. He produced a widely used measure of internal control. Many studies have found a correlation between scoring high on internal control and subjective well-being. Control does not appear in the Big Five, but is quite close to the dimension of conscientiousness, with its facets of dutifulness, achievement, striving, self-discipline and deliberation, all of which are aspects of trying to control events (Furnham, 1997). Internal control has consistently been found to be a predictor of happiness. Lu et al. (1997) used a sample of 494 adults in Taiwan and found that internal control correlated with happiness (using a Chinese version of the OHI). Furthermore this held up after extraversion, neuroticism, demographic variables and negative life events had been taken into account.

This is all the opposite side of the theory of "learned helplessness", used to explain the outlook of depressed individuals, which claimed that depressed individuals had found that they could not obtain desirable goals or prevent undesirable events, and that this was due to themselves. It is well-known that depressed individuals have a certain way of attributing the cause of bad events—by thinking that they caused them themselves, and that these will keep on happening, and will occur in other spheres (Abramson et al., 1978). It is not known whether the negative cognitions cause the negative emotions or the other way round; nevertheless modification of negative cognitions is used as part of cognitive therapy for depression. We have found that happy people have similar but positive responses to good events—that they caused them themselves, and that these will continue to occur and in different spheres (Argyle et al., 1989).

Grob et al. (1996) carried out a study with 3844 adolescents in 14 countries. It was found that "control expectations" correlated .35 with positive attitude to life, and this was found uniformly in all 14 cultures. Control expectations also had a high correlation with self-esteem (.82), which we discuss below. Lachman and Weaver (1998), in another large study of 3485 adults, found that a scale of "mastery" was strongly correlated with life satisfaction, and with depression (negatively) and health. Self-reported "constraints" had the opposite effect.

Their effects were stronger for people with lower incomes, and the lower well-being of lower-class individuals could partly be explained by their lower mastery and greater perceived constraints (see page 134 and Figure 9.3). These class differences may be due to real experiences of lack of control of working-class individuals (Kohn and Schooler, 1982).

Job satisfaction research has found that having a sense of autonomy, being able to do the work in your own way, is an important source of such satisfaction. Sheldon et al. (1996) carried out a diary study with 60 subjects. They found a "good day" was when they felt autonomous and competent in their daily activities.

Optimism

The "Pollyanna" principle describes those individuals who look on the bright side. They are optimistic about the future, recall only good things in the past, and have a positive view of others, and produce pleasanter items in free association tests; they experience more pleasant stimuli and judge more stimuli to be pleasant (Matlin and Gawron, 1979). This fits other findings about the links between emotion and cognition. For example we remember things better that are associated with our present mood, so when happy we recall happy events better (Teasdale and Russell, 1983). Happy people are the opposite of depressed ones in this respect, as the latter are pessimistic and look on the black side of things, recalling unhappy memories.

We saw earlier that most people have a positive view of the world, but some have a more positive view than others. An approach to optimism was developed by Scheier and Carver (1985) who saw it as a generalised expectation that future events will be positive, and they developed the Life Orientation Test (LOT) to measure it. This has been widely found to correlate with happiness; Hills and Argyle (2001) found a correlation of .75 (see Table 10.2). It has also been found to correlate with maintaining well-being in the face of stress.

There may be a certain amount of self-deception here (Taylor and Brown, 1988). We discussed this in Chapter 4 and concluded that positive illusions are common and are generally beneficial for happiness.

Optimism appears to be a part of subjective well-being which has strong effects on health and mental health. Sweetman et al. (1993) found that among a sample of lawyers optimism was the best predictor of general well-being, better than hardiness or attributional style. Lai and Wong (1998) working in Hong Kong found that the unemployed had higher GHQ scores, but not if they were high in optimism. Segerstrom et al. (1998) found for law students that those high in optimism at time 1 had more active immune systems at time 2, and that this was partly due to their having more positive moods, perceiving less stress and not using avoidance methods of coping.

Several investigators have found that optimism consists of two somewhat independent factors, optimism and pessimism; that while both correlate with other aspects of well-being, the pessimism factor does so more strongly (negatively). Robinson-Wheeler et al. (1997) found that only the pessimism factor predicted psychological and physical health; Chang et al. (1997) found that pessimism only had a partial correlation with the BDI.

There are several ways of "thinking positively". One is having ruminations with a positive content, and attributing good and not bad events to self, which Argyle et al. (1989) found happy people tend to do. Another is having a good sense of humour, which enables people to "see the funny side of things", having an ironic view of life, which makes bad things seem good (see page 62).

Purpose in Life

Measures of purpose in life, PIL, are strongly correlated with happiness. As we show in the next chapter religion is one source of it, but religion is not the only source of purpose in life, there is also work and career, making money, looking after the family, political parties, voluntary work and other leisure activities, for example.

Just having long-term plans or goals gives people a sense of meaning in life. Victor Frankl (1959) was famous for surviving concentration camp, and helping others to do the same, by finding a goal to pursue should they get out; this might be caring for another person, writing a book, or completing some other task. Later he developed this into a form of therapy, "logotherapy", which consisted of helping people find the goals they might pursue, which would then give meaning to their lives.

Having a sense of "meaning and purpose" is a rather vague and mysterious entity. Its absence is clearer. Freedman (1978) reported on the results of a *Psychology Today* survey in which it was found that people were happier if they felt that their lives had meaning, a direction and they had confidence in their guiding values. Here is what one of them said:

> My life has been terrific the last few years—lots of money, women, friends, all sorts of activities and travel. My job is good and I am good at it. There is even a good future—I will probably be promoted this year and make lots more money and have freedom to do what I want. But it all seems to lack any significance for me. Where is my life leading, why am I doing what I am doing? I have the feeling that I am being carried along without ever making any real decisions or knowing what my goals are. It's sort of like getting on a road and driving along fine but not knowing why you chose that a particular road or where it is leading.
>
> (Argyle, 1987, p. 123, from Freedman, 1978, pp. 195–196)

Battista and Almond (1973) constructed a measure of purpose in life, their Life Regard Inventory, to measure purpose in the sense of having a set of life goals and the extent to which they had been fulfilled; this has been widely used.

A later version was used by Van Ranst and Marcoen (1997); an example of the goals part is "I have found a really significant meaning for leading my life", and for fulfilment "I have a real passion in my life". They gave this test to a large group of young people, and another group of older ones who were mostly married and in professional careers, or had been. The second group had higher scores on both parts than the first. A group of problem students in Bangladesh were found to have much lower scores (60) compared with other students (88) (Rahman and Khaléque, 1996). We shall describe Paloutzian and Ellison's Existential Well-Being scale in the next chapter; it has similar items such as "I feel that there is some real purpose in my life".

Cantor and Sanderson (1999) argue that "participating in valued activities and working towards personal goals" is important for well-being. They broaden the concept of purpose and goals to include "valued activities". These goals and activities enhance well-being in several ways: (1) by giving a sense of personal agency and purpose, produced by valued and challenging activities, and lacking in the depressed; (2) giving structure and meaning to daily life; (3) by giving help coping with problems and adversity in daily life, which may lead to renewed commitment; and (4) by strengthening social relationships and leading to more social participation. There is more effect on well-being when the activities are freely chosen, when goals are realistic, the goals are consistent with each other, and when people manage to spend a lot of time in goal-relevant activities.

McGregor and Little (1998) report a way of studying goals, by asking people to list "personal projects" and rate them on scales. In two studies they asked 327 subjects to rate 10 personal projects each, on 35 scales. Happiness was correlated with a factor of "efficacy" consisting of lack of difficulty, stress or time pressure, plus positive outcomes and control.

Sheldon and Elliot (1999) proposed that "goal self-concordance" would be important; by this they mean believing in the importance of goals and choosing them for fun and enjoyment rather than goals being externally imposed or followed to avoid guilt or anxiety. These authors confirmed a causal model where goal self-concordance leads to greater effort, to goal attainment and to enhance well-being (Figure 10.2).

A problem about goals is that when the gap between goals and achievement

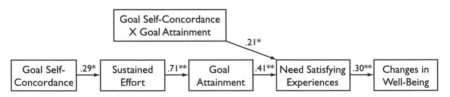

Figure 10.2 Study 3 structural equation model: Theoretically central paths and parameter estimates (Sheldon and Elliot, 1999)

$*p < .05, **p < .01.$

is too great then individuals are discontented, as we saw earlier (page 48). Emmons (1986) asked 40 subjects to rate 15 kinds of personal striving on 16 scales each. He found that life satisfaction was greater and negative affect less if future success was thought to be likely. Again it is desirable to have goals that are realistic, but above all it is good to have goals at all and to take part in activities which are valued. One reason for this is that such valued goals and activities are part of the self-image, and lead to self-esteem.

Resources

Resources make some activities more possible and help in the attainment of goals. Resources include money, social support, social skills, and power. We interpreted the benefits of social relationships earlier in terms of their value as resources for social support for example (see page 74).

Personality qualities can be seen as resources in the same way. Intelligence had a small correlation with happiness, .13 in the Campbell et al. (1976) study, and it could be due to social class or occupation. Physical attractiveness has a stronger effect, at least for young women; it leads to more popularity with the opposite sex, and also with teachers and employers, and it leads to upward mobility (Argyle, 1994).

Social skills are very important. Argyle and Lu (1990) found that extraverts are happier because of their assertiveness, and later we found that happiness is related to cooperativeness, leadership and heterosexual skills (Argyle et al., 1995). These skills are important because they enable us to have the desired relations with others. Individuals who are unrewarding or otherwise lack social skills are likely to be isolated and lonely.

However, Diener and Fujita (1995) found that resources affected well-being only when they were relevant to goals. For example money affected well-being most for those individuals who wanted to be rich.

THE EFFECT OF AGE

Some big international surveys, over many countries and with over 100,000 subjects, have found that life satisfaction increases with age (e.g. Cantril, 1965), for men more than for women (World Values Study Group, 1994), and this pattern has also been found for positive affect. Job satisfaction shows a similar rise with age (Kalleberg and Loscocco, 1983). These increases could be due to historical, that is generational, differences, and be due to life becoming "worse", less satisfying, throughout the world, so that older people continue to be happier.

This issue can be settled by longitudinal studies, of the same individuals over time, and there are one or two of these. For positive affect Helson and Lohnen (1998) report such a study of 80 women, and the spouses of 20 of them, from the age of 27 to 52, using the Adjective Check List. As shown in Figure 10.3 there was a definite rise in positive affect between 27 and 43 and a fall in negative affect; the smaller number of male subjects showed the same pattern. This is a unique demonstration of the effects of age on positive affect.

Several studies have found that positive affect, like satisfaction, increases for men but declines for women. Mroczak and Kolanz (1998) with a large American sample, examined the effect of age when many other variables were controlled. However, the increase in positive affect held up only for male introverts. The decline in negative affect in women worked only for married women.

A number of studies have examined satisfaction with different domains in relation to age, for example Butt and Beiser (1987) who used 13,858 subjects in 13 countries.

- *Income* rises with age as does satisfaction with it; free income increases when the children grow up, but falls for most after retirement.
- *Health* is less good for the old, especially for the very old.
- *Social relationships.* Satisfaction with these rises with age in most countries, but marital satisfaction has two low points for many—when there are small children and when these become adolescents (see page 82).
- *Job satisfaction* was highest in the middle age groups for the Butt and Beiser study, but increased with age in other studies (Kalleberg and Loscocco, 1983). Retirement naturally leads to loss of job satisfaction for most.
- *Leisure.* Exercise and many other forms of active leisure decline with age, and older people go to fewer parties and other forms of enjoyable social life. For old people walking is the main form of exercise, and they watch TV and read more.
- *Physical attractiveness* is of modest importance for well-being, though more important for women. However, this factor inevitably declines with age.

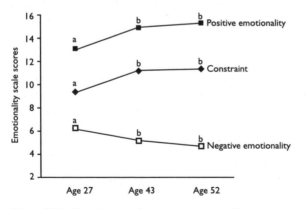

Figure 10.3 Mean levels of positive emotionality, negative emotionality, and constraint at three ages for women (N = 80) (Helson and Lohnen, 1998)
Means differ at $p < .05$.

- *Religion* is another modest source of well-being. It is more important for the elderly, and satisfaction from religion increases with age.
- *Fear of ageing* increases with age, and is a source of low subjective well-being (Klemmack and Roff, 1984). This is partly a fear of declining health and attractiveness, of loneliness and of death.

What is the explanation of these age changes? To start with, studies such as that shown in Figure 10.3 have found that there are real effects here and that the results are not due to historical or cultural changes. It was once thought that there was declining emotionality with age, but we have seen that positive affect increases while negative affect falls. If there is increased satisfaction, as some studies have found, this may be due to the gap becoming smaller between what people want to do or have and what they have already, as Campbell et al. (1976) found for aspirations for housing and neighbourhood. Could the results be due to real differences in life conditions at different ages? These and other studies have shown that older people are worse off in several ways, with less money for some, though they also have less demands on it, worse health, and they are more likely to be widowed or divorced. Yet they are more satisfied, even with the material conditions of life and with relationships (Butt and Beiser, 1987). Another explanation is that older people in some way "adapt" or "adjust" to their situation. The way this might be done is by being able to regulate their positive experiences by selecting people and situations that will bring about positive moods (Diener and Suh, 1997b; Mroczak and Kolanz, 1998). We described this kind of person–situation interaction before.

GENDER DIFFERENCES

There have been many studies of gender differences in happiness. Wood et al. (1989) carried out a meta-analysis of 93 studies, mostly done in the USA. They found that women were on average a little happier than men (not much, 7% of a standard deviation), had a little more positive affect (also 7%) and life satisfaction (3%). However, for a group of studies of "general evaluation" men were more positive. These weak positive effects were a little stronger for married people (8%). And as we saw earlier men become happier with age than women.

There is a much stronger effect for depression, anxiety and negative emotions in general. Women are twice as likely to become depressed as men, 50% more likely to suffer from anxiety or neurosis, and they experience more negative emotions in everyday life. This gender difference is less for members of ethnic and traditional cultures (Nolen-Hoeksema and Rusting, 1999). This does not contradict the overall higher happiness of women because the clinically depressed are a small proportion of the total.

Women experience stronger emotions than men, both positive and negative. Diener et al. (1985) found an average intensity of 4.34 for women and 3.88 for men on a scale from 1 to 6. This may be because females are socialised to be more expressive, or because they are more involved with social relationships. Other explanations are focused on the greater levels of depression in women. It has been suggested that could be partly due to the high level of sexual and physiological abuse among women, or to the high level of empathy in women, making them responsive to the distress of others, or the coping style of ruminating about negative events that Nolen-Hoeksema (1991) has found in women. She asked people "What do you do when you feel depressed?" Women were most likely to have a good cry or a good moan with their friends—a "ruminating" form of coping which may make things worse. This goes against the usual theory that catharsis in therapy is good for people. Men were more likely to engage in physical activity, such as a run or a game of squash, which had the effect of distracting them from their troubles, as well as giving them the benefits of exercise, a powerful source of good moods. Drinking with their mates is another.

The sources of happiness are different for the two sexes. Men are more affected by their jobs, and by economic satisfaction, and with themselves. Women are more affected by their children and the health of their family, and are more self-critical. For men being tall is good, for women it is not, provided they are near the norm (5'8"). For women physical attractiveness is very important, and being overweight is very bad. Fewer women over 45 are judged attractive by others, so this is a source of dissatisfaction for many.

The extent of gender differences varies with the culture. In Taiwan the happiness of men depends primarily on satisfaction at work while that of women depends more on satisfaction with and the happiness of their families (Lu, 2000).

CONCLUSIONS

There are happy people in the sense that measures of happiness are very stable over time, that different aspects of subjective well-being correlate, and that twin studies show a genetic basis for it. Happiness, and especially positive affect, correlate strongly with extraversion, negative affect with neuroticism. These effects are partly due to extraverts being more responsive to rewards, neurotics to punishment, and partly to the seeking and avoidance of situations. Positive affect is less stable, more affected by situational factors than negative emotions are.

There are correlations of well-being with various cognitive aspects of personality; these can be seen as being parts of well-being, in a wider sense; this was Ryff's approach. There are strong links between happiness and internal control, self-esteem, optimism and purpose in life. Purpose in life is given by commitment to goals, which are realistic and for which there are resources.

Some investigators have concluded that personality is a greater determinant of happiness than race, social class, money, social relationships, work, leisure, religion or other environmental variables (Diener et al., 1999). We have examined most of these in previous chapters and we have confirmed that some of them do have quite a strong effect on happiness.

Personality and situation both affect happiness, and they interact, in the sense that some kinds of person are more responsive to pleasant situations, and also in the sense that happiness is achieved partly through the choice and manipulation of situations and relationships. It is also known that individuals with social anxiety or lack of social skills avoid many social situations that others find enjoyable.

Satisfaction and positive affect increase slightly with age, negative affect decreases, both more for men. This increase is despite the lower incomes and worse health of older people, probably because over time they can adjust to their situation. Gender differences in happiness are small, but women are slightly happier than men, though also more likely to suffer from depression. Women experience both kinds of affect more strongly.

Chapter 11

Religion

INTRODUCTION

In this chapter we shall ask how much effect religion has on happiness, which aspects of religion produce such effects, which groups of people benefit most from religion, and which aspects of well-being are most affected.

GENERAL HAPPINESS SURVEYS

General surveys show a definite, though weak, effect of religion on happiness. It is assumed that this is due to religion influencing happiness rather than the other way round, as there is no reason to expect happy people to turn to religion, in fact the reverse seems more likely. Inglehart (1990) combined a number of Eurobarometer surveys of 14 European countries, giving a total subject sample of 163,000. He found that 85% of those who said they went to church once a week or more were "very satisfied" with life, compared with 82% of those who went occasionally, and 77% of those who never went at all.

Witter et al. (1985) carried out a meta-analysis of 56 American surveys and found a similar positive but modest result. The overall correlation between religion and well-being was .16, though the size of this effect increased with age. However, this effect has declined historically. They also found that the effect of religion on happiness was greater for religious activity rather than other measures of religiosity. Some other American studies have involved large national samples, repeated measures over time, and have controlled for a number of demographic variables such as education, age and occupation. The effect of religion on happiness and other aspects of well-being is still found, after all these variables have been controlled. However, this is quite a small effect, but we shall see later that the effect of religion on health is greater, as is its effect on joy at the time.

Surveys from round the world are reported by Veenhoven (1994) and these show that the effect of religion on well-being is stronger in American than in

European surveys, and that the effect is greatest for older people, Blacks, women and Protestants.

We shall see later that religion affects happiness most for those who are socially isolated, and that the church community is very cohesive and support- ive. This suggests that one way that religion benefits people is through social support from other members of their church. However, this is not the only way that religion is beneficial. Pollner (1989) found that with social support held constant, reported closeness to God, having an image of God as a friend, was associated with happiness. There may be a third factor, having firm beliefs. Ellison (1991) found that this influenced happiness after both social support and private devotions had been held constant. In another study Ellison et al. (1989) had found that church attendance and private devotions affect well-being, but via their effect on beliefs. What we will do now is to consider these three aspects of religion separately to see how much they affect well-being, and which aspects of well-being.

There has been research interest in another religious variable "spiritual well- being". Paloutzian and Ellison (1982) introduced a measure of this with two components. "Religious well-being" was about having a satisfying relationship with God, and "existential well-being" referred to having life satisfaction and purpose. The first part of this corresponds to our relation with God category, the second to our purpose in life dimension, dealt with before. Examples of the items are given in Table 11.1. Genia (1996) found that spiritual well-being, and especially the religious well-being component, were correlated strongly with intrinsic religiosity. By this is meant serious commitment to religion as an end in itself.

Measures of purpose in life, PIL, are strongly correlated with happiness. Religion is one source of it. "Strict" churches, such as evangelical and charis- matic churches, give clear guides to what their members should do, thus provid- ing a guide to life. This may explain their attractiveness; strict churches are expanding their membership in many parts of the world (Argyle, 2000). Emmons (1999) argues that spiritual goals are just the kind of goals found to be associated with well-being, i.e. are rated as highly valued, attainable, instru- mental and not conflicting (see our page 139). Emmons (1986) used a different

Table 11.1 Religious and spiritual well-being scales

Religious
1. I believe that God loves me and cares about me.
2. I feel most fulfilled when I'm in close contact with God.

Spiritual
1. I believe that there is some real purpose for my life.
2. I don't enjoy much about life.

Source: Paloutzian and Ellison (1982).

method of assessing inner commitment to religion—asking subjects for their goals and then coding them for religious content; he was thus able to measure religious strivings. He saw these as consisting of two kinds of transcendence—having goals beyond the self, and seeking a closer relation with a higher power. They correlated with subjective well-being. I will put this too under the heading of "relation with God", though it also contains an additional striving component.

EFFECT OF CHURCH ATTENDANCE

We saw in the meta-analysis by Witter and colleagues (1985) that church attendance was consistently the strongest correlate of various aspects of happiness and well-being. In a recent American area study of 627 in Dayton, Ohio, Poloma and Pendleton (1991) found that church attendance correlated with life satisfaction, happiness and existential well-being more than other religious variables such as prayer and beliefs, though not as much as "religious satisfaction". We shall see later that church attendance is also the strongest predictor of health.

The effect is strongest for the elderly; Table 11.2 gives some of the results of the study by Moberg and Taves (1965) of 1343 individuals aged 65+ in Minnesota. The "index of adjustment" used here was really an early happiness scale. It can be seen that the benefits of greater church involvement were more

Table 11.2 Scores on an index of adjustment, and church membership

	Church leaders	Other church members	Non-church members
Married	15	15	12
Widowed	15	11	7
Single	12	8	5
65–70	18	14	10
71–79	15	12	7
80 +	13	8	6
Fully employed	18	18	17
Partly employed	16	16	13
Fully retired	15	12	7
Health (self-rated)			
Excellent	17	14	13
Good	15	14	11
Fair	17	6	8
More active in religious organisations than in 50s	16	13	9
Less active	14	11	7

Source: Moberg and Taves (1965).

striking for those who were single, retired, old or in poor health. This suggests that the benefits of church may be due to the social support it provides. It is found that church communities are very close; Kaldor (1994) studying church attenders in Australia found that 24% said that their closest friends belonged to their church, and another 46% had some close friends in it. These percentages were higher for Pentecostalists and other small Protestant bodies. Ellison and George (1994) found a strong correlation between church attendance and number of ties outside the family, frequency of social contact, and an index of received social support. The four kinds of support particularly affected were giving presents, business or financial advice, home maintenance or repairs, and shopping or errands.

I have argued elsewhere (Argyle, 2000) that religion is in some ways a social phenomenon. Very close bonds are formed between members, perhaps because of their shared beliefs, perhaps because shared rituals are a bonding experience. In addition religious experiences have a strong pro-social component. The effect of shared rituals could be through what Turner (1969) called the state of "communitas", which he found in some primitive rituals. This is an ideal and ecstatic state of love, harmony, equality and social union, among those taking part in the ritual. The relation with God is a further way in which religion is a social phenomenon.

THE RELATION WITH GOD

We saw earlier that church attendance and social support is not the only way in which religion can enhance well-being. Pollner (1989) found that reported "closeness to God" correlated .16 with happiness and satisfaction when church attendance had been controlled. Ellison et al. (1989) found that "devotional intensity" (frequent prayer and feeling close to God) was the strongest religious predictor of life satisfaction. Poloma and Pendleton (1991) found that peak experiences and prayer experience were the best predictors of well-being, especially existential well-being. Other studies have found that existential well-being (meaning and purpose) is the aspect of SWB most influenced by religion (e.g. Chamberlain and Zika, 1988). Kirkpatrick (1992) suggested that the relation with God via prayer, private devotions and religious experiences, can be experienced in much the same way as relations with humans, and can give similar benefits.

Frequency of personal prayer has been found to be the strongest predictor of well-being. Maltby et al. (1999) gave a number of measures of religiosity to 474 British students and found that it was the best predictor of low depression and anxiety, and of high self-esteem.

However, the effect of religiosity on subjective well-being is stronger for Black Americans; for black males it was a major predictor, with a regression weight of .41. This was no greater for the poor and uneducated so did not appear to be due to deprivation; it was more that for members of this group religion was central to their way of life (St. George and McNamara, 1984).

BELIEFS

The third way in which religion may affect well-being is via beliefs. Ellison (1991) found that having firm beliefs, sometimes called "existential certainty", correlated with life satisfaction, independently of both church attendance and private devotions. In another study Ellison et al. (1989) found that attendance and private devotions had their effect on well-being via their impact on beliefs. Certainty of beliefs is found to be advantageous, producing existential well-being. This may explain the popularity of "strict" churches in the USA and some other parts of the world. Kelley (1972) compared the membership statistics of strict and liberal branches of the same denominations in America and found that in every case the strict branches had expanded while the liberal ones had contracted.

Belief in an after-life is beneficial, especially to those about to go there—who are old, ill or in danger in war. However, religious beliefs are more than assent to verbal propositions ("Do you believe in God?"). This is the tip of the iceberg; the hidden parts are the emotional commitment and way of life associated with the beliefs (Argyle, 2000). This is similar to the measures of "meaning and purpose", which have been devised in happiness research. An example is Battista and Almond's (1973) Life Regard Inventory. It is this aspect of well-being which is most strongly associated with religion. On the religious side of the equation are measures of "existential well-being", which are not very different.

Ellison et al. (1989) found that beliefs were the most important source of happiness, in that both church attendance and relation to God had their influence through their effect on beliefs. Dull and Skokan (1995) have suggested how beliefs have their effect. It may be through their effect on perceptions of control, self-enhancement and optimism, which Taylor and Brown (1988) showed were good for well-being. Beliefs can also give meaning to events, for example by showing that they are not random, and that personal growth is possible after negative events.

Conclusions on happiness

Religion has overall a modest positive effect on happiness, but this is greater for the elderly and members of strict churches, there is most impact on existential well-being, and for devotional intensity/closeness to God, but there are also clear effects of church attendance and beliefs.

THE EFFECT OF RELIGION ON HEALTH

Religion and health have long been connected; for thousands of years one of the main purposes of religion was curing illness. Okun et al. (1984) carried out a meta-analysis between health and happiness and found an overall correlation of .32; this was stronger for women and when subjective measures of health were used, but it doesn't tell us which caused which. We shall see that subjective reports of health are often not at all the same as objective assessments of health. Mortality is a highly objective measure. Comstock and Partridge (1972) found the death rates from a number of diseases for church-goers and others (Table 11.3). It can be seen that those who went to church had much lower death rates from these diseases. Could these results be due to the infirm being unable to get to church? No, because similar results have been obtained for the religious commitment of students and for rates of church membership in different areas.

Another way of tackling the problem is by studying the longevity of church members and others. Hummer et al. (1999) used data from the American National Health Interview Survey, 22,800 individuals in all, over an 8-year period; in this time 2016 died and it was calculated that church-goers at age 20 had 7 years greater life expectancy than others. The corresponding gap for American blacks was 14 years. There was a gap of 4.4 years for the whole sample between those who went less than once a week and those who never went at all. This advantage in favour of church-goers was found to be partly due to better health behaviour, partly due to better social support. "Religion, like socioecomomic status, might best be conceptualised as a "fundamental cause" of mortality, because it allows for access to important resources" (Hummer et al., 1999, p. 283).

This study did not separate members of different churches, but earlier studies had found that the difference is greatest for Seventh Day Adventists, Mormons, Orthodox Jews and the Amish, probably because of the greater strictness of these bodies about health behaviour (Jarvis and Northcott, 1987; Levin, 1994).

The most obvious explanation of all this is that the "health behaviour" of church members is better, i.e. they drink less, smoke less, etc. Table 11.3 also

Table 11.3 Mortality rates of regular church-goers and others (per 1000 over 5 years in most cases)

	Once a week or more	Less than once a week
Heart disease	38	89
Emphysema (3 years)	18	52
Cirrhosis (3 years)	5	25
Cancer of the cervix	13	17
Suicide (6 years)	11	29

Source: Comstock and Partridge (1972).

supports this: church goers had lower rates of death from cirrhosis of the liver (due to alcohol), emphysema (due to smoking), cancer of the cervix (partly due to promiscuity), and heart disease (partly due to smoking and diet). The longest living religious groups have strict rules about all these kinds of behaviour.

However, this is not the whole explanation of the benefits of religion for health; it will not explain the benefits for members of mainstream churches which make little or no demands for good health behaviour. A second factor is social support, which we have seen is exceptionally strong in churches and which is well known to be good for health. Berkman and Syme (1979) found massive effects of social support on death rates, and one of the effective forms of social support here was church membership (see page 88).

However, there are still health benefits from religion after health behaviour and social support have been controlled, and this was confirmed by Hummer et al. (1999). We know that stress impairs the immune system and that positive moods and close relations enhance it. Religion would be expected to benefit the immune system through these different aspects of peace of mind and reduced stress, the relation with God and the positive moods induced by church services (Dull and Skokan, 1995; McFadden and Levin, 1996).

Attempts are often made to cure people of physical illnesses by healing services. Many claim that they can heal people or that they have been healed in this way, but does it really work? Several careful follow-up studies have been done; for example Glik (1986) interviewed 176 individuals who had attended charismatic and other healing groups, and compared them with 137 who had received regular primary care. Those who had been to the religious healing groups reported feeling better than those getting the regular medical care, they reported better health behaviour, and their general well-being was greater, but there was no diference in the actual symptoms reported. Idler (1995) studied 286 who had become ill, many with disabilities; some had sought help from religion and some had found it. Their greater subjective health was due to thinking of their inner spiritual self, to which the body is irrelevant, and which included their emotional well-being, relations with others, a non-physical self that was well even if their body was not. There was no change in their actual physical condition. Several studies have found however that subjective health can predict reduced mortality even with physical health held constant (Idler and Benyamini, 1997).

Much use is made of prayer, for the health of self or others. Poloma and Pendleton (1991) found that 73% of the Ohio sample thought prayer could help cure illness, and 34% claimed to have experienced this. We shall discuss prayer further in the next section, on the effect of religion for mental illness. However, it is certainly possible that the kind of peace of mind and positive outlook that religion can produce may have bodily effects.

THE EFFECT OF RELIGION ON MENTAL HEALTH

The literature reports both positive and apparently negative findings here. However, Batson et al. (1993) analysed 115 American studies, which had used self-report measures of depression and other aspects of mental health. They had often used several measures of religiosity. The majority of these studies found a positive correlation between intrinsic religiosity and mental health, but a negative correlation with extrinsic religiosity. (This is going to church as a means to an end, such as making friends or other benefits.) Later studies, using larger samples and better measures, have found the same. For example Idler (1987) studied 2811 elderly people in New Haven and found that depression was lower for those who went to church or who worshipped in private.

Being religious can buffer the effects of stress. Park et al. (1990) found that students high in intrinsic religiosity did not feel depressed, anxious or lower in self-esteem following negative life events. For Protestants this worked even for uncontrollable life events; for Catholics only for controllable ones. And amazingly the Protestants felt less depressed than before these negative events.

The social support given by church congregations is probably one reason for these benefits of religon, and we saw above how churches are major sources of social support. Many studies have shown the benefits of these kinds of social support for mental health.

Religion does not seem to prevent major, that is psychotic, illness, indeed there are many patients with a religious content to their illness, such as thinking they are important religious figures. Rokeach (1981) carried out a study of three patients who each thought they were Jesus. There is a puzzle about the personalities of religious leaders, especially the gurus who start new religious movements. They often go through a period of near or actual insanity before producing their new vision; if this appeals to and meets the needs of their potential followers the guru becomes a successful religious leader (Storr, 1996). Many important religious leaders have shown some signs of insanity; however, they are quite different from real patients—they were sufficiently sane to lead large groups, and their ideas had an appeal to large numbers of others, not just themselves.

Durkheim (1897) thought that Protestants had a higher suicide rate than Catholics, because they have a closer social network. This higher suicide rate for Protestants was found in earlier European studies, though there is little difference now. However, religious commitment in general is certainly correlated with lower rates of suicide. Comstock and Partridge (1972; and see our Table 11.3) found that for those going to church once or more times per week the suicide rate was 0.45 per 1000 while for those who never went it was 2.1. Social cohesion is probably the main reason for this: suicide rates have been found to be lower for those churches and those communities with stronger social networks and lower divorce rates (Beit-Hallahmi and Argyle, 1997).

Sect members are another problem. They may seem crazy, yet joining these groups is often beneficial, since they offer a haven from the world, strong social support and strong discipline. When young people join who have dropped out and taken to drugs, their condition improves. There are also costs—separation from family and friends, giving up career for the time being at least, in some cases giving up sex or having marriage arranged, acceptance of strict sometimes tyrannical discipline, and being compelled to do menial work such as selling flowers. There is also a cost to their families, who can't understand what has happened to their children and whom they may not be allowed to visit.

MARITAL HAPPINESS

Most religions value marriage and the family, and Christianity is no exception. Does this result in happier marriages? In the West at least it does result in lower divorce rates. Heaton and Goodman (1985) combined several American national sample surveys to examine the effects both of denomination and church attendance (Table 11.4). For each denomination the divorce rate was much lower for regular church attenders, and the rate of divorce was lowest for Catholics and Mormons. In another study Call and Heaton (1997) studied the break-up rate for 4587 couples over a period of 5 years. The best predictor of couples staying together was regular and joint church attendance. Others have found that intrinsic religiosity is a further predictor. On the other hand if husbands and wives go to different churches things are much worse. Catholic–Protestant couples are twice as likely to get divorced as pairs of Protestants or pairs of Catholics, and the Catholic–Mormon combination is even worse. Since all these groups are an favour of family and against divorce, there must be some other reason for same-faith couples to stick together. Marital success is predicted by taking part in joint leisure activities in general, but the effect of shared church is particularly strong. This may be due to the same process that makes church communities so cohesive and supportive—their shared beliefs, and taking part in shared rituals. In addition same-faith couples belong to this same cohesive group and have its social support.

But is marital happiness affected by religion? Some investigators have found that religious couples reported more sexual satisfaction in marriage; there is

Table 11.4 Divorce rates by church and attendance

	Catholic		Liberal Protestant		Conservative Protestant		Mormons	
	High	Low	High	Low	High	Low	High	Low
Percentage divorced	13.3	30.4	24.0	32.3	20.3	37.4	12.7	23.9

Source: Heaton and Goodman (1985).

certainly no inhibition of sexual activity (Hood et al., 1996). Several kinds of research have found a link between religion and sex. The shared religion perhaps creates an additional emotional intimacy. However, these were all correlational studies; Booth et al. (1997) carried out a careful longitudinal study of 1005 married people and found that over a 12-year period increases in religious activity did not lead to increased marital happiness or decreased conflict, though it did lead to slightly less thinking about divorce. On the other hand increased marital happiness led to increased church attendance. If this result applies more generally, it looks as if church enables couples to stick together but not necessarily by increasing their marital happiness.

POSITIVE EMOTIONS

Church services and other religious activities can give rise to quite strong positive emotions, which may or may not be reflected in general measures of happiness. In a survey of the emotions produced by different leisure activities the present author found that church scored high on joy, less than dancing, about the same as music (Argyle, 1996). We investigated further the nature of these positive emotions in church. Argyle and Hills (2000) tested 300 adults in Oxfordshire and found three factors in their religious affect, as shown in Table 11.5. This shows some of the classical features of religious experience, such as transcendence (factor 1) and mystical or immanent (factor 3). In addition there is a strong social factor (2). There are joy or other well-being elements in each of the factors. However, in this sample the church members scored no higher than others on the Oxford Happiness Inventory; belonging to sports clubs did. A possible explanation is that most church goers do this once a week, while sports players may do it every day; frequency of positive moods is a more important source of happiness than intensity, according to Diener et al. (1985).

In the study of more intense religious experiences, usually occurring rarely and in isolation, it is found that positive feelings result. Hay (1990) found in a sample of adults in Nottingham that 61% said that they were "at peace or restored, happy/elated, or uplifted/awestruck". Greeley (1975) found that those who had classic mystical experiences, described as "being bathed in light" were later in state of positive affect. Pahnke (1966) induced religious experience by means of drugs and the effects on positive outlook were still there 6 months afterwards, described as "joy, blessedness and peace". We have seen that prayer produces enhanced happiness and existential well-being; Poloma and Pendleton (1991) found that this was greatest when religious experiences occurred during prayer, and that these were brought on by meditative prayer. Religious conversion also produces marked positive feelings, for a time. In cases of sudden conversion, it is found that those concerned have often been through a period of guilt, depression or personal stress, discontent with the self, loss of meaning in life, "existential crisis", for some time (Ullman, 1982). After conversion it is

Table 11.5 Factor analysis of the religious affect scale

Item	Item label	$F_1{}^a$	F_2	F_3
G19	Contact with God	.82		
G25	Being at peace with God	.80		
G12	Feeling supported and helped	.74		
G11	Feeling uplifted	.72		
G13	Feeling loved	.72	.46	
G14	Feeling "at home"	.72		
G03	Refreshment	.68		
G07	Obtaining guidance	.66		
G09	Joy/elation	.65		
G05	Positive feeling about life	.65		
G20	Calmness	.62		.48
G16	Excitement	.59		
G04	Quieting of the mind	.57		.52
G18	Enjoying company of others present		.81	
G22	Being united with other people		.78	
G23	Being part of a family		.75	
G06	Opportunities to help others		.61	
G02	Taking part in a shared performance		.61	
G17	Enjoying familiar practices		.57	
G15	Experiencing a unifying vision	.49	.49	
G01	Timelessness			.78
G08	Loss of sense of self			.66
G21	Bodily well-being			.56
G24	Being bathed in warmth and light		.49	.56
G10	Glimpsing another world			.54
Cronbach's alpha		.95	.95	.79
Variance explained		49.6%	7.0%	6.1%

Source: Argyle and Hills (2000).

Notes
All factor loadings ≥ .45 are shown.
^{a} Factor labels: F_1, transcendent; F_2, social; F_3 immanent.

found that they have a stronger sense of meaning and purpose (Paloutzian, 1981), and may regard themselves as reborn and a new kind of person. They also see themselves as members of a new group, which has been very welcoming.

Conversion can happen at revivals, but these can have negative effects too. A number of individuals become emotionally disturbed by them, and may become mental patients. During the Millerite revival in New England in the nineteenth century, nearly a quarter of local mental hospital admissions were said to be due to "religious excitement" (Stone, 1934). Similar effects have been reported for revivals in developing countries where behaviour at revivals can be very violent. The emotions aroused by these events may be positive, but they are also at a very high level of arousal, which is too much for some. In Jerusalem a number of visitors become emotionally disturbed simply by the strong religious presence of holy places and religious symbolism, and end up in the hospital ward kept for those with the "Jerusalem syndrome".

NEGATIVE AFFECT

Fear of death

There are several kinds of negative emotion that religion may be able to alleviate. Fear of death (FOD) is a widespread human problem, thought by anthropologists to be one of the main roots of religion. Does religion with its belief in an after-life, relieve this fear? Many correlational studies have been carried out and most of them find the expected correlation. Intrinsic religiosity has a negative correlation with FOD of .4 to .5, but those high in extrinsic religiosity have a greater fear. This does not show that religion leads to less fear of death. Some dramatic experiments have been carried out in which FOD has been aroused experimentally by showing slides of corpses, playing dirge-like music, and telling subjects about the dangers of dying from accidents or diseases. It was found that for those subjects who were already believers this experience produced greater belief in the after-life and reduced FOD, but for those who had a weak belief in the after-life there was no change (Osarchuk and Tate, 1973). This kind of research is now regarded as unethical and can't be done again; unfortunately weaker versions of it have not been successful.

Certainly the belief in heaven is very widespread. In one survey 100% of the over-90s believed. And elderly fundamentalists are found to be looking forward to death, saying for example "it will be wonderful" (Swenson, 1961).

Guilt feelings

A central part of Christian thinking and practice is based on the idea that people can be saved from their sins. If guilt feelings can be regarded as a subjective appraisal of sins, this means relieving their guilt feelings. Protestant fundamentalists place a lot of emphasis on saving from sins, and being born again. Is this successful? There are puzzling findings here. On one hand members of this group are found to have strong guilt feelings, and to have experienced more early traumas, such as severe punishment or child abuse (Strozier, 1994). These guilt feelings are partly induced by the conversion techniques that have often been used, where those attending are made to feel guilty. In previous centuries they were made to feel terrified of going to Hell. On the other hand fundamentalists are found to score high on measures of optimism and other aspects of well-being, and this seems to be due to their certainty of beliefs (Sethi and Seligman, 1993). We have just seen that after sudden conversions, which are common in this group, those converted often do feel much better, and think that their problems have been taken away.

Deprivation

Freud and Marx are the best known exponents of the idea that religion is a kind of projective response to deprivation in this world, and there have been several other versions. A lot of findings in the psychology of religion are consistent with this idea. There is more religious activity of some kinds among the poor, uneducated, ethnic minority groups, unmarried, old, ill and those afflicted by famine and oppression (Beit-Hallahmi and Argyle, 1997). Millennial religious movements, which predict the imminent end of the world as we know it, are found in deprived and hungry developing country groups. The form of being saved in some of these cases is being saved from colonial oppression. This does not of course prove that religion saves people from these troubles, but it may make them feel better about things. The main objection to the theory is that there are plenty of prosperous individuals who are not evidently deprived at all, who are actively religious, so it can only explain some aspects of religion. The theory is somewhat tautological in deciding which groups are supposed to be deprived, which may be done on the basis of their religiosity; for example in some studies the greater religiosity of women has been explained by saying that they are a deprived group.

Stress

Being religious can buffer stress, i.e. remove its adverse effects. This is especially true of uncontrollable life events, for which there is no human solution. McIntosh et al. (1993) studied 124 individuals who had experienced the death of a child. Regular church attenders reported more social support and finding meaning in their loss. Thinking and talking about things from a religious point of view led to reduced distress 18 months later. Siegel and Kendall (1990) found that while bereavement led to more depression, particularly for men, this was much less for widowed men who belonged to a church or temple. Indeed there can be "stress-induced growth", where distress leads to favourable results, by means of positive reinterpretation of events, acceptance, emotional social support and religious coping, to which we turn next. Such stress-related growth is more likely in those with intrinsic religiosity (Park et al. 1996).

By "coping" is meant ways of thinking or behaving which reduce the effects of stress; religious coping is when religious thoughts or behaviour are used in this way. Pargament (1997) reviewed 130 studies of religious coping and found that in 34% of them positive results were reported, and found that the most successful kinds of religious coping were perceiving help or guidance from God, "collaborative coping" in which God is a partner in decisions, "benevolent reframing" in which negative events are seen in a more positive way as the will of God, and seeking support from clergy or congregation.

CONCLUSIONS

Religion produces positive effects on subjective well-being, especially on existential well-being, but also on general happiness, mental and physical health; the greatest effect is on the latter. One of the main processes responsible is the strong social support given by church groups, which provide many kinds of emotional and practical help. Strength of beliefs, "existential certainty", is a second process, not only in relation to belief in the after life but in providing meaning and purpose. The relation with God, experienced in prayer and religious experiences, operates as a kind of supportive social relationship.

The benefits for physical health and mortality are due to an additional process—the better "health behaviour" of church members, though church members and those attending healing services also simply feel better. Mental health is helped by various coping processes that make stress-induced growth more likely.

Religious services arouse strong positive emotions, through the shared emotions produced by music and the positive message. Religious rituals also generate prosocial feelings, and a sense of union with the others present. This is one of the ways in which religion is a social phenomenon. The benefits of religion for well-being are greatest for those most involved, for the elderly and for fundamentalists, because of their certainty of beliefs.

Chapter 12

National differences in happiness

International social surveys have shown large differences in the average happiness and satisfaction of nations. Part of the evidence that these differences are genuine comes from findings about the correlates, perhaps causes, of national happiness—average income, individualism and social equality for example. This is potentially of great practical importance, as it may suggest how whole countries might be made happier. We will consider another possible explanation, that there are different social norms for whether happiness should be expressed, and this may influence how questions about happiness are answered. So we turn to objective measures. We also look at ethnic differences within countries, and at the subjective well-being scores of different countries. Finally we ask if there have been any historical changes in happiness.

INTERNATIONAL HAPPINESS SURVEYS

A good example is the World Values Study Group (1994) survey of 41 countries. Life satisfaction was assessed by a single question, answered on a 10-point scale, positive and negative affect were assessed from five questions each, and "hedonic balance" was calculated from positive affect (PA) minus negative affect (NA). There were about 1000 respondents in each country (Table 12.1). It can be seen that there is quite a large range, in life satisfaction, from 5.03 for Bulgaria to 8.39 for Switzerland. The highest PA was for Sweden (3.63), the lowest Japan (1.12). NA was lowest for Switzerland (0.24) and highest for Turkey (2.50). Countries are not very consistent on these different measures; for example Switzerland had the highest satisfaction but quite low PA, while Turkey and Nigeria had high PA but quite low satisfaction.

Market Opinion and Research International carried out a survey of 54 countries, including a one-question happiness measure (Worcester, 1998). The ordering of countries was very similar to that found in the World Values study. The happiest countries were Iceland, Sweden, Netherlands, Denmark, Australia, Ireland and Switzerland. The least happy were again Bulgaria and parts of the

Table 12.1 Subjective well-being values of nations

Nation	Life satisfaction	Hedonic balance	Positive affect	Negative affect
Bulgaria	5.03	0.91	1.93	1.01
Russia	5.37	0.29	1.69	1.41
Belarus	5.52	0.77	2.12	1.35
Latvia	5.70	0.92	2.00	1.08
Romania	5.88	0.71	2.34	1.63
Estonia	6.00	0.76	2.05	1.28
Lithuania	6.01	0.60	1.86	1.26
Hungary	6.03	0.85	1.96	1.11
India	6.21	0.33	1.41	1.09
South Africa	6.22	1.15	2.59	1.44
Slovenia	6.29	1.53	2.33	0.80
Czech Republic	6.30	0.76	1.84	1.08
Nigeria	6.40	1.56	2.92	1.36
Turkey	6.41	0.59	3.09	2.50
Japan	6.53	0.39	1.12	0.72
Poland	6.64	1.24	2.45	1.21
South Korea	6.69	—	—	—
East Germany	6.72	1.25	3.05	1.80
France	6.76	1.33	2.34	1.01
China	7.05	1.26	2.34	1.08
Portugal	7.10	1.33	2.27	0.94
Spain	7.13	0.70	1.59	0.89
West Germany	7.22	1.43	3.23	1.79
Italy	7.24	1.21	2.04	0.84
Argentina	7.25	1.26	2.45	1.19
Brazil	7.39	1.18	2.85	1.68
Mexico	7.41	1.38	2.68	1.30
Britain	7.48	1.64	2.89	1.25
Chile	7.55	1.03	2.78	1.75
Belgium	7.67	1.54	2.46	0.93
Finland	7.68	1.18	2.33	1.15
Norway	7.68	1.59	2.54	0.95
United States	7.71	2.21	3.49	1.27
Austria	7.74	1.77	2.90	1.13
Netherlands	7.84	1.81	2.91	1.10
Ireland	7.87	1.99	2.89	0.90
Canada	7.88	2.31	3.47	1.15
Sweden	7.97	2.90	3.63	0.73
Iceland	8.02	2.50	3.29	0.78
Denmark	8.16	1.90	2.83	0.93
Switzerland	8.39	1.14	1.39	0.24

Source: World Values Study Group (1994).

Note
Values are weighted to achieve probability samples of nations, and respondents with apparent data errors were dropped before analyses.

former USSR. Britain came 9th out of 54, compared with 14 out of 41 in the World Values survey for satisfaction, and 11 out of 41 for PA.

Comprehensive annual surveys have been carried out in European countries by the Eurobarometer. The results for being very satisfied or being very happy between 1974 and 1983 are shown in Figure 12.1. It can be seen that those in the Netherlands and Denmark claim to have been much happier and more satisfied than those in Italy, France and Germany. There is a large fall in satisfaction in Belgium over this period, which was a time of unusual economic recession. Britain fell a little below the mean with about 25% very happy, 35% very satisfied. The main difference between these results and those of the other surveys is that the gap between countries is much greater.

However, there are some surprises with the results of these surveys. Why are the Icelanders so happy, why does Scandinavia always come out so high, while Italy, France and Germany come out quite low? In the Eurobarometer survey about 45% of the Dutch were very happy, but only 5% of the Italians; 55% of Danes were very satisfied with their lives in general, but only 10% of Italians and 15% of French. These results are hard to believe, and give some cause for concern about their validity.

In other fields of psychology it is not the custom to measure anything by a single, direct question. Usually questions are indirect so that respondents do not know what the "right" answer is, and usually a number of questions are used, which have been shown to form a factor, sampling responses over the whole domain being assessed. We would not measure racial prejudice by one question like "Do you hate black people?"

There is a psychological measurement which has a lot of questions, and does not mention happiness, yet correlates quite well with happiness. This is the Eysenck Personality Questionnaire (Eysenck, 1976) which has been used in samples of students in many countries, and some of the results are shown in Table 12.4 (page 193). Neuroticism is closely related to anxiety, and can be regarded as measure of negative affect. Extraversion is correlated with happiness and can be regarded as an index of happiness. Furthermore these scales consist of many questions, and do not ask about happiness—they can be regarded as good indirect measures of it, and may be less liable to errors of self-presentation or cultural norms about expressing happiness.

Extraversion is very high for the USA, and a little less for Australia, Britain and Canada, but also for the European countries. However, Nigeria, India and Israel come out even higher. China is very low, as in the other surveys. Neuroticism is high in all industrialised countries, though lower in Germany and Canada, and lower still in Israel and Nigeria. We might have more faith in these figures if they fitted into a pattern of empirical relationships. Lynn (1981) tested several theories about the causes of national differences in personality, measured by social indicators. He found that neuroticism, which we are taking as an index of negative affect, was greater in all Middle Eastern Arab countries, which he put down to rapid social change and disruption of traditional way of life.

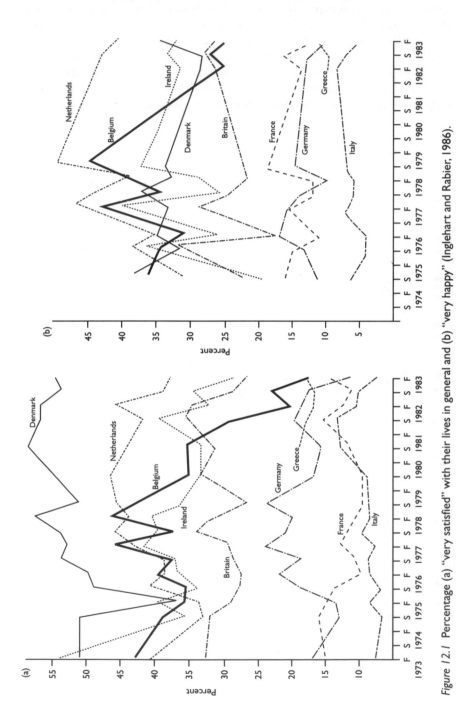

Figure 12.1 Percentage (a) "very satisfied" with their lives in general and (b) "very happy" (Inglehart and Rabier, 1986).

Neuroticism was also higher for all Latin American countries (with the exception of Brazil), which he put down to the political conflict and revolutions. And he found that in the countries defeated in World War II there was a rise in neuroticism levels until 1965, when they returned to normal (Figure 12.2). Extraversion, which we are taking as a measure of happiness, was high in the USA, Australia and Canada, which Lynn puts down to selection, extraverts being more likely to emigrate, together with extraversion being higher in more affluent countries.

Emigration rates could be used as a behavioural measure, not depending on self-report, of the relative happiness of different countries, assuming that people know which countries are happiest, though it may be they go primarily to places where they will not be persecuted and where they can find jobs.

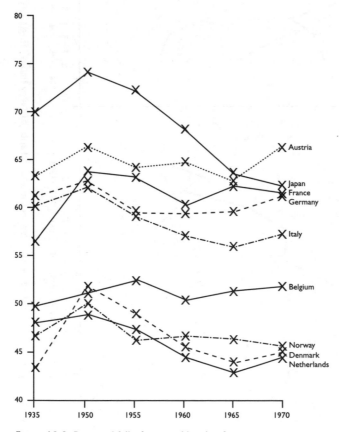

Figure 12.2 Rise and fall of national levels of neuroticism in nations suffering military defeat in World War II (Lynn, 1981).

INCOME AND WEALTH

Income has consistently been found to correlate with average satisfaction. We looked at research on this issue in Chapter 9: we saw that average national satisfaction correlated with average income at about .70, which is much greater than within-country correlations. The reason for this difference in the apparent effects of income is partly that within-country differences are dominated by individual differences, in personality for example, and partly because between-country effects are partly due to collective goods, such as facilities for health, education and leisure.

Diener et al. (1995) used the 41 nations covered in the World Values Survey; mean purchasing power correlated .69 with life satisfaction, .29 with PA and −.41 with NA. Rich countries such as Switzerland, Canada and the USA are satisfied, whereas poor countries like Bulgaria, Russia and China are not. Some studies found that the effect of income levelled off above middle incomes, but other studies did not. Income is the strongest predictor of satisfaction, but it is not the only one.

We saw that this is partly because income meets basic needs, for food, shelter, clothes, etc., but that income continues to give satisfaction after these needs have been satisfied. Diener (1995) combined 14 objective indicators of domains of well-being. As Figure 12.3 shows, the size of this index increased with income, but only up to a value of $3000 p.a. in 1981 US dollars, after which it levelled off. This index included a lot more than satisfaction of material need, so it looks as if money satisfies other needs too, but only up to quite a low level of income. This is similar to the relation found between individual income and happiness within countries.

More money brings other good things, such as health facilities, education and leisure facilities of all kinds. Diener and Diener (1995) also found that richer countries have greater longevity, less infant mortality, less crime, cleaner water and more food. However, purchasing power led to increases in SWB, which were linear and in this study did not level off. They found that per capita GNP and average purchasing power still had some correlation with satisfaction with basic need fulfilment held constant. We may be able to find out what these other needs are.

There are other features of nations that correlate with life satisfaction, such as individualism, human rights and income equality. However, these are all correlated with national income—richer countries have more of them. But which is the fundamental cause of national satisfaction?

Not all individuals and not all countries place great value on money. Lynn and Martin (1995) found that poorer countries were much more aggressively competitive, and concluded that they valued money more than those in richer

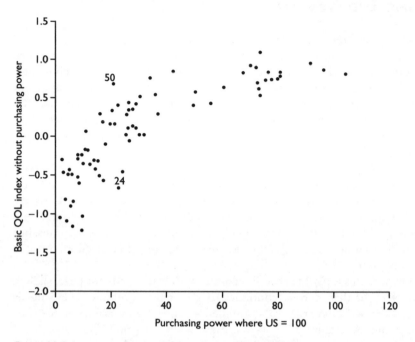

Figure 12.3 Income and basic QOL variables (Diener, 1995).

countries. Oishi et al. (1999) found that financial satisfaction was more strongly correlated with life satisfaction in poorer countries, whereas home satisfaction is a better predictor in richer countries. Inglehart (1971) proposed that in affluent societies people come to value non-material goals as much as or more than material ones. These may be wanting a friendlier and less impersonal society, one that honours ideas more than money, freedom of speech, widespread participation in decision making, environmental issues and the quality of life. It is found that young people, and professional middle classes, value such goals more than economic growth, strong defence or maintaining order (Inglehart, 1971). We shall see shortly that some of these are found to be predictors of national happiness. However, we should not underestimate the interest in money and material things among the members of rich societies. But there has to be some restraint on satisfying individual needs, or there will be social chaos. This is what moral rules are all about, their purpose is the welfare of all, and the basic rules are culturally universal; cooperation and concern for others are essential to society (Argyle, 2000).

Individualism

The distinction between individualism and collectivism was introduced to describe some of the differences between the cultures of East and West, for example China and the USA. In collectivist cultures "individuals may be induced to subordinate their own goals to the goals of some collective, which is usually a stable in-group (e.g. family, band, tribe)" (Triandis et al., 1988). There is a high level of cohesion, conformity and cooperation within groups such as families, and there is concern for group harmony. In individualist societies on the other hand people are more loosely attached to a number of different groups, and there is less conformity, cooperation and social support. In collectivist societies self-definition is mainly in terms of group membership: "Who am I?" leads to answers such as "a member of the volley ball team", while in individualist societies the answer is more like "I am an extravert" (Markus and Kitayama, 1991).

Hofstede (1980) measured the average individualism of 40 countries by the answers to four questions about work, such as "How important is it to you to have considerable freedom to adapt your own approach to the job?" This measure only gets at work aspects of collectivism, and this is not the same as family collectivism, which is central in China. On this scale the USA, Australia and Britain valued individual autonomy most; Venezuela, Columbia and Pakistan the least. This measure has been widely used, and Hofstede found that it correlated with GNP at .82, and also with economic development, social mobility, loss of traditional agriculture, growth of industry and urbanisation, and smaller families. Industrialised countries score high on individualism.

Diener et al. (1995) used additional measures of individualism, including individualism–collectivism ratings of countries by Triandis. They found a correlation with SWB of .77. So both income and individualism are strong correlates and possibly causes of subjective well-being. If income is held constant, the correlation of average happiness with individualism fell, from .55 to .05, in a study by Veenhoven (2000). However, if rich and poor nations are separated, Veenhoven found that the correlation with happiness was positive for the rich nations and negative for the poor ones. For countries that are prosperous, the freedom of individualism is best, but for nations that are poor, the mutual help and social support of collectivism is best. We will look again at the rewards and costs of individualism later in the chapter when we come to look at objective indicators of well-being.

Self-esteem is valued more in individualist cultures, where it is more strongly related to life satisfaction; in collectivist cultures the correlation is much lower, and for women in some cultures there is no relation (Diener and Diener, 1995).

Equality and income dispersion

Income equality can be assessed by calculating the ratio of average incomes of the richest 20% and the poorest 20%. This ratio is 26.1 for Brazil, followed by Botswana and Costa Rica; the most equal countries are Hungary (3.0), Poland (3.6), Japan (4.3) and Sweden (4.6) (Argyle, 1994). Equality has a quite strong correlation with subjective well-being; Diener et al. (1995) found this to be .48, Veenhoven and Ehrhardt (1995) found it .64. However, if income is held constant, the effect of income dispersion is much smaller or vanishes, because rich countries are also more egalitarian. In some studies the relationship was reversed, so that more unequal countries were happier. Diener and Oishi (in press) suggest this may be because eastern European countries are egalitarian, but unhappy for other reasons, while South American countries are unequal and happy, also for other reasons. However, within countries there is more variation in satisfaction when incomes are more unequal (Veenhoven, 1993).

Clark (2000) analysed six waves of British panel surveys, containing 10,000 respondents. He too found evidence that people may prefer inequality. GHQ scores were lower when there was more income inequality within respondents' own reference groups (i.e. those of similar job, income, etc.), though this effect decreased with income, and if they had more experience of varying income—perhaps because this suggested opportunity of improvement. They also liked inequality among those in lower income categories, but disliked it in higher income categories.

HUMAN RIGHTS, DEMOCRACY AND INTERPERSONAL TRUST

Diener et al. (1995) found that combined measures of several kinds of human rights correlated .48 with satisfaction, but again this disappeared when income was held constant because richer countries have better human rights. However, Veenhoven (2000) found that although political and personal freedom could be explained by wealth, economic freedom could not. By economic freedom he meant freedom from excessive taxes, and scope for free enterprise and money transfer. Political freedom was about free speech, human rights and free elections. Personal freedom was about religion, travel, marriage and sexuality. He then looked at rich and poor countries separately, and found that overall freedom correlated with national happiness .49, but for the poor countries it was non-significant. Evidently freedom only makes people happy when they are in a position to make use of it.

Frey and Stutzer (2000) compared the 26 Swiss cantons, which vary a lot in how much their residents can take part in democratic institutions. This had quite a strong effect on average happiness reported in those cantons.

In their book *The Civic Culture*, Almond and Verba (1963) report surveys of various aspects of social and political participation and trust in government in five countries in 1959–60. They found that the USA and Britain were high in trust while Germany and France were very low at that time. Inglehart and Rabier (1986) report a later survey, and the results of both are given in Table 12.2. Other sociological studies found a very low level of interpersonal trust in Italy and to a lesser extent in France; there was a modest correlation between national scores on trust and SWB, so this may explain the relatively low satisfaction scores of Italy and France. Germany also had quite a low trust level at the time, and had problems over the East–West divide; Schmitt and Maes (1998) found that for both West and East Germans negative emotions were related to envy and perceived unfairness, though these feelings were much stronger in East Germany.

We showed above that neuroticism, an index of anxiety, was greater in Arab and Latin American countries, probably because of the political instability. Ouweneel and Veenhoven (1994) found that happiness was greater when there was more political participation, and less civil disorder and conflict. They also found that happiness was lower if there were other risks, from floods, wars, earthquakes, or famine. Schyns (1998) found a low level of satisfaction in countries undergoing rapid change, such as Korea, South Africa and the Philippines. We saw in Table 12.1 (page 179) that the least happy countries are Bulgaria, Russia, and Rumania, all countries with very weak democratic institutions, as well as low standards of living.

External threats also affect happiness. Landau et al. (1998) report 203 Israeli surveys that show the effects of national stress. When this was high there was a substantial decline in average happiness, surprisingly a decline in health worries, and a small decline in estimated ability to cope.

We saw in Chapter 11 that religion is a source of happiness and other aspects of well-being, mainly through the support of the religious community.

Table 12.2 Interpersonal trust, by nationality, in 1959–60 and 1981

1959–60 (Civic Culture Study)		1981 (World Values Survey)	
United States	55	Denmark	66
Great Britain	49	The Netherlands	58
Mexico	30	Great Britain	57
Germany	19	Northern Ireland	57
Italy	7	Ireland	55
		Spain	48
		United States	47
		Germany	45
		Belgium	42
		Italy	39
		France	36

Sources: Almond and Verba (1963); Inglehart and Rabier (1986).

Countries differ greatly in the amount of church membership, and this may well be a factor in national differences in happiness. There is lower divorce rate in Italy, Greece and Portugal, all Catholic countries. Religion could explain the surprisingly high level of happiness in South America and Nigeria, and the high level in the USA compared with Europe, the former being countries where churches are very active, and the low level of happiness in China and Russia where religion is discouraged.

Ethnic differences

There have been many comparisons of blacks and whites, especially in the USA. Campbell et al. (1976) found that 18% of blacks said they were very happy compared with 32% of whites, and similar results have been obtained in other countries. Stock et al. (1985) did a meta-analysis of 54 such American studies and found that there was a small difference, that decreased with age of subjects. In the US this gap has narrowed during recent decades. On the other hand during the 1980s black Americans became objectively worse off, in terms of income, education and health; meanwhile their life satisfaction increased, though not their happiness (Adams, 1997). Blanchflower and Oswald (1999) found that black Americans became a little happier over this period, but were still below whites in this respect.

However, much of this black–white difference can be explained by differences in income, occupational status, and employment; if these are held constant the difference due to race is even smaller. Blanchflower and Oswald (1999) carried out an analysis of data for 100,000 people in the USA and Britain, and calculated the effects of race on happiness translated into economic terms. Being black was still equivalent to a salary loss, of $30,000 p.a., though this was less than the costs of being unemployed or being widowed.

Being black does not have the expected effect on self-esteem. Campbell et al. (1976) found in the USA that 32% of blacks and 50% of whites had high self-esteem but black children are often found to have higher self-esteem than whites, especially if they go to segregated schools where they do not meet any white children. The same causal factors affect the happiness of blacks and whites; however, Burton et al. (1993) found that while marriage and employment were good for the happiness of blacks and whites, the combination of the two roles was particularly beneficial for blacks.

In South Africa white South Africans are most satisfied and most optimistic, followed by coloured and Indian South Africans, and then by indigenous Africans. On the other hand whites were the least confident of a happy future for all races in South Africa (Harris, 1997).

It has often been found that immigrant ethnic groups are unhappy and suffer from mental disorder. This is not always true. Chinese and Japanese Americans have high self-esteem, probably because of their stable families and the social cohesion of the ethnic group (Cockerham, 1981). The same applies to

American Indians, until they come into contact with white urban culture and compete, unsuccessfully, for jobs and income; they are then likely to become depressed and mentally disturbed (Fuchs and Havighurst, 1973).

COULD APPARENT NATIONAL DIFFERENCES BE DUE TO DIFFERENT SOCIAL NORMS?

We have seen that there are apparently quite large differences in national happiness and satisfaction between countries that are similar in prosperity and political institutions. Is Denmark really so much happier than Italy for example? Are South American countries really much happier than Japan? Figure 12.1 (page 181) showed some very dubious differences between European countries. These differences are sometimes said to be due to "cultural" differences, but what are they? Perhaps there are cultural differences in ways of thinking, including ways of answering questions.

Countries and groups with a positive happiness bias

1. It has been suggested that the high satisfaction and happiness scores in the USA are partly due to the social norms that demand the appearance of cheerfulness. Suh (in press) concluded that North Americans have more positive self-views, exhibit more self-serving biases and engage in more self-enhancement than East Asians. Ostroot and Snyder (1985) thought that the difference in satisfaction between the Americans and the French was due to the "rosy outlook" of the former. They found that Americans also rated the satisfaction of other countries more highly than the French did. There is a self-presentation effect too—younger Americans report more happiness and less depression in interviews compared with questionnaires, older ones do not—the young are expected to be happy (Diener and Suh, 1999).
2. In parts of Africa and India depression is rarely reported, people do not report feelings of depression, sadness, guilt or inadequacy. However, studies with the "Present State Examination" have found that many African patients have bodily feelings of tiredness, weakness, headaches, loss of appetite, insomnia and loss of interest in sex or people (Marsella, 1980). Self-report measures of their happiness would be misleading.
3. In Japan it is not socially acceptable to show negative facial expression in public, one should smile. This was found by Friesen (1972) in a famous experiment in which Japanese subjects who had been shown a disgusting film smiled when interviewed about it; the American subjects still looked disgusted.
4. Harris and Lipian (1989) interviewed English boys who were just starting at boarding school at age 8 or 13. Some of them felt very distressed, anxious

or homesick, but most said that they were able to conceal their feelings, because otherwise they would be teased or ridiculed. I have been told that this ban on admitting unhappiness extends to letters home.

5. Hochschild (1983) showed how air hostesses had to keep up a convincing expression of cheerfulness and positive attitudes towards passengers no matter how badly behaved they were. The training course includes modelling and trying out the proper expressions for dealing with aggravating passengers.

Countries and groups with a negative happiness bias

There are places where happiness is concealed.

1. The Ifaluk tribe live on a small Pacific island. In this culture looking happy is not socially acceptable since it suggests that an individual is too pleased with him- or herself, may show off; others are then angry and the person who was looking happy becomes anxious (Lutz, 1988).
2. In China people focus more on negative events, are less optimistic than Americans, and it is important to have a modest demeanour (Lee and Seligman, 1997). The Chinese, like the ancient Greeks, fear punishment by fate if they are too happy.

Some of this can be described in terms of "display rules", the kind of rules that prescribe for example what emotion it is right to display at weddings or funerals. On some occasions people manage to look happy whether they are feeling happy or not. The non-verbal expression of emotion may well extend to the verbal responses to questionnaires.

Saarni (1979) has shown that children learn which is the most advantageous facial expression to show. In one study children were asked to choose the last frame in a series of pictured episodes. With increasing age there was a greater tendency not to choose the face corresponding to the emotion experienced, though some did this by age 7. The reasons they gave for concealment were avoiding trouble (44%), maintaining self-esteem (30%), not hurting other's feelings (19%) and politeness (8%). Learning to control the expression of fear or distress is part of male socialisation in many cultures, including painful male initiation rites in primitive societies.

Emotional socialisation takes place in several ways, including modelling of parents and others, and exposure to emotional expressions. American children learn how to act "cool" and not be "square" or shy from watching TV soap operas. In working-class Baltimore children are frequently exposed to anger and aggression; in more middle-class circles they are protected from such negative emotions, and see only happy, loving faces (Gordon, 1989). In the USA "children may be encouraged to smile and laugh and to seek out fun situations . . . and that seeking pleasurable situations is a good thing . . . and they may be taught to identify a feeling of arousal in a positive way" (Diener and Suh, 1999). In the Confucian cultures of Southeast Asia negative emotions are seen as neutral, while in South America they are seen as very undesirable. In Elizabethan England "melancholy" was regarded as a desirable state of mind—especially for poets and intellectuals.

These are examples of different social norms for the expression of well-being, which may well affect responses to interviews. An international survey of students asked people what degrees of pleasant and unpleasant affect they regarded as "desirable and appropriate", on five items for each. There were quite large differences for ideal satisfaction: on the 7-point Satisfaction with Life Scale, Australia came top with 6.23 and China last with 4.00. There were similar differences for pleasant affect, though Greece was now highest (6.38) and China lowest again (4.47); there was some variation in the desirability of negative affect: Puerto Rica found it least desirable (2.30) and Hungary the most (4.32). The South American countries valued positive affect a lot, China very little. Norms for satisfaction may not affect satisfaction, it could be the other way round—if things are bad it is better not to aim too high. Nevertheless it does seem a real possibility that this is part of the explanation of national differences.

The correlation between national life satisfaction and average ideal level of satisfaction is .73, and with income controlled was still .68 (Diener et al., 1999). In collectivist cultures life satisfaction is correlated with norms for valuing this variable (.35) while in individualist cultures it is not (.16), it depends more on affect balance (.56) (see page 179). Clearly some of the national differences in affect as well as satisfaction can be explained in terms of these cultural norms. Suh (in press) found that in those cultures where high life satisfaction was ideal, satisfaction was more strongly correlated with satisfaction in the most satisfying domains—perhaps they have learnt how to look on the bright side.

If part of the reported differences in national happiness are due to norms or other aspects of the culture, are there really differences in happiness or not? It seems likely that the differences are exaggerated. However, a positive bias in the expression of positive emotion for example would be expected to feed back onto the experience of the emotion, thus creating a real difference.

OBJECTIVE INDICATORS OF NATIONAL WELL-BEING

Objective indicators can be used for measuring national differences in well-being, and this avoids problems of translating questions, or cultural differences in styles of answering. Objective indicators can also be used for looking at quality of life in the past, when no social surveys had been carried out.

Some measures have been directed to measuring satisfaction. One of these is the United Nations Human Development Index (1990), which is a combination of gross national product, life expectancy and average years of education.

As we showed in Chapter 1 there are many such objective indicators that can be used. Britain recently adopted a list of 14 of them, thought to be desirable goals of government, which included clean rivers and number of surviving species of birds. Lists of objective indicators for well-being appear to be very arbitrary. Becker et al. (1987) found that for 329 American cities, 134 of them could come first depending on different weighting of the indicators.

Diener (1995) proposed a "values based index" with measures for seven value areas which he believed are widespread. These are listed, together with his chosen measures for less developed countries and for advanced countries in Table 12.3. These values and the measures chosen for them are arbitrary, though some have more face validity than others. Offer (2001) observes that the advanced index includes items such as per capita Nobel prize winners, and signing of major environmental treaties, which are not really measures of well-being, while subjective well-being is not an objective measure. Nevertheless this measure has interesting relations with SWB.

Some of these items are measures of unhappiness, or negative affect. Suicide is related to depression, and alcoholism to anxiety, so we have possible objective measures of the two main negative emotions. Table 12.4 gives the measures for a number of countries. These figures are quite illuminating; they show for example that Britain has lower rates of both compared with the USA, Canada and Australia, that the European countries scored high on both and Sweden and Denmark high on suicide. There is a third negative emotion, anger, and this can

Table 12.3 Value regions and basic and advanced Quality of Life indices variables

Mastery	
Basic	Basic physical need fulfillment
Advanced	Physicians per capita
Affective autonomy	
Basic	Suicide rate
Advanced	Subjective well-being
Intellectual autonomy	
Basic	Literacy rate
Advanced	College/university attendance
Egalitarian commitment	
Basic	Gross human rights violations
Advanced	Income equality (GINI)
Harmony	
Basic	Deforestation
Advanced	Major environmental treaties
Conservatism	
Basic	Homicide rate
Advanced	Monetary savings rate
Hierarchy	
Basic	Purchasing parity power
Advanced	Per capita income

Source: Diener (1995).

Table 12.4 National average medium of neuroticism, extraversion, and rates of suicide and alcoholism

	Neuroticism	Extraversion	Suicide	Alcoholism
United Kingdom	14.9	18.0	8.9	5.2
USA	15.0	21.7	12.3	11.2
Australia	15.5	19.3	11.6	7.4
Canada	12.7	18.0	17.6	8.7
Sweden	—	—	19.4	5.1
Denmark	—	—	31.6	8.4
France	15.1	17.7	22.7	22.6
Germany	13.6	18.4	20.7	23.8
Italy	16.6	18.4	8.3	32.4
Japan	16.7	16.5	19.4	14.2
China	14.4	13.7	18.9	12.4
Russia	18.0	16.1	—	—
Brazil	14.8	17.6	3.3	8.3
India	15.2	22.7	—	—
Nigeria	9.4	24.4	—	—

Source: Lynn and Martin (1995).

be indexed from the homicide rates. This is very low in most countries, but very high in Mexico, Puerto Rica, Brazil, and the USA, which has 12 times the British rate.

Lester (2000) carried out a similar study of objective indicators for 32 countries and found a "neuroticism" factor composed of national rates of suicide, alcohol consumpton, accidents, divorce and crime. If we take the factor scores as measures of unhappiness the least unhappy industrialised countries were Britain, followed by Japan, USA, Canada and Australia. Denmark and France were more unhappy, Hungary the most. There were also low unhappiness levels for Egypt, Turkey, Israel, and Singapore.

Other social indicators can be seen as causes of well-being. Unemployment is a major cause of unhappiness: within Europe it is high in France, Italy, Ireland, Germany and Sweden, low in the Netherlands, Denmark and Belgium, moderately low in Britain. There are also big differences in unemployment benefits as a percentage of average income: these are very high for the Netherlands, quite high for Spain and Denmark (Gallie and Paugam, 2000). There are differences in the nature of work, reflected in job satisfaction that is found. Overall job satisfaction is high in the Netherlands, Belgium, Luxemborg and Denmark, but low in Greece, France, Portugal, Ireland and Spain (Smulders et al., 1996).

Family breakdown is another major cause of unhappiness. The percentage of families that break up is large in Sweden (46%), Denmark, Britain, Belgium, France and Germany, but low in Italy, Portugal and Greece, though divorce may be replaced by separation in these Catholic countries. Another index of social cohesion and support is the percentage who see friends or relatives most days: this is high in Ireland (71.3%), France, Spain and Greece, but low in the Netherlands (19.3%), Germany and Denmark (Gallie and Paugam, 2000).

Objective indicators show that there is a negative side to individualism: countries high in this dimension have higher suicide rates and higher divorce rates. They have a faster pace of life, as assessed from walking speed and other measures (Levine and Norenzayan, 1999); they also have higher rates of death from coronary heart disease. Lynn (1981) found a dimension of anxiety, one of the main negative emotions, based on a number of indices such as suicide rates, deaths from cirrhosis, motor accidents, homicides, and hypertension, and rates of alcoholism, coronaries, cigarette consumption, calorie intake and mental illness. There was a correlation of .67 between the anxiety factor and economic growth (Lynn, 1971). Some of these differences are very great, five times as many heart attacks, ten times as many suicides in the more anxious countries, and all these measures correlated together to make up a single factor. Lester (2000) found a similar "neuroticism" factor (page 193). Again a number of collectivist third world countries had quite low scores. These differences are not all clearly shown in the negative affect scores shown in Table 12.1 (page 179), but this is arguably a less accurate index of the negative side of individualism as it is based on self-report.

It might have been expected that members of collectivist societies would be happier, because of the greater social cohesion and social support; this could certainly explain why they have better health, especially fewer heart attacks and much lower suicide rates, since these are both strongly affected by social support (e.g. Triandis et al., 1988). The effects of divorce of parents on the well-being of their children are less in collectivist cultures, because other people look after the children (Gohm et al., 1998). The explanation of the apparently lower happiness in collectivist cultures is probably the lack of freedom from family, which can be very oppressive, with the demands for filial obedience and demands to look after older relatives and work in the family business. Sastry and Ross (1998) studied the levels of perceived control in Asian and other Americans and in Asian countries. The level of control was considerably lower for Asians, and it had less effect on distress. Black Americans had low control too, but it *did* affect distress. It is argued that while control can lead to effectiveness and active problem-solving, for Asians it is sanctioned because it is related to the pursuit of self-interest not that of the community or family. Members of individualist societies may be happier because they are wealthier, and because they are more free than members of collectivist cultures, but they are also under a lot more stress and are more anxious, and yet say they are happy partly because of their social norms.

HAPPINESS IN PARTICULAR COUNTRIES

Britain has quite high satisfaction and positive affect (Table 12.1, page 179) and there has been a small rise in satisfaction. There is a low alcoholism rate, a low suicide rate, relatively small numbers in prison, and until recently a low crime rate, adding up to a low unhappiness score based on objective indicatora; there is also a low level of anxiety on questionnaire measures. Among other objective indicators, there is now a high divorce rate, but unemployment is less than in many other industrial countries. Economic prosperity has risen, individualism is high.

USA has high satisfaction, a little more than Britain's, and high positive affect, though it has fallen slightly, and has a high extraversion score. This high level of satisfaction can partly be accounted for by strong norms for feeling and expressing positive affect (Diener et al., 1995); there is a positive bias towards reporting well-being. The USA is high in economic indicators and in the components of individualism, but there are racial problems and high rates of alcoholism, suicide, homicides and number of prisoners, making up a neuroticism score higher than Britain's. We have noted the decline in marriage and in social networks.

Australia always comes out at or near the top of happiness surveys, and has a high extraversion score. It also comes out top for ideal level of life satisfaction and of positive affect, and this is in tune with the widespread Australian belief that this is "the happy country"; it looks as if there is a positive bias for reporting well-being here too. It has a low suicide rate. It scores high on objective indicators, such as economic prosperity and in individualism, much the same as the USA or Britain; in addition it has "the good weather".

Sweden and Denmark usually come out at or near the top of national happiness scores. They are high in satisfaction, positive affect and job satisfaction, low in negative affect; they are both low in anxiety and neuroticism, but they have high suicide rates, and Denmark has quite a high unhappiness rate based on social indicators, between France and Belgium. Sweden and Denmark have high norms for positive affect, and this may explain the high level of self-reported well-being. They are quite prosperous and have a high level of equality and democratic institutions. There is low unemployment in Denmark, high in Sweden, but a high divorce rate in both.

France, Germany and Italy usually come out quite low in SWB measures, sometimes very low, well below Britain or the USA, and less than their economic level would predict. It is not clear whether the apparently low level of well-being is correct; extraversion is high, and may be a better measure, and the norms are high. Job satisfaction is low in France and Germany and there are above average rates of alcoholism, suicide and anxiety. Objective indicators show a high level of economic prosperity and a high level of the individualism measures, apart from inequality in former East Germany. But there is a high level of unemployment in all three countries, divorce is high in France and

Germany. One theory is that the level of trust in these countries is low; contact with friends is high in France but low in Germany.

Japan scores much lower in satisfaction and positive affect than would be expected from the high economic prosperity. Norms are low for satisfaction, and a lot of negative affect is acceptable. There are high levels of suicide, anxiety and neuroticism, and the latter was very high after World War II. The Japanese appear to be under a lot of stress, though the hot summers may also be a factor. Work is the main preoccupation and leisure satisfaction is low.

China comes out low in satisfaction, though higher in positive affect. Mainland China is very low in extraversion, but this is not true of Taiwan. There is a high suicide rate. Norms are very low, little is expected, and SWB is not salient. There are norms against too much expression of happiness, which may extend to answering survey questions. The causes of happiness are different, since this is a collectivist culture, and happiness depends on good relations in the family. Taiwan is much happier, more than the USA; it is also much more prosperous than the mainland.

South American countries, such as Brazil, Peru, Puerto Rica and Chile, have quite high satisfaction and positive affect scores, more than Europe, and more than would be expected from the average income, and extraversion is high. Chile in particular is very high in satisfaction and positive affect. This may be due to the high norms for satisfaction and PA. Neuroticism is very high, apart from Brazil. Objective indicators are unfavourable—low prosperity, high inequality and political instability. Suicide rate is low, perhaps because of the high level of religious activity.

African countries, like Ghana and Nigeria have rather low satisfaction, but higher positive affect, and quite low norms; extraversion is high. Objective indicators are poor—economically low, high inequality, political instability. There has been believed to be a happy "African personality", though this has yet to be demonstrated. Religion is very active, especially in West Africa.

Russia. The countries of the former Soviet Union are very low in satisfaction, and in positive affect. There is a high neuroticism score. We have seen that this may be partly due to the low norms for expressing positive feelings, or lack of socialisation for thinking positively. Objective indicators are not good—poverty, lack of democratic institutions, and political instability. The cold weather may be a factor too. Markham (1942) did find a small correlation between national anxiety levels and cold winters, but a larger one with hot summers.

The sources for this section are Table 12.1, norms from Diener (1995), International College Student Data (1995, cited by Diener and Suh, 1999), Lynn (1981), Lynn and Martin (1995).

HISTORICAL CHANGES IN HAPPINESS

Has the world become any happier? Looking back at Figure 9.1 (page 133) we saw that over the 40 or so years in which happiness and satisfaction surveys have been done, Americans have become much richer but not more satisfied with life, and this may apply to other countries too. We saw in Chapter 9 that this could be explained in terms of rising aspirations for material way of life—though it is still difficult to say whether Americans are more satisfied or happier than before or not. We saw that Belgians have become much less satisfied with their lives. There was economic depression and high unemployment in Belgium at this time (Table 12.1, page 179), though this was also the case in other European countries (Inglehart and Rabier, 1986).

Blanchflower and Oswald (1999) carried out an intensive study of 100,000 people in Britain and the USA at five periods from the 1970s to the 1990s. They were able to hold a number of demographic variables constant. In Britain, when demographic variables are held constant, there has been a small increase in life satisfaction; on the other hand unemployment and marital break-ups have increased, which have negative effects. In the USA happiness has slightly decreased, and this is partly due to the increased unemployment and marital failures. In addition men have become more happy, women less, and blacks have become happier, whites less so. In a similar study Blanchflower and Oswald (1997) had found that young people under 30 were happier in 1990 than in 1972, and that it was the unmarried young who gained most.

Meanwhile Americans were marrying later, and more were divorcing; the children of divorced parents are found to be more emotionally disturbed. Myers (1999) thinks this accounts for the increasing rates of depression, suicide and crime. Changes in American society can be interpreted as increasing individualism; there has been a decline of social networks and participation, such as voluntary work, leisure groups, and fewer people vote (Putnam, 2000).

These studies show that it is possible to study historical changes in happiness and satisfaction, but only over the past 40 years, when survey data is available. There is a further problem. Despite the great economic and other changes during this period, there has been very little change in reported satisfaction with life. We have already cast doubt on whether the apparent international differences are genuine, we may now doubt whether the lack of historical changes is genuine.

There is another way of tackling historical changes, by using objective social indicators. We have seen that income, health, and similar variables are good predictors of subjective well-being, so again it is reasonable to use such indicators as indices of satisfaction. Furthermore the data is available over a longer historical period than the last 40 years. Jordan (1992) studied the quality of life of British children in the nineteenth century. He used three groups of variables: (1) health: mortality rate and four other measures; (2) economic: GNP per capita and four other measures; (3) social: education, literacy and household size. He was able to find figures for every year. A brief index was constructed by using only the one indicator in each group that predicted the others best. As Figure 12.4 shows, all four measures increased during the period 1815–1914.

Jordan (1993) carried out a similar study of the quality of life of British adults during the nineteenth century. He used measures in three domains: (1) economic: wages and four other measures; (2) social: literacy, alcohol consumption, birth rate, rainfall and house building; (3) health: death rate, January temperature, and tea consumption. Again measures were found for each year. These indices are ingenious, but rather arbitrary. Statistical analysis showed that the components of each sub-index correlated well together, and that the overall well-being score was predicted best by the social index, least well by health. The

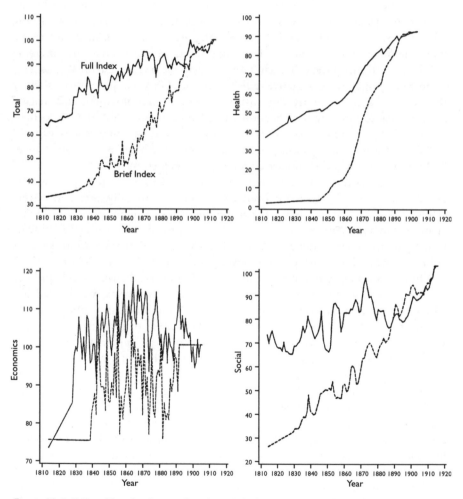

Figure 12.4 Full and brief indexes of quality of life for Victorian children (Jordan, 1992).

results show that there was a general increase in quality of life during the century up to 1900, followed by a fall.

If we accept such measures as indices of well-being, it is possible to test theories about how changes in society produce well-being. Frey and Song (1997) did this for 263 Chinese cities. They used the United Nations Human Development Index, consisting of life expectancy, literacy and GNP per person. Several theories were tested about the causes of development measured in this way. The strongest predictor was state investment, followed by foreign penetration. Industrial employment increased economic output but reduced health and literacy. Population growth had negative effects.

If we want to go further back in history other measures must be found. The content analysis of literary sources is one such measure. Mayer (1994) counted emotion terms in the Old Testament and other works, and found that over 12 centuries happiness terms increased, while other emotions did not.

CONCLUSIONS

A number of international surveys of average national happiness and life satisfaction have been carried out, and they show large differences between countries. These differences can partly be explained by economic differences such as average income; the reason for this is that money satisfies basic needs, though only up to a fraction of average US incomes. Satisfaction also correlates with individualism, though this is highly correlated with income, and affects the happiness of rich nations only, so that it is difficult to separate them. Low income dispersion also correlates with national happiness, but the reverse is sometimes found, as in Britain. Human rights and democratic institutions are correlated with income, but only for rich countries. There are ethnic differences in satisfaction within countries, but these are smaller when variables such as occupation are controlled.

An alternative explanation of national differences is in terms of social norms—and the socialisation of children to express or conceal emotions; this is confirmed by surveys of what is thought to be the ideal level of satisfaction and affect.

Although the surveys show clear national differences in happiness, the interpretation of these results is no longer clear. An alternative method is to use measures that are longer and less direct than the single items used so far. Much can be learnt from the use of objective indicators, such as depression and suicide rates. These have also been used to study historical changes.

Chapter 13

Happiness enhancement

LABORATORY MOOD INDUCTION

A number of methods have been used for inducing moods such as elation, depression and anxiety in the laboratory; it is elation, or positive moods, that we are interested in here. We now know how well these methods work, in terms of how large the average mood change is, how many subjects respond to them, and how long the mood lasts.

The first method to be widely used was that devised by Velten (1968). Subjects are asked to read silently then aloud a list of statements of the kind "I really do feel good", and "I *am* elated about things", and try to put themselves in the mood suggested. At first there was a list of 60 of these, but later it was shortened to 25. In a meta-analysis, Westermann et al. (1996) reanalysed 46 studies using this method and found that there was a mood change with an effect size of .38 (this is a proportion of a standard deviation) (see Table 13.1). In another meta-analysis Gerrards–Hesse, Spies, and Hesse (1994) found that on average 67% of subjects had their moods changed by this method. There is no doubt that it works; however, the elevated mood produced does not last very long, 10–15 minutes according to Frost and Green (1982). It has been objected that the Velten method only produces descriptions of emotions that subjects think they

Table 13.1 Effect of different methods of mood induction

Film/story +	.73
Film/story	.53
Gift	.38
Velten	.38
Imagination	.36
Feedback	.33
Music +	.33
Music	.32
Social interaction	.27
Facial expression	.19

Source: Westermann et al. (1996).

are expected to be feeling, and that any apparent change in mood is due to "demand characteristics". However, it has been found that the Velten method produces responses on an adjective check list that are different from what subjects imagined they would feel (Finegan and Seligman, 1995). In addition the method produces behavioural responses as well as self-report ones, as will be described shortly (Westermann et al., 1996).

A lot of other methods of mood induction in the lab have been studied. The average effect sizes found in a meta-analysis are given in Table 13.1. The most effective method, we now know, is the "film/story" one. This consists of showing an emotionally arousing film or asking subjects to read an emotionally arousing story. They may also be asked to get involved in the story and the feelings expressed; this is an additional bit of mood manipulation and is shown as " + " in Table 13.1; when this is used the effect is much greater (.73 versus .53). Films for positive mood induction may consist of extracts from Peter Sellars, John Cleese and others, sometimes of "out-takes"—discarded sequences where the actor has lost control. The materials used are very funny, and we saw in Chapter 5 how humour has immediate positive effect on mood. The film/ story method has a high success rate, especially with the added instruction, when it works with everyone. These percentages of success are taken from another meta-analysis by Gerrards–Hesse et al. (1994).

Music was found to be a powerful method in early studies, but overall has an effect size of only .32, though it has an 83% success rate, depending on the music used. Clark (1983) produced large effects, and I have heard his tapes, which were a very cheerful Haydn trumpet concerto for positive mood, and a Prokofiev suite played at half speed for depression induction—used for research purposes, not a usual form of therapy. Part of the problem is that different kinds of music appeal to different people (Carter et al., 1995).

The next most successful method is a gift, usually an unexpected gift of a chocolate bar, a can of coke, or a coin (.38), though no doubt larger gifts would have greater effects. By "imagination" is meant asking subjects to spend some time, sometimes 20 minutes, remembering a happy event "in as much detail as possible"; the effect is greater if concrete images are called up. We described this kind of research in Chapter 3. We have found that the effect is greater if people do this in pairs and tell each other about these happy events, and if they are pairs of friends (Argyle et al., 1989). "Feedback" means giving positive feedback about how well subjects are alleged to have done on some test or task. In real life outside the lab success at exams or in getting promotion are of course major sources of joy. The "social interaction" manipulation that has been used has consisted of meeting an experimental confederate who is very cheerful, or being given the opportunity to "help" someone who needs it. This has had rather small effects on mood (.27) but these are rather mild kinds of rewarding social interaction and much stronger ones could be devised. Schachter and Singer (1962) in a classic experiment used a really manic confederate to arouse positive moods. "Facial expression" refers to facial feedback experiments by

Laird (1984) and others in which subjects are asked to arrange their faces in expressions corresponding to positive emotions. It is interesting that there is an effect, but it is weaker than other methods.

We have seen how strong the overall effects of these methods are and how many subjects respond. The next question is how long do these induced moods last? This is most important since it affects whether these means of mood induction would be of any practical use or not. It is usually found that the Velten method has rather short-lived effects, about 10–15 minutes as Frost and Green (1982) found. However, Sinclair et al. (1994) devised a strengthened version of the Velten, in which there were 60 items, and an incubation period for subjects to get into the right mood; the effects lasted for 35 minutes. Small gifts have very short-term effects too; perhaps large gifts would do better. Showing films has longer-lasting effects.

Exercise was not included in the lists of mood induction methods above. However, as we have seen a 10-minute brisk walk has positive effects on mood, which last for 2 hours (see page 113), and more demanding exercise has effects that last for the whole day, even to the next. It is one of the easiest and most effective methods of inducing positive moods. Another method not included in the list above is the use of drugs, not normally possible in laboratory experiments, though the author has used alcohol (in small doses) for this purpose. As we have seen, Prozac and other anti-depressants can enhance positive moods (page 213), and their merits as a means of happiness therapy will be discussed below. However, for more enduring moods we have to turn to stronger life events and pleasant activities, occurring outside the lab, which will be discussed shortly.

Similar mood induction studies with depression find that this is easier to induce than happiness: the average effect size was .53 compared with .41 for happiness. The most effective methods were again film/story + , followed by telling people that they have failed at a test, imagination and Velten. Manipulation of facial expression was no good at all and no acceptable negative equivalent for gifts has been devised (Westermann et al., 1996). Fines are of course often used to punish people.

Not all subjects are influenced by these procedures, some are more affected than others. We saw in Chapter 10 that extraverts are more influenced by positive mood inductions and those high on neuroticism are more influenced by negative ones. We gave this as part of the explanation of the happiness of extraverts and the unhappiness of neurotics.

POSITIVE LIFE EVENTS

The mood induction procedures we have just looked at enhance positive moods but not by very much and not for very long. We now turn to events and activities that occur naturally and which may have a stronger impact. Stressful life events are a familiar and much studied source of unhappiness, mental and physical ill-health. Do positive life events (PLEs) have similar effects in the opposite direction? The kind of positive events we have in mind are sport and exercise, social events, success and recognition at work, concerts and church services, meetings of leisure groups, and sexual intercourse. Most of these cannot be arranged in the lab. They are very different from stressful life events, which are like accidents, uninvited and unexpected. Some PLEs are accidental, such as gifts, invitations, unexpected meetings with friends, success, falling in love. Some PLEs (as I shall call them) are like this, but more often they are sought and planned, or are part of a regular way of life, as with Saturday football or dances.

Table 13.2 shows how a number of PLEs were rated by Oxford students. The second part of the table is a similar set of ratings by a sample of American students. Some PLEs are quite infrequent, as with summer holidays, or very rare, as with getting married or having a baby; others happen all the time, such as watching TV or going for a run. Some are intense, such as sexual intercourse, others are not intense at all, as with watching TV. Some are more than intense, they are major life changes, such as getting married, getting a new job, and religious conversion; they will affect future PLEs.

We need to know what the effects are of these events, and how long the effects last. Mood induction techniques were disappointing in having such a short-term impact, but some of the other PLEs, such as exercise, are much better. Some of them could be built into schemes of happiness therapy or enhancement.

Much research on PLEs has treated them quantitatively, and added up their frequency. However, they are not all the same, they have a very different quality, as we have seen when we looked at the different kinds in earlier chapters.

- *Social events.* There are many kinds of these. Being in love is a source of intense joy, and increased self-esteem; being with friends produces companionship and positive feelings, sometimes admiration; family life is a great source of happiness. All these relations involve regular and usually frequent encounters.
- *Sport and exercise* produce positive moods and greater happiness when done regularly, and the effect may last to the next day. The quality of experience is of increased arousal, and self-esteem, as well as enjoyment of the social relations involved.
- *Religion* and *music* are quite intense for those involved, including other-worldly feelings of loss of sense of self, timelessness, glimpsing another world. And the groups in question are very supportive.
- *Leisure groups* of other kinds are a source of PLEs; sometimes several aspects of the experience combine, as with dancing which involves music, exercise and social interaction.
- *Work.* Positive experiences here are mainly reported for success and recognition, though job satisfaction studies find that intrinsic satisfaction comes from use of skills and social satisfaction from relations with workmates.

Table 13.2 Positive life events: Oxford students

Falling in love	78.0
Passing an examination or gaining a qualification	75.5
Recovering from a serious illness	72.1
Going on holiday	68.9
Making it up after an argument with your husband/wife or boy/girlfriend	66.0
Getting married or engaged	65.0
Birth of a child	64.6
Winning a lot of money	64.4
Getting promoted at work or getting a pay rise	59.9
Going out with or visiting friends	58.0
Getting a new job	56.1

Source: Henderson, Argyle, and Furnham (1984).

Positive life events: American students

Event type	Objectivity rating	Goodness rating
Got into graduate school	1.32	0.64
Promotion/raise	1.38	0.64
Marriage (mine)	1.11	0.72
Parent got raise or promotion	1.41	0.76
Received an award or public recognition for achievement other than grades	1.27	0.76
Engagement (mine)	1.28	0.86
Received a 4.5 (B +) or higher average for a semester of college	1.23	0.97
Received an unexpected (but welcome) call from an old friend	1.66	1.02
Best friend got married	1.18	1.07
Sibling got married	1.16	1.07
Parents took you on a vacation	1.39	1.14
Got a car	1.23	1.16
Became an aunt/uncle	1.32	1.20
Parent/relative gave you a start in business or a job	1.61	1.27
Got a pet	1.16	1.42
Played on an athletic team	1.25	1.53
Parents gave me a major gift (over $1000 value)	1.36	1.58
Joined a club or group	1.38	1.60
Began a hobby	1.55	1.61
Engaged in a certain art or craft for leisure	1.91	1.64
M	1.36	1.13

Source: Magnus, Diener, Fujita, and Payot (1993).

- *Watching TV* is a great enigma. It is done so much that it must be rewarding, but research finds that it produces only weak positive moods, and that watchers are often half asleep. However the moods it produces are positive, and followers of soap operas may gain some imaginary friends.
- *Holidays*, though not frequent, can be looked forward to, and are great sources of relaxation, adventure, sex or religious pilgrimage, according to taste.

The causes of positive life events

Stressful life events are usually seen as uncontrollable accidents, though in fact they are partly due to features of persons and features of their life situation and life style.

Certain aspects of personality affect PLEs. Headey et al. (1985) in a longitudinal study in Australia found that extraverts were more likely to have such experiences at work and with friends, and Magnus et al. (1993) found the same in a longitudinal American study. In both of these investigations it was found that neuroticism predisposed people to negative life events. Extraversion also predisposes people to having positive reactions even to negative events. Personality acts in several ways—it can lead people to choose or avoid certain situations, it can also lead to people interpreting situations in different ways, it can lead to people changing situations, in this case so that they are more positive. Another feature of individuals that affects their PLEs is the amount of social support they have. Meehan et al. (1993) found that high-school pupils with good social support experienced more PLEs and appreciated them more.

Different sections of the community have different frequencies of events; working-class people have more which are due to poverty, unemployment, trouble with the law, etc., and this can explain differences in well-being (Argyle, 1994). Working-class people are in worse mental health and are less happy than middle-class ones; this can partly be explained by the higher rate of stressful life events for the working class. There are also differences in PLEs. Middle-class people enjoy much better leisure activities, especially exercise and social clubs, go to church more, and have more friends (Argyle, 1996). There are also some class differences in personality that are relevant. Middle-class individuals are stronger in internal control, as the result of different patterns of socialisation, and this enables them to control or think they can control what happens to them (Kohn and Schooler, 1982). Married individuals are happier than unmarried, as we have seen. The married are likely to enjoy much more sex, more social interaction and companionship, than those living alone.

We looked at the effects of positive mood induction in the lab, we now turn to the effects of real-life PLEs. These tend to be stronger and hence likely to have greater effects. However, the research is different, as it is rarely experimental, and depends on weaker designs, though there have been a number of longitudinal studies, which are nearly as good as experiments.

Diener, Sandvik, and Pavot (1991) found that the percentage of time that individuals were experiencing positive affect correlated with happiness at about .50, while the average intensity of positive affect when they were feeling happy correlated at only .25. They concluded that intensity is relatively unimportant, and report that intense positive experiences occur only on 2.6% of days. I am not convinced of this: a lot of people have sexual intercourse more often than once in 38 days (i.e. 2.6% of days), some go to church once a week, or engage in vigorous exercise every day, all sources of fairly intense PLEs.

In case there is any doubt that PLEs make people happy we turn to one or two field experiments in which PLEs have been manipulated. Reich and Zautra (1981) carried out a field experiment in which they asked one group of subjects to choose from a longer list 12 activities that they regarded as highly pleasurable but which they had not done for 2 weeks, and another group to choose 2 such activities. These included sporting, academic, cultural and social activities. Forty-eight subjects agreed to perform these activities during the next 2 weeks. It was found that members of both groups had higher scores for quality of life and pleasantness than before and than a control group. It made no difference whether they did 2 or 12.

A number of other field experiments have been done in which subjects agreed to carry out serious exercise for a period, for example regular running, jogging or swimming for some weeks. This is found to have strong effects on happiness, health and mental health (see Chapter 8).

Other research has used longitudinal methods, with naturally occurring PLEs. Headey et al. (1985), in their longitudinal study of 600 Australians, found that PLEs in the spheres of friendship and work were not only predicted by extraversion and led to enhanced subjective well-being, but also led to higher levels of extraversion, in a "chain of well-being" (Figure 13.1).

All the investigations mentioned so far were with normal subjects. PLEs have also been found to be good for patients suffering from depression. Needles and Abramson (1990) found that depressives who experienced PLEs and who made positive attributions for them had reduced levels of hopelessness and remission of depressive symptoms.

PLEs are also good for physical health. Caputo et al. (1998) found that PLEs predicted reduced blood pressure and hence reduced risk of hypertension in adolescents. Brown and McGill (1989) found that PLEs led to improved physical health, but only in individuals with high self-esteem; it is suggested that PLEs for people with low self-esteem are inconsistent with their self-image.

We shall see in the next section how increasing PLEs has been used success-fully as a method of enhancing happiness both for depressed patients and for normal people.

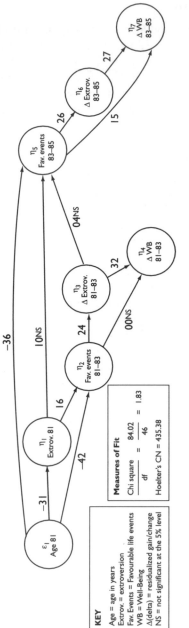
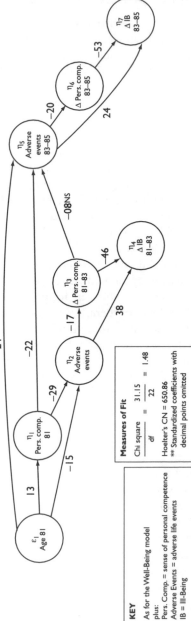

Figure 13.1 Chains of well-being and ill-being (Headey et al., 1985).

HAPPINESS THERAPY

Regular positive mood induction

We have just seen that positive moods are produced by pleasant activities and events such as seeing friends, taking exercise, eating out and sexual activity. Some of these lead to a good mood for the rest of the day, sometimes to the next day (Stone and Neale, 1984). It follows that if you engage in such mood induction every day, or even twice a day, a good mood can be kept up all the time. Two easy ways of enhancing mood are exercise and music. Some individuals jog or swim every day, and many listen to music of their choice daily. A few take part in religious services twice a day.

We also saw that there is some variability in the activities that work best for different individuals, so the right ones need to be found. An American friend starts the day by going for a run across the Nevada desert, accompanied by his wife or by music on his walkman, while enjoying the spectacular sight of the sun rising over the desert, and I have on occasion joined him. This is a very powerful piece of mood induction, including exercise, wife or music, and sunrise. He has a very good breakfast too.

Depressed and other unhappy people report fewer pleasant activities, and Lewinsohn proposed that depression is caused by insufficient positive reinforcement. This can happen for various reasons including lack of social skills. A form of therapy was devised to enable depressed patients to have more positive activities, though this can equally be used for non-patients. Clients are asked to keep daily records for a month of positive events, from a list of 320, and their daily mood. Of these 49 were found to be associated with a good mood for the day for 10% of their subjects, and these are given in Table 13.3. Computer analysis then shows which activities have the most positive effect, and patients are encouraged to engage in them more often (Lewinsohn et al., 1982). They are persuaded to do this in various ways, including small increases between sessions, rewarding them by more therapist time, and teaching them to reward themselves, for example by food or other treats. Turner et al. (1979) found that this was successful in lifting the depression of a group of depressed university staff and students. Reich and Zautra (1981) as we have seen were also successful with a group of students who were not patients.

More recently Lewinsohn and others have incorporated pleasant activities into more elaborate packages of treatment, which are described later. The Lewinsohn and Gotlib (1995) "Coping with Depression" course includes increased positive activities, and also social skills training and self-control therapy, which includes self-reinforcement, problem-solving therapy, relaxation, stopping negative thoughts and setting realistic goals. This method has been found successful with depressed adults and adolescents, but has not been used with non-patients (Lewinsohn and Gotlib, 1995).

The Fordyce (1983) happiness programme has been used with community

Table 13.3 Pleasant activities that affect mood for the whole day

Social interaction
1 being with happy people
2 having people show interest in what you have said
3 being with friends
4 being noticed as sexually attractive
5 kissing
6 watching people
7 having a frank and open conversation
8 being told I am loved
9 expressing my love to someone
10 petting, necking
11 being with someone I love
12 complimenting or praising someone
13 having coffee, tea, a Coke, and so on with friends
14 being popular at a gathering
15 having a lively talk
16 listening to the radio
17 seeing old friends
18 being asked for my help or advice
19 amusing people
20 having sexual relationships with a partner of the opposite sex
21 meeting someone new of the same sex

Incompatible with depression
22 laughing
23 being relaxed
24 thinking about something good in the future
25 thinking about people I like
26 seeing beautiful scenery
27 breathing clean air
28 having peace and quiet
29 sitting in the sun
30 wearing clean clothes
31 having spare time
32 sleeping soundly at night
33 listening to music
34 smiling at people
35 seeing good things happen to my family or friends
36 feeling the presence of the Lord in my life
37 watching wild animals

Self-efficacy
38 doing a project in my own way
39 reading stories, novels, poems, or plays
40 planning or organising something
41 driving skilfully
42 saying something clearly
43 planning trips or vacations
44 learning to do something new
45 being complimented or told I have done well
46 doing a job well

Miscellaneous
47 eating good meals
48 going to a restaurant
49 being with animals

Source: Lewinsohn and Graf (1973).

college non-patients. The cognitive components were listed before. In addition a number of behavioural and social skill components are included:

- spend more time socialising
- strengthen your closest relationships
- develop an outgoing, social personality
- be a better friend
- become more active
- become involved with meaningful work.

As before clients are asked to concentrate on one element for a day at a time; the overall package, including the cognitive parts, has been very successful. However, we do not know how important each of these various elements is in making people happier.

Cognitive therapy

"Cognitive therapy is a complex collection of techniques that share the goal of making interpretations of events rational and realistic" (Rehm, 1990). It was developed for mental patients, including patients suffering from depression. Many people have serious depression, about 9% of those who go to see the doctor for example, while 12–17% have a life-time risk of major depression, and many more of minor degrees of depression (Angst, 1997). So we can take note of methods that are able to increase the happiness of the depressed, though we also want to know whether they also work for those who are not clinically depressed, i.e. normals who want to be happier.

We have seen in earlier chapters that happy people think differently from unhappy ones in a number of ways. They have a positive view of everything, realistic goals and a purpose in life, can see the funny side of things, do not blame themselves when bad things happen, and believe they can control what happens. Several theories in clinical psychology have suggested that depression is caused by negative and irrational ways of thinking, and forms of cognitive therapy have been devised to correct them. Some of these negative ways of thinking used by depressed patients overlap with the ways that unhappy people have been found to think in the happiness research tradition.

Forms of cognitive therapy have been used for normals, with success. Lichter et al. (1980) devised a course of eight 2-hour sessions over 4 weeks, focusing on improving insight and understanding and correcting irrational beliefs. Those trained in this way improved in happiness and satisfaction, as shown in Figure 13.2.

Fava et al. (1998), working in Italy, used the six dimensions of happiness listed by Ryff (1989)—self-acceptance, positive relations with others, autonomy, environmental mastery, purpose in life, and personal growth. This course is unusual in that it focuses on positive thinking. Clients kept diaries of positive episodes and anything that interrupted these, and were then guided to progress along all six dimensions. Ten individuals who did this course gained more in well-being than another ten who had more orthodox cognitive therapy, though they improved too.

There have been many studies of cognitive therapy for depressed patients. The Lewinsohn and Gotlib (1995) "Coping With Depression" course, using 12 sessions over 7 weeks, includes some cognitive components, such as realistic goals and reducing negative thinking, as well as the positive activities described already.

The Fordyce (1977) package, for non-patients, his "Personal Happiness Enhancement Program" with 14 components, includes several cognitive components:

- work on a healthy personality
- lower expectations and aspirations
- develop positive, optimistic thinking
- value happiness
- get better organised and plan things
- develop "present orientation"
- reduce negative feelings
- stop worrying.

The therapy consists of working on the 14 areas one at a time for each day for 6 weeks. This course has been very successful: out of 338 students 69% became happier, and with 226 more adults 81% reported gains of happiness (Fordyce, 1983).

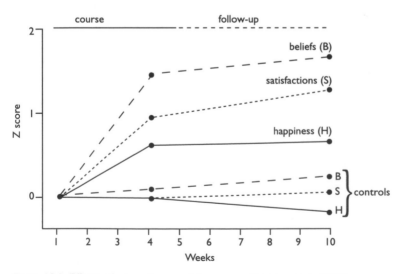

Figure 13.2 Effects of a happiness training course (Lichter et al., 1980).

A number of studies have compared the efficacy of cognitive and other therapies for depressed patients. It is certainly more successful than no treatment, it is usually better than placebo controls (e.g. an inactive drug), it does better than behaviour therapy, and about the same as drugs, although drugs are better for those severely depressed (Rehm, 1995).

Social skills training

We saw in Chapter 6 that relationships are a very important source of happiness—especially marriage and other close relations, friends, and people at work. Difficulty in establishing or keeping these relationships is a major source of unhappiness. Argyle and Lu (1990) found that part of the explanation for the happiness of extraverts was their greater social skills, particularly their assertiveness and cooperativeness. Depressed patients and many other mental patients have been found to display defective social skills such as low rewardingness (Hollin and Trower, 1986). Social skills training (SST) can help with these skills. For those who can't make friends the training can also include non-verbal communication, verbal communication, rewardingness, better understanding of social situations and relationships. Those who have friends but still feel lonely can benefit from more self-disclosure. Marital therapy and marital enrichment can include rewardingness, and also training in resolving conflicts by negotiation. There are many more detailed aspects of marital skills, which can be taught (Argyle, 1994).

SST has been widely used for depressed and other patients, alone or as part of a larger package of the kind that were described above. Considerable success has been reported, and the benefits have been found to last for 1- or 2-year follow-up periods. SST is included in larger packages of treatment. The Lewinsohn and Gotlib (1995) "Coping with Depression" course includes:

- conversational skills
- making friends
- negotiation
- assertiveness
- clearer communication.

This forms a large part of a package which has been found to be very successful with depressed patients: a high rate of recovery was reported at a 2-year follow-up (Hops and Lewinsohn, 1995). Other schemes have focused on marital and family skills.

Drugs

We saw earlier that drugs can be used to relieve anxiety and depression, and to produce positive emotions such as excitement. Depressed and other mental patients are widely treated in this way and this creates the possibility that non-patients might be made happier by the same drugs. Alcohol is widely used by non-patients, and is successful in relieving tension and anxiety for many, though too much of it can of course be disastrous.

Prozac is used a lot for depressed patients, and is also prescribed for many who are not really depressed, though it is suspected that quite a proportion of the normal population are somewhat depressed. It caught on in the USA in particular after it was introduced in 1983, and has received a lot of magazine coverage, because for some it makes them feel "better than well", "more alive", perhaps because of an American desire for hope and optimism, as compared with what was seen as European fatalism and pessimism (Healy, 1997). Prozac works by concentrating serotonin in certain parts of the brain, and also endorphins and dopamine. The main problem is that for quite a proportion of individuals it has no effect at all, or makes them feel worse, so 20% at least give up. And 54% report side-effects, which are quite serious, particularly:

- loss of sexual desire (25–35%)
- nausea (21%)
- headaches (20%)
- insomnia (14%)
- drowsiness (17%)
- and a few commit suicide (about 3.5%), but this happens to depressives in general (Fieve, 1994).

Figures on the side effects like these are widely reported but they have been challenged in the courts by the manufacturers of Prozac. And it should be said that all anti-depressant drugs have side-effects; those from Prozac are less than for the others. Furthermore an overdose is not fatal, and this drug is not addictive.

As forms of treatment for depression Prozac and other antidepressants are successful for many of those who take them, about the same as cognitive therapy, though the combination of the two is better. In a meta-analysis of controlled trials comparing Prozac with a placebo, Greenberg et al. (1994) found an effect size of .40, which means that two-thirds of treated patients did better than those not treated. Prozac is however about 33% more expensive than cognitive behaviour therapy (Antonuccio et al., 1997). And patients have to keep on taking it, a tablet a day indefinitely, or the depression returns; they are not actually cured (James, 1997).

I conclude that Prozac and other antidepressants, despite their evident success with many patients, cannot be recommended as a means of making the world happier—because of the side-effects, the failure rate, and the expense.

CONCLUSIONS

Mood induction experiments in the lab find that positive moods can be produced by exposure to happy films or stories, music, and other methods, but the mood does not last long. Exercise does better, as do other positive life events, from social relations, work or leisure for example. Their frequency and their intensity are both important, and if regularly repeated lead to happiness and to personality changes. They also lead to better mental and physical health.

Happiness therapy, for normals and depressed patients, can be carried out by increasing the number of positive life events. Cognitive therapy is successful with both normals and patients, and has been elaborated in happiness enhancement programmes. Social skills training is successful alone and as part of these packages. Antidepressant drugs like Prozac are successful with over half of patients, but have bad side-effects for many.

Another, and probably better, way of enhancing happiness is through changes in lifestyle, making use of the causes of happiness discussed in this book. This will be dealt with in the next chapter.

Chapter 14

The effects of positive moods and happiness

Mood induction experiments have also been used to study the *effects* of happiness and good moods. Other methods have been used too, such as the effect of positive life events. We were asking in Chapter 3 what is the biological function of positive moods and happiness. Perhaps we can learn more about this by finding what people do when they are in these conditions.

SOCIABILITY

Some mood induction experiments found that when positive moods have been induced in subjects they feel very sociable. Cunningham (1988) induced such moods, and found that students expressed more interest in taking part in social, prosocial, and strenuous leisure and general activities, but not in intimate, non-social or antisocial activities. They also said that when they were happy they were likely to be with someone they loved, or friends or with happy people—though these might have been causes of their happiness. Kammann and Flett (1983) found that happy people said that they felt closer to others, felt loved and trusted, were interested in others and did not feel lonely.

Happy people not only have more social interaction with others, but it is also of a higher quality. Berry and Hansen (1996) asked 105 students to keep social diaries for a week. Those with higher scores on positive affect had more frequent social encounters, spent more time on them, and found them more enjoyable; the encounters were more directed to leisure than work. In a laboratory study female students were paired at random and those with higher PA scores found these encounters more enjoyable, pleasant, satisfying and relaxing, and they liked one another more; they rated the quality of interaction higher. Their behaviour was rated as open warm, friendly, empathic and generous. Other studies have found that when in a good mood people are more cooperative, for example they negotiate in a way that produces maximum gains for both sides, as a result of more flexible behaviour, better problem-solving and a better understanding of the situation (Forgas, 1998; Isen, 1987).

When people are in a positive mood they have a less cautious social style, for example making requests directly, whereas those in a negative mood put more work into constructing elaborate and indirect requests (Forgas, 1999). When others make requests, subjects in a good mood are more likely to comply, especially when the request was impolite.

Couples coming out of a happy movie, or who had seen one in the lab, evaluated their relationships more positively, and reported greater admiration for each other and more self-disclosure, than couples coming out of sad movies (Forgas et al., 1994). This may be because those in positive moods are also sexually aroused more readily (Mitchell, 1998).

Several studies have shown that happy people like others more; they are also liked more by others, who will spend more time with them, sit nearer, say they would like to meet them again, compared with depressed individuals for example (Howes and Hokanson, 1979). Happy people get on better with their children, and happy mothers more often say they like their adolescent children. Happy people are more likely to get married (page 79).

The most remarkable effect in the social sphere is that when individuals have had a lot of positive life events they become more extraverted, which in turn makes them happier, as Headey and Wearing (1992) found in their longitudinal study in Australia.

HELPING AND ALTRUISM

Several experiments have found that positive mood induction can lead to subjects agreeing to minor altruistic acts in the lab such as helping another student, and picking up dropped papers (Isen, 1987). Positive mood induction can lead to more serious help than this; O'Malley and Andrews (1983) found that 47% of subjects who had been put in a good mood by recalling happy past events offered to give blood, compared with 17% in a control condition. It works for children too: Isen and Levin (1972) found that children who had been allowed to win at bowling gave three times as much to poor children. Baumann et al. (1981) found that children could be made more generous to poor children by mood induction, but they also rewarded themselves more, by helping themselves to candy. On sunny days waitresses get bigger tips. In another kind of study Rimland (1982) found a strong correlation between ratings of happiness and of unselfishness for 2000 people.

Happy people are found to be more interested in other people and with social problems, less with their personal problems or inner world. It is sometimes thought that political activity is motivated by discontent, but happy people are not deficient in voting; they do not take part in violent protests, but they do join community organisations a lot.

Why do positive moods lead to altruism? There are several possibilities. Happy people may know that helping is rewarding and they want to maintain their positive mood; Isen and Simmonds (1978) found that subjects were less likely to help if they were told this would put them in a bad mood; however, a very weak form of mood induction had been used—finding a dime in a telephone box. And Manucia et al. (1984) found that beliefs about mood lability affected the impact of negative but not of positive moods on helping. Good moods make people like others more. Cheerful subjects may want to redress the balance in happiness between themselves and others. Good moods may make them remember the rewarding aspects of helping (Batson, 1995).

WORK PERFORMANCE

As we saw in Chapter 7 there is a modest correlation between job satisfaction and rate of work, some of it probably due to job satisfaction affecting work. Several studies have found that happy individuals are more effective, as astronauts and in naval training. The effect is greater for both "altruism" and "compliance" at work. There is a clear effect of job satisfaction on (lower) labour turnover, and a smaller one on absenteeism.

There is no sign of happy people being idle, as some theories would predict. When in a good mood people become very active socially, wanting to meet new people, wanting to be helpful, and seeking out leisure activities.

Do positive moods affect happiness?

We will look both at the effects of positive mood induction in the lab, and at the effects of real-life positive life events (PLEs). These tend to be stronger and hence likely to have greater effects. However, the research is different, as it is rarely experimental, and depends on weaker designs, though there have been a number of longitudinal studies, which are nearly as good as experiments.

To start with, good moods have several positive features—seeing the good side of things, such as having positive views of others, engaging in pleasant reminiscences, generally having a rosier outlook (Veenhoven, 1988). Diener et al. (1991) found that the percentage of time that individuals were experiencing positive affect correlated with happiness at about .50, while the average intensity of positive affect when they were feeling happy correlated at only .25. In case there is any doubt that PLEs make people happy we cited field experiments in which PLEs have been manipulated, as by Reich and Zautra (1981). A number of other field experiments have been done in which subjects agreed to carry out serious exercise for a period, for example regular running, jogging or swimming for some weeks. This is found to have strong effects on happiness, as well as on health and mental health (see Chapter 8).

Other research has used longitudinal methods, with naturally occurring PLEs. Headey and Wearing (1992) carried out repeated measures of 600 Australians, measuring their happiness and other attributes every 2 years. They found that PLEs in the spheres of friendship and work led to enhanced subjective well–being, and also led to higher levels of extraversion. All the investigations mentioned so far were with normal subjects. PLEs have also been found to be good for patients suffering from depression, as we shall see below.

Induced good moods have an effect on the self–concept, people think better of themselves, especially about aspects of themselves that are less stable or about which they are uncertain (Sedikides, 1995).

WAYS OF THINKING

A lot of mood induction experiments have studied the effects of moods on how people think and solve problems. The findings appear at first sight to be contradictory. Children who have been put in a positive mood can do sums faster, 50% faster in one experiment (Bryan and Bryan, 1991). In another experiment Clark and Isen (1982) found that subjects ranked fictitious cars for which nine kinds of data were given in 11.1 minutes compared with 19.6 for controls. They found that subjects were also better at solving a problem of attaching a candle to a wall given a box of drawing pins and a book of matches. The solution was to use the drawing pin box as a base, pinned to the wall. This was solved by 75% of those who had seen a funny film. compared with 13% of those who had seen a non–humorous film and 13% who had seen no film. Subjects in a good mood do better at problems that need a creative solution, and can think of more examples of a category, including more unusual examples (Greene and Noice, 1988). They do better on measures of creativity (Adaman and Blaney, 1995).

But in other experiments those in a positive mood do worse. In a syllogism task they were less successful, perhaps because they did them faster and drew fewer diagrams; those in a positive mood got an average of 3.24 right in 10 minutes compared with 5.56 for controls; they had put less time and effort into it (Melton, 1995). It appears that when in a positive mood subjects do worse if there is a easier way of doing things, in which case they use stereotypes and the most available information, but do less hard thinking, less analytic work (Bless et al., 1996; Isen, 1987). However, Bodenhausen et al. (1994) found that the positive–mood subjects did not make more use of stereotypes if told that they would be accountable for their social judgements. In judging social situations those in good moods have a greater "fundamental attribution error", i.e. they attribute more to the person, less to the situation, they are using the more obvious source of information (Forgas, 1998).

The explanation of this apparent lack of effort on the part of people in a good mood may be that they normally have no need to solve any problems, they want things to stay as they are. Schwarz (1990) said "they have little need to engage in cognitive effort unless it is required by currently active goals". It is unhappy people who need to do something. The reason for the greater creativity of those in good moods may be that the cognitive system becomes more relaxed so that more diverse associations can be made. The greater use of top-down general ideas enables subjects to go beyond the information given (Bless et al., 1996).

The main effects of positive mood on thinking are that people think faster, and are more creative, but depend more on stereotypes and easily available information, and do less careful, logical thinking.

HEALTH

Many studies have looked at the correlation between happiness and various measures of health. In a meta-analysis Okun et al. (1984) found an average correlation between happiness and health of .32. This was stronger for women and for old people, and if measures of subjective health were used. Negative affect has a stronger connection than this with poor health.

The relation is stronger with self-rated, or subjective health, as opposed to health rated by the doctor for example (Okun and George, 1984). And the relation with self-rated health is much less if neuroticism is held constant; so the explanation is partly that neurotic individuals are unhappy and think they are in bad health; or as Okun and George put it "Self-health is a proxy for emotional as well as physical health" (pp. 532–539). It has been suggested that unhappy people have a low threshold for pain or minor symptoms, and are ready to decide that they are "ill". Positive affect at time 1 predicts fewer health complaints 3 months later (Brenner, 1973). Some studies have found a relation between subjective well-being and real physical health, and the link between satisfaction and health remains after variables like social status and income have been held constant (Edwards and Klemmack, 1973).

But does happiness cause health or does health cause happiness? Longitudinal studies have shown causal effects of satisfaction on health. Wickrama et al. (1995) found in a study of 310 married couples that the reported health of husbands was predicted better by their work satisfaction (especially if they were committed to occupational success), whereas the health of wives was predicted better by parental satisfaction (especially if they were involved with parenting). Attempts to solve the causation problem by causal modelling have found both directions operating; one of these directions is of subjective well-being affecting health (Feist et al. 1995).

There is nothing imaginary or subjective about living and dying, and it has been found that happy people live longer. Deeg and van Zonneveld (1989) studied a sample of 3149 Dutch people aged 65 or over, controlled for a range of demographic variables, and found that 70-year-old men lived on average 20 months longer if they were one standard deviation above average for happiness; the effect for women was smaller. We saw earlier that church members live several years longer than non-members, as do those who take regular exercise. However, church and exercise are factors that affect both happiness and health, and these findings do not show a direct relation between them.

How does happiness affect health? Stone et al. (1987) found in a longitudinal study that good moods elevated the immune system and negative moods depressed it; it took 3–5 days before the appearance or non-appearance of any symptoms. Caputo et al. (1998) found that PLEs predicted reduced blood pressure and hence reduced risk of hypertension in adolescents. Happiness may operate at a more psychological level too. Brown and McGill (1989) found that positive life events led to improved health in high-school girls, but only if they had high self-esteem too. Weisenberg et al. (1998) found that after seeing a humorous film subjects could stand more pain, 51 minutes with a hand in cold water, compared with only 31 minutes after a sad film.

MENTAL HEALTH

We saw in Chapter 2 how the absence of depression and other negative emotions is part of subjective well-being. Many studies have shown how there is a strong negative relation between depression in particular and measures of happiness and satisfaction (Veenhoven, 1994). In their Australian study, Headey and Wearing (1992) found that life satisfaction and positive affect correlated with depression and anxiety as follows:

	Depression	Anxiety
Life satisfaction	−.59	−.39
Positive affect	−.35	−.23

As we said before, these negative emotions are distinct from positive affect and satisfaction, but they have quite strong negative correlations with them.

Does happiness prevent people from becoming depressed; can it cure depression? Several studies have shown that happiness acts as a buffer for stress. Verkley and Stolk (1989) found that happy individuals coped better with being unemployed for example. Needles and Abramson (1990) followed a group of depressed students over 6 weeks and found that the occurrence of positive life events resulted in reduced hopelessness and depression, but only if they also had a positive attributional style. In Chapter 13 we looked at forms of treatment in which PLEs are generated, and which have had some success.

PLEs certainly affect depression. Davis and Leonard (1999) studied 1089 students and found that the frequency and the intensity of PLEs correlated with (the absence of) depression. Stressful life events can have positive effects in the form of "stress-related growth". This is more likely to happen if there have also been recent PLEs (Park et al., 1996).

Trope et al. (2000) found that induced positive moods made subjects more able and willing to deal with negative information about themselves—they could react constructively to criticism.

CONCLUSIONS

In Chapter 3 we discussed the issue of why there are positive emotions, and cited the answer offered by Fredrickson (1998). She suggested that positive moods provide occasions for play (hence learning skills), exploration, reflection and integration, and social bonding. Our examination of the effects of positive moods in this chapter confirms that all this happens, but that the most striking effects of happiness and positive moods are in the domain of social behaviour. Good moods produce social behaviour that is warm, positive and generous, resulting in mutual liking.

There are other benefits that can be looked at in terms of resources—enhancing health and mental health. There are some other effects, such as more work and more creative thinking, that may build other resources. But the main effect of positive moods is happiness, which is an end in itself.

Chapter 15

Conclusions

We have seen in the course of this book that happiness is a major dimension of human experience, including positive mood, satisfaction with life, and cognitions such as optimism and self-esteem. There has been extensive research on the causes of happiness, and we now have a very good idea what they are. This research consists partly of big social surveys, sometimes of many countries, and also of longitudinal and "quasi-experimental" studies which can tease out the direction of causation.

Happiness is partly caused by objective features of life such as wealth, employment, and marriage, but also by subjective factors such as how we perceive those conditions, for example comparison with others and adaptation. Another cause of happiness is having the right kind of personality, but this can be changed by life experiences.

We saw in Chapter 13 that positive moods can be induced by a variety of activities, and that it is possible to enhance happiness by therapy, social skills training or drugs. It is strongly affected by "positive life events", and this has become the basis of methods of happiness therapy. Such positive events can be built into a changed way of life, making use of the causes of happiness which have been shown to be important; therapy or drugs will then be unnecessary.

MONEY

Many people assume that money is the key to greater happiness. In fact for most people money has a very small effect on happiness, because their basic needs are satisfied already, and there are other, much more important, causes of happiness, of which they are not aware. The belief that money will bring happiness is an illusion; the reason is perhaps that we buy things because we think we will like them, that they will give us pleasure, but in fact they may make very little difference to our lives.

What research shows is that for poor people, and those in poor countries, money does make a difference to their happiness. For everyone else the effect is small, because money is spent on bigger or better cars, houses, holidays, etc., and this doesn't do much for us. This is not always the case: it is possible to spend money on objects or activities that are life-enhancing. Research also shows a substantial difference in average happiness between rich and poor countries, and this is probably because richer countries have better public facilities for education, medicine, leisure, security and the rest. An unsolved research problem is why there has been almost no increase in satisfaction or happiness as a result of massive historical changes in average incomes. This is probably due to rising expectations: where once people aspired to owning a bicycle now they want two cars. There are differences in happiness between rich and poor within countries, especially in countries where there are large social differences. This is not only due to the rich people spending more money; they also have more satisfying jobs, better leisure, more enduring social relationships.

When individuals suddenly get rich, for example by winning the Lottery, the prizes may be so large this it disrupts their lives, by giving up their jobs, moving to a new neighbourhood and social circle with different ways of life, abandoning old ways and friends and not being accepted by the new group.

LEISURE

It is difficult to become better paid or richer, and the stress of doing so can make people ill. Leisure on the other hand is largely under our own individual control—it is done in our "free" time. Most of the pleasant activities chosen by those undergoing pleasant activity therapy are forms of leisure. And we have seen that certain kinds of leisure do lead to positive affect, happiness and to good mental and physical health. Physical exercise is the quickest way of acquiring a good mood, and if done regularly the benefits go a lot further than that, up to relieving at any rate milder forms of depression, and promoting length of life. Music has been found to be another easy way of inducing positive moods, and the moods induced by music have a depth and intensity like those due to religion. The most popular form of leisure now is watching TV, but this is found to do no more than induce a weak positive mood.

We know that many individuals do not take advantage of their free time to take part in beneficial kinds of leisure. The unemployed and the elderly may do little more than watch TV and read the paper. They may say that shortage of money stops them engaging in leisure, but this is really a minor problem since much leisure is free or almost so—voluntary work, gardening, listening to music, church, reading and study, running and walking, for example.

Lack of facilities is a more important obstacle, though local government does a lot to build swimming pools, tennis courts, ice rinks, ski slopes and sports halls. This is also done by private enterprise—there is money in providing leisure; there is also work, since leisure creates it. It is found that people are much less likely to visit sports facilities when these are any distance away.

Another obstacle is lack of skill to do these things; this is important for music and most sports. Often people find out about sporting or cultural activities, and acquire the skills, at school and even more at college. Those who do not go to college are less likely to do so and there is a class difference in leisure activities.

WORK

Most people like their jobs, though a minority do not; another minority like them very much indeed. Most of them do not realise that their work is a major source of satisfaction, though they may do so if they lose their jobs. Most lottery winners give up their work voluntarily, so they lose their job satisfaction too. Work is not only free, you get paid for doing it, though a number work without being paid, as with voluntary work, and some of the retired who love their work and can't stop.

Job satisfaction research has found the kinds of work that are most satisfying. Again pay is of minor importance, though workers are very upset if they are paid less than others doing similar work. Job status is a factor in job satisfaction, including pay, rank, level of skill and conditions of work. Work is enjoyed more if it involves a variety of skills, there is autonomy, and the completion of meaningful tasks. The social aspects of work are very important, small cooperative groups and teams are best, together with supportive supervisors. Job satisfaction has some positive effects, such as making workers more cooperative and reducing absenteeism and labour turnover.

Conditions of work have improved enormously since the days of assembly lines and early textile mills; however, new technology is sometimes making things worse again, with reduced autonomy and social contacts.

Unemployment and fear of unemployment are a major cause of unhappiness. Experiments in encouraging the unemployed to do voluntary work or participate in sports training have shown positive results. These are two examples of the value of serious and satisfying leisure; they can provide some of the satisfactions of work.

The retired are happier than the unemployed, though they too are "unemployed". They say that they miss the work itself and their workmates. Many forms of leisure are suitable for the retired—easier exercise, some kinds of voluntary work, hobbies such as bird-watching and archaeology, reading and study.

SOCIAL RELATIONSHIPS

This is probably the greatest single cause of happiness and other aspects of well-being. Simply being with friends and those we love puts us in a good mood. They are a major source of positive life events, are chosen for pleasant activities therapy. Friends are very important but how do we find and keep them? Part of the answer lies in social skills training, described in Chapter 13, part of it lies in joining leisure groups, since it is here that others with similar interests can be found.

Romantic love is the source of the greatest joy, while it lasts. Marriage is a very strong source of well-being, including mental and physical health. Many marriages now break up and this is a great source of unhappiness in the modern world, both for the couples and for their children. Marital guidance and therapy have been found to be effective and could be made more widely available. Bereavement is another source of unhappiness, showing how much has been lost.

Children are a great source of fun and joy, but also of conflict and distress, at certain periods of family life, such as when they are adolescents. The wider family is a source of much help and other social support, particularly in collectivist cultures like China, but also in the West.

An increasing proportion of individuals in Britain live alone, because they are single, widowed or divorced, and many of them are also retired. Social isolation can be avoided by involvement in leisure activities that are conducted in groups, and these offer a range of intimate and other relationships, such as church, drama and voluntary work.

PERSONALITY

There are definitely happy people, just as there are depressed ones. There is a partial genetic basis to happiness and there are links with some personality traits. Some of these too are partly innate, but this does not mean that individual happiness is unchangeable. One of the most important is extraversion, and this is increased by regular positive experiences with friends and at work. Other personal properties, such as social skills, can be trained.

Extraverts tend to be happier than introverts, and they experience more positive affect. Since this is a statistical relationship it is no surprise that there are some happy introverts too—they are individuals who score on other sources of happiness. Those high on emotional stability tend to be happier than those high in neuroticism, who have more negative affect.

There are several cognitive aspects of personality, what might be called thinking styles, which are also related to happiness. Some of them make up what used to be called the "Pollyanna principle" of looking on the bright side. They include internal control—the belief that future events can be controlled, optimism, self-esteem and purpose in life. All are highly correlated with happiness measures, indeed so strongly that they could be seen as aspects of happiness.

Purpose in life and a sense of meaning can be generated by commitment to goals, if these are realistic and if there are resources to reach them. One form of therapy is based on choosing suitable goals.

Religion is another source of meaning and purpose, as of confidence in the future, and it has modest positive effects on happiness. The main benefits of religion come from the social support of the church community, the positive moods produced by services, and the health benefits due to less drinking, smoking and the rest.

Intelligence has almost no effect on happiness. However, social skills does, since it enables people to establish and maintain relationships and to cope with and enjoy social situations. Sense of humour is another; humour is one of the easiest ways of inducing positive moods, maintaining positive bonds and reducing interpersonal conflicts within groups. Humour works by suggesting a second meaning or way of looking at something, where the less obvious one is more irreverent. Being able to see the funny side of things makes them less threatening, so sense of humour enables us to cope with stress. It needs a special skill to do this.

NATIONAL DIFFERENCES

There have been social surveys of many countries, which appear to find large national differences in average happiness. Since these surveys have used one or very few questions, and since some of the findings seem unlikely, it seems possible that various biases in ways of answering such questions may be interfering with the results. More limited surveys with longer measuring instruments have obtained quite different results. Another approach is to use objective social indicators; so unhappiness can be assessed from rates of suicide, mental illness, alcoholism, possibly from major causes like divorce rates and unemployment. However, measures of happiness or positive affect are more difficult to find. Objective social indicators also make it possible to study historical change in happiness, which has not been found feasible from social surveys.

IS THERE A THEORY OF HAPPINESS?

The research on happiness has not been theory-driven, though there has been debate over the explanation of particular findings. And some of them probably need more than one theory to explain them. We know that sport and exercise are good for inducing positive moods and other aspects of happiness. This seems to be partly due to a direct physiological effect, activation of endorphins, but also to an effect on self-esteem, and an effect of doing it with other people. Here are three theories for a start.

Physiological explanations

Positive moods are produced by neurotransmitters such as dopamine and serotonin. These can be activated by drugs, but also by goal-related activity. Sport and exercise produce "runner's high", due to the activation of endorphins.

Other positive moods can be produced by drugs: alcohol reduces anxiety, marijuana generates excitement. These different emotions can also be produced without drugs, and can be equally intense. It seems likely however that the emotions produced by success or music for example will activate the same brain areas that are stimulated directly by drugs.

Social activity and relationships

We have seen that love is a great source of joy, and all social relationships affect happiness; extraverts are happy, because of their superior social skills and their frequent social activity. The enjoyment of social relations is one of the main reasons for the satisfactions of leisure—put people in a good mood and they seek more social activity. So there is a close link between happiness and sociability, but what is it? It could be due to the satisfaction of social needs, to meeting self-esteem needs, or recalling the close relationships of childhood; social psychology has not decided.

Satisfying objective needs

There is some support for this theory: money does make people happy, if they are very poor, or live in a very poor country, so does having a house, a job, a spouse, good health; these are all sources of happiness. However, the effects are very weak for most people, and as we see shortly satisfaction with any of these is dependent on various cognitive factors, such as comparison with the past or with others. And there are important sources of happiness that seem to have nothing to do with satisfying needs—the benefits of music and religion for example, of doing voluntary work and most other forms of leisure. Needs theory can only be made to work here by inventing lots of new needs; it has never been suggested that there is a need for music.

Cognitive factors in happiness

Satisfaction with life is judged to be greater if comparisons are made with those who are worse off; however, people can often choose their own targets for comparison, and happy people can gain from upward comparison. A gap between attainments and goals can have a negative effect. There can be adaptation to both good and bad life experiences, though for some this fails. Emotional state affects judged satisfaction, since it is taken as immediate evidence of well-being. Looking on the bright side affects happiness, and is due to personality variables of positive thinking style, including optimism and sense of humour. Many have positive illusions and think things are better than they are.

There is a whole bundle of cognitive processes here, all of them affecting judgements of satisfaction or happiness, and all working in complex ways. They underline the finding that judged happiness does not reflect an individual's actual situation in a simple or direct way. People may be unhappy, not because of any real deprivations or disasters, but because of the way they are looking at things. Happiness therapy courses have a substantial component of cognitive therapy, to teach clients how to see things more positively.

Goals, activity and self-esteem

There is a group of processes here that we have not touched on yet in this section. Job satisfaction depends on use of skills, and successful task perform-ance. The same is true of sport and other forms of leisure. There is "intrinsic satisfaction" from doing these things, apart from any external rewards. Part of the satisfaction may come from self needs, pleasure at using the skills, attaining the goals. We have seen that happiness is enhanced by commitment to goals that are attainable and that are valued; such goals, like the ego-ideal, are in a sense part of the self, and give self-esteem. These theories have not been well spelt out yet, but they may account for important sources of happiness.

SHOULD WE BE PROMOTING HAPPINESS?

Is happiness really so important, or are there more important goals for the human race? Would we prefer the famous composers to have been happier but not to have produced any music? As well as musical creativity there are many other fields of human striving—science, sport, social welfare, for example, where those involved value what they are doing rather than any happiness it will generate. In fact it does generate a lot of happiness, especially if they succeed in these goals; we know this from research on job satisfaction. Perhaps future happiness research will pay more attention to the quality of happiness as well as its extent or its intensity.

We value human creativity, but we have seen that one effect of positive mood induction is greater creativity of some kinds. We value human striving and aspiration, and are not attracted by the vision of the future of our race by Fukuyama (1992) in his book *The End of History and the Last Man*. He thought that when all our work is done by computers and other machines all we will have to do is lie in the sun like dogs. However, experiments on the induction of positive moods show that positive moods do not make people lie in the sun, rather they want to engage in sociability, altruism, and building resources by work, exploration and reflection. This may be the biological point of happiness, that it leads, not to quiescence, but to building resources and social bonds.

So we should be in favour of individuals seeking the happiness of themselves and others, and they can do so by making use of the research summarised in the earlier part of this chapter. It is sometimes said that you can't seek happiness, it has to come as a by-product of other activities. But depressed patients certainly seek happiness for themselves, and mental health workers seek it for them, successfully, and there seems to be no objection to that. Normal, non-patients are seeking it all the time too, though they may not know the true causes and so may not do it very effectively.

What can governments do about increasing happiness? It is often assumed that one of the main goals of government is to make the population richer, though other goals are recognised, such as education and health. Social indicators research has introduced the study of lists of these desirable goals, and some governments do continuous research to see how they are doing. Nothing is said about making people happier. If this became a prime goal of government, what might they do differently? They would give some priority to leisure facilities and training, especially for the working class, to reducing unemployment and to increasing job satisfaction, to enhancing social relationships by provision of social skills training, more marriage guidance, more care for the socially isolated. The list of social indicators could be extended to include some of these sources of happiness.

References

Abramson, L. Y., Seligman, M. E. P., & Teasdale, J. D. (1978). Learned helplessness in humans: critique and reformulation. *Journal of Abnormal Psychology, 87*, 49–74.

Adaman, J. E., & Blaney, P. H. (1995). The effects of musical mood induction on creativity. *Journal of Creative Behavior, 29*, 95–108.

Adams, M. (1968). *Kinship in an Urban Setting.* Chicago: Markham.

Adams, V. H. (1997). A paradox in African American quality of life. *Social Indicators Research, 42*, 205–219.

Aldwin, C. M. (1994). *Stress, Coping and Development: An Integrative Perspective.* New York: Guilford Press.

Alfonso, V. C., Allinson, D. B., Rader, D. E., & Gorman, B. S. (1996). The Extended Satisfaction With Life Scale: development and psychometric properties. *Social Indicators Research, 38*, 275–301.

Almond, G., & Verba, S. (1963). *The Civic Culture.* Princeton, NJ: Princeton University Press.

Altman, I., & Wohlwill, J. F. (Eds.). (1983). *Behavior and the Natural Environment.* New York: Plenum.

American Academy of Physical Education. (1984). *Exercise and Health.* Champaign, IL: Human Kinetics.

Andrews, F. M., & McKennell, A. K. (1980). Measures of self-reported well-being: their affective, cognitive and other components. *Social Indicators Research, 8*, 127–155.

Andrews, F. M., & Withey, S. B. (1976). *Social Indicators of Well-Being.* New York and London: Plenum.

Angst, J. (1997). Epidemiology of depression. In A. Honig & N. M. Van Praag (Eds.), *Depression: Psychopathological and Therapeutic Advances* (pp. 17–29). Chichester, UK: Wiley.

Antonuccio, D. O., Thomas, M., & Danton, W. G. (1997). A cost-effectiveness analysis of cognitive-behavioral therapy and fluoxetine (Prozac) in the treatment of depression. *Behavior Therapy, 28*, 187–210.

Apte, M. L. (1985). *Humor and Laughter: An Anthropological Approach.* Ithaca, NY: Cornell University Press.

Apter, M. J. (1982). *The Experience of Motivation: The Theory of Psychological Reversal.* London: Academic Press.

Argyle, M. (1987). *The Psychology of Happiness.* London: Methuen.

Argyle, M. (1988). *Bodily Communication* (2nd ed.). London: Methuen.

Argyle, M. (1989). *The Social Psychology of Work* (2nd ed.). London: Penguin.

Argyle, M. (1994). *The Psychology of Social Class*. London: Routledge.

Argyle, M. (1996). *The Social Psychology of Leisure*. London: Routledge.

Argyle, M. (2000). *Psychology and Religion: An Introduction*. London: Routledge.

Argyle, M., & Crossland, J. (1987). The dimensions of positive emotions. *British Journal of Social Psychology, 26*, 127–137.

Argyle, M., & Dean, J. (1965). Eye-contact, distance and affiliation. *Sociometry, 28*, 289–304.

Argyle, M., & Furnham, A. (1982). The ecology of relationships: choice of situation as a function of relationship. *British Journal of Social Psychology, 21*, 259–262.

Argyle, M., & Furnham, A. (1983). Sources of satisfaction and conflict in long-term relationships. *Journal of Marriage and the Family, 45*, 481–493.

Argyle, M., & Henderson, M. (1985). *The Anatomy of Relationships*. Harmondsworth, UK: Penguin.

Argyle, M., & Hills, P. (2000). Religious experiences and their relationships with happiness and personality. *International Journal for the Psychology of Religion, 10*, 157–172.

Argyle, M., & Lu, L. (1990). The happiness of extraverts. *Personality and Individual Differences, 11*, 1011–1017.

Argyle, M., & Martin, M. (1991). The psychological causes of happiness. In F. Strack, M. Argyle, & N. Schwarz (Eds.), *Subjective Well-Being* (pp. 77–100). Oxford, UK: Pergamon.

Argyle, M., Martin, M., & Crossland, J. (1989). Happiness as a function of personality and social encounters. In J. P. Forgas & J. M. Innes (Eds.), *Recent Advances in Social Psychology: An International Perspective* (pp. 189–203). North Holland: Elsevier.

Argyle, M., Martin, M., & Lu, L. (1995). Testing for stress and happiness: the role of social and cognitive factors. In C. D. Spielberger & I. G. Sarason (Eds.), *Stress and Emotion* (Vol. 15, pp. 173–187). Washington, DC: Taylor & Francis.

Arrindell, W. A., Hatzichristou, C., Wensink, J., Rosenberg, E., van Twillert, B., Stedema, J., & Meijer, D. (1997). Dimensions of national culture as predictors of cross-national differences in subjective well-being. *Personality and Individual Differences, 23*, 37–53.

Arvey, R. D., McCall, B. P., Bouchard, T. J., Taubman, P., & Cavanaugh, M. A. (1994). Genetic influences on job satisfaction and work values. *Personality and Individual Differences, 17*, 21–33.

Avner, Z., Gorenstein, E., & Mons, A. (1986). Adolescents' evaluation of teachers using disparaging humour. *Educational Psychology, 6*, 37–44.

Bachorowsky, J.-A., & Braaten, E. B. (1994). Emotional intensity: Measurement and theoretical implications. *Personality and Individual Differences, 17*, 191–199.

Balatsky, G., & Diener, E. (1993). Subjective well-being among Russian students. *Social Indicators Research, 28*, 225–243.

Bandura, A. (1977). Self-efficacy: toward a unifying theory of behavioral change. *Psychological Review, 84*, 191–215.

Banks, M. H., & Jackson, P. R. (1982). Unemployment and risk of minor psychiatry disorder in young people: cross sectional and longitudinal evidence. *Psychological Medicine, 12*, 789–798.

Barschak, E. (1951). A study of happiness and unhappiness in childhood and adolescence of girls in different cultures. *Journal of Psychology, 32*, 173–215.

Bateman, T. S., & Organ, D. W. (1983). Job satisfaction and the good soldier: the relationship between affect and employee "citizenship". *Academy of Management Journal, 26*, 587–595.

Batson, C. D. (1987). Prosocial motivation: is it ever truly altruistic? *Advances in Experimental Social Psychology, 20,* 65–122.

Batson, C. D. (1995). Prosocial motivation: why do we help others? In A. Tesser (Ed.), *Advanced Social Psychology.* (pp. 333–381). New York: McGraw-Hill.

Batson, C. D., Schoenrade, P., & Ventis, W. L. (1993). *Religion and the Individual.* New York: Oxford University Press.

Battista, J., & Almond, R. (1973). The development of meaning in life. *Psychiatry, 36,* 409–427.

Baumann, D. J., Cialdini, R. B., & Kemrick, D. T. (1981). Altruism as hedonism: helping and self-gratification as equivalent responses. *Journal of Personality and Social Psychology, 40,* 1039–1046.

Beck, A. T. (1976). *Cognitive Therapy and the Emotional Disorders.* New York: International Universities Press.

Becker, R. A., Denby, L., McGill, R., & Wilks, A. R. (1987). Analysis of data from the Places Rated Almanac. *The American Statistician, 41,* 169–186.

Beehr, T. A. (1986). The process of retirement: a review and recomendations for future investigation. *Personel Psychology, 39,* 31–55.

Beit-Hallahmi, B., & Argyle, M. (1997). *The Psychology of Religious Behaviour, Belief and Experience.* London: Routledge.

Bell, N. J., McGhee, P. E., & Duffy, N. S. (1986). Interpersonal competence, social assertiveness and the development of humour. *British Journal of Developmental Psychology, 4,* 51–55.

Berkman, L. F., & Syme, S. L. (1979). Social networks, host resistance, and mortality: a nine-year follow-up study of Alameda county residents. *American Journal of Epidemiology, 109,* 186–204.

Berkowitz, L., Fraser, C., Treasure, F. P., & Cochran, S. (1987). Pay equity, job qualifications, and comparison in pay satisfaction. *Journal of Applied Psychology, 72,* 544–551.

Berry, D. S., & Hansen, J. S. (1996). Positive affect, negative affect, and social interaction. *Journal of Personality and Social Psychology, 71,* 796–809.

Berry, D. S., & Willingham, J. K. (1997). Affective traits, responses to conflict, and satisfaction in romantic relationships. *Journal of Research in Personality, 31,* 564–576.

Biddle, S., & Mutrie, N. (1991). *Psychology of Physical Activity and Exercise.* London: Springer-Verlag.

Birdi, K. S., Warr, P. B., & Oswald, A. (1995). Age differences in three components of employee well-being. *Applied Psychology: An International Review, 44,* 345–373.

Blanchflower, D. G., & Oswald, A. J. (1997). *The rising well-being of the young.* Cambridge, MA: National Bureau of Economic Research.

Blanchflower, D. G., & Oswald, A. J. (1999). *Well-being over time in Britain and the USA.* Warwick, UK: University of Warwick.

Blauner, R. (1960). Work satisfaction and industrial trends in modern society. In W. Galenson & S. M. Lipset (Eds.), *Labor and Trade Unions* (pp. 339–360). New York: Wiley.

Blaxter, M. (1990). *Health and Lifestyle.* London: Tavistock/Routledge.

Bless, H., Clore, G. L., Schwarz, N., Golisano, V., Rabe, C., & Wolk, M. (1996). Mood and the use of scripts: does a happy mood really lead to mindlessness? *Journal of Personality and Social Psychology, 71,* 665–679.

Bloch, S., Browning, S., & McGrath, G. (1983). Humour in group psychotherapy. *British Journal of Medical Psychology, 56,* 89–97.

Bodenhausen, G. V., Kramer, G. P., & Suesser, K. (1994). Happiness and stereotypic thinking in social judgment. *Journal of Personality and Social Psychology, 66*, 621–632.

Bolger, N., & Eckenrode, J. (1992). Social relations, personality and anxiety during a major stressful event. *Journal of Personality and Social Psychology, 23*, 586–604.

Booth, A., Johnson, D. R., Branaman, A., & Sica, A. (1997). Belief and behavior: does religion matter in today's marriage? *Journal of Marriage and the Family, 57*, 661–671.

Bortz, W. M., Angwin, P., Mefford, I. N., Boarder, M. R., Noyce, N., & Barchas, J. D. (1981). Catecholamines, dopamine, and endorphin levels during a major stressful event. *New England Journal of Medicine, 305*, 466–467.

Boskin, J. (1966, May 1). Good-by Mr Bones. *New York Times Magazine*, p. 30.

Bourhis, R. Y., Gadfield, N. J., Giles, H., & Tajfel, H. (1977). Context and ethnic humour in intergroup relations. In A. J. Chapman & H. C. Foot (Eds.), *It's a Funny Thing, Humour* (pp. 261–266). Oxford, UK: Pergamon.

Boyd-Wilson, B. M., Walkey, F. H., McClure, J. & Green, D. E. (2000). Do we need positive illusions to carry out plans? Illusion and instrumental coping. *Personality and Individual Differences, 29*, 1141–52.

Bradburn, N. M. (1969). *The Structure of Psychological Well-Being*. Chicago: Aldine.

Bradford, H. F. (1987). Neurotransmitters and neuromodulators. In R. L. Gregory (Ed.), *The Oxford Companion to the Mind* (pp. 550–560). Oxford, UK: Oxford University Press.

Brandstatter, H. (1991). Emotions in everyday life situations: time sampling of subjective experience. In F. Strack, M. Argyle, & N. Schwarz (Eds.), *Subjective Well-Being* (pp. 173–192). Oxford, UK: Pergamon.

Bremner, J., & Roodenburg, H. (Eds.). (1997). *A Cultural History of Humour*. Cambridge, UK: Polity Press.

Brenner, M. (1973). *Mental Illness and the Economy*. Cambridge, MA: Harvard University Press.

Brickman, P., Coates, D., & Janoff-Bulman, R. (1978). Lottery winners and accident victims: is happiness relative? *Journal of Personality and Social Psychology, 36*, 917–927.

Brown, G. W., & Harris, T. (1978). *Social Origins of Depression*. London: Tavistock.

Brown, J. D. (1986). Evaluations of self and others: self enhancement biases in social judgments. *Social Cognition, 4*, 353–376.

Brown, J. D., & McGill, K. L. (1989). The cost of good fortune: when positive life events produce negative health influences. *Journal of Personality and Social Psychology, 57*, 1103–1110.

Brown, R. (1995). *Prejudice: Its Social Psychology*. Oxford, UK: Blackwell.

Brown, R. J. (1978). Divided we fall: an analysis of relations between sections of a factory work-force. In H. Tajfel (Ed.), *Differentiation Between Social Groups* (pp. 395–429). London: Academic Press.

Browne, M. A., & Mahoney, M. J. (1984). Sport psychology. *Annual Review of Psychology, 35*, 605–625.

Brunstein, J. C., Schultheiss, O. C., & Graessman, R. (1998). Personal goals and well-being: the moderating role of motive dispositions. *Journal of Personality and Social Psychology, 75*, 494–508.

Bryan, T., & Bryan, J. (1991). Positive mood and math performance. *Journal of Learning Disabilities, 24*, 490–494.

Bryant, J., & Zillman, D. (1984). Using television to relieve boredom as a function of induced excitational states. *Journal of Broadcasting, 28*, 1–20.

Burchell, B. (2000). *Work intensification and the quality of working life*. Paper presented at the third conference of the International Society for Quality of Life Studies, Girona, Spain.

Burton, R. P. D., Rushing, B., Ritter, C., & Rakocy, A. (1993). Roles, race and subjective well-being: a longitudinal analysis of elderly men. *Social Indicators Research, 28*, 137–156.

Butt, D. S., & Beiser, M. (1987). Successful aging: a theme for international psychology. *Psychology and Aging, 2*, 87–94.

Buunk, B. P., Collins, R. L., Taylor, S. E., VanYperen, N. W., & Dakof, G. A. (1990). The affective consequences of social comparison: either direction has its ups and downs. *Journal of Personality and Social Psychology, 59*, 1238–1249.

Call, V. R. A., & Heaton, T. B. (1997). Religious influence on marital stability. *Journal for the Scientific Study of Religion, 36*, 382–392.

Campbell, A. (1981). *The Sense of Well-Being in America*. New York: McGraw-Hill.

Campbell, A., Converse, P. E., & Rogers, W. L. (1976). *The Quality of American Life*. New York: Sage.

Campbell, W. K., Sedikedes, C., & Bosson, J. (1994). Romantic involvement, self-discrepancy and psychological well-being: a preliminary investigation. *Personal Relationships, 1*, 399–404.

Camras, L. A., Holland, J. M., & Patterson, M. J. (1993). Facial expression. In M. Lewis & J. M. Haviland (Eds.), *Handbook of Emotion* (pp. 119–208). New York: Guilford Press.

Cantor, N., & Sanderson, C. A. (1999). Life task satisfaction and well-being. In D. Kahneman, E. Diener, & N. Schwarz (Eds.), *Understanding Quality of Life* (pp. 230–243). New York: Russell Sage.

Cantril, H. (1965). *The Pattern of Human Concerns*. New Brunswick, NJ: Rutgers University Press.

Caplan, R. D., Cobb, S., French, J. R. P., van Harrison, R., & Pinneau, S. R. (1975). *Job Demands and Worker Health*. Ann Arbor, MI: Institute for Social Research, University of Michigan.

Caputo, J. L., Rudolph, D. L., & Morgan, D. W. (1998). Influence of positive events on blood pressure in adolescents. *Journal of Behavioral Medicine, 21*, 115–129.

Carsten, J. M., & Spector, P. E. (1987). Unemployment, job satisfaction, and employee turnover: a meta-analytic test of the Muchinsky model. *Journal of Applied Psychology, 72*, 374–381.

Carter, F. A., Wilson, J. S., Lawson, R. H., & Bulik, C. M. (1995). Mood induction procedure: importance of individualising music. *Behaviour Change, 12*, 159–161.

Carter, H., & Glick, P. C. (1970). *Marriage and Divorce: A Social and Economic Study*. Cambridge, MA: Harvard University Press.

Carver, C. S., & White, T. L. (1994). Behavioral inhibition, behavioral activation, and affective responses to impending reward and punishment: the BIS and BAS scales. *Journal of Personality and Social Psychology, 67*, 319–333.

Chamberlain, K., & Zika, S. (1988). Religiosity, life meaning and well-being. *Journal for the Scientific Study of Religion, 27*, 411–420.

Chamberlain, K., & Zika, S. (1992). Stability and change in subjective well-being over short time periods. *Social Indicators Research, 26*, 101–117.

Chan, R., & Joseph, S. (2000). Dimensions of personality, domains of aspiration, and subjective well-being. *Personality and Individual Differences, 28*, 347–354.

Chang, E. C., Maydeu-Olivares, A., & D'Zurilla, T. T. (1997). Optimism and pessimism as partially independent constructs: relationship to positive and negative affectivity and psychological well-being. *Personality and Individual Differences, 23*, 433–440.

Chapman, A. J. (1976). Social aspects of humorous laughter. In A. J. Chapman, & H. C. Foot (Eds.) *Humour and Laughter: Theory, Research and Applications*. Chichester, UK: Wiley

Chapman, A. J., & Foot, H. C. (Eds.). (1976). *Humour and Laughter: Theory, Research and Applications*. Chichester, UK: Wiley.

Cheung, K. (1997). Relationships among satisfaction, commitment, and performance: a group level analysis. *Applied Psychology: An International Review, 46*, 199–206.

Clark, A. (1998a). *What makes a good job? Evidence from OECD countries*. Document de Recherche, Laboratoire d'Economie d'Orleans, France.

Clark, A., Oswald, A., & Warr, P. (1996). Is job satisfaction U-shaped in age? *Journal of Occupational and Organizational Psychology, 69*, 57–81.

Clark, A. E. (1996). *Job satisfaction and gender: why are women so happy at work?* DEELSA, France.

Clark, A. E. (1998b). *The positive externalities of higher unemployment: evidence from household data*. CRNS and LEO-CRESEP, France.

Clark, A. E. (2000). *Inequality-aversion or inequality-loving*. Paper presented at the Nuffield College conference on Well-Being.

Clark, A. E., & Oswald, A. J. (1996). Satisfaction and comparison income. *Journal of Public Economics, 61*, 359–381.

Clark, D. M. (1983). On the induction of depressed mood in the laboratory: evaluation and comparison of the Velten and musical procedures. *Advances in Behaviour Research and Therapy, 5*, 24–49.

Clark, M. S., & Isen, A. M. (1982). Toward understanding the relationship between feeling states and social behavior. In A. Hastorf & A. M. Isen (Eds.), *Cognitive Social Psychology* (pp. 73–108). New York: Elsevier.

Clark, M. S., & Reis, H. T. (1988). Interpersonal processes in close relationships. *Annual Review of Psychology, 39*, 609–672.

Clark, R. A., & Sensibar, M. R. (1955). The relationship between symbolic and manifest projections of sexuality with some incidental correlates. *Journal of Abnormal and Social Psychology, 50*, 327–334.

Cobb, S., & Kasl, S. V. (1977). *Termination: The Consequences of Job Loss*. Cincinnati, OH: US Dept of Health, Education and Welfare.

Cochrane, R. (1988). Marriage, separation and divorce. In S. Fisher & J. Reason (Eds.), *Handbook of Life Stress, Cognition and Health* (pp. 137–160). Chichester, UK: Wiley.

Cockerham, W. C. (1981). *Sociology of Mental Disorder*. Englewood Cliffs, NJ: Prentice-Hall.

Cohan, C. L., & Bradbury, T. N. (1997). Negative life events, marital interaction, and the longitudinal course of newlywed marriage. *Journal of Personality and Social Psychology, 73*, 114–128.

Collinson, D. L. (1988). "Engineering humour": masculinity, joking and conflict in shop-floor relations. *Organization Studies, 9*, 181–199.

Compton, W. C. (1992). Are positive illusions necessary for self-esteem? *Personality and Individual Differences, 13*, 1343–1344.

Compton, W. C., Smith, M. L., Cornish, K. A., & Qualls, D. L. (1996). Factor structure of mental health measures. *Journal of Personality and Social Psychology, 71*, 406–413.

Comstock, G. W., & Partridge, K. B. (1972). Church attendance and health. *Journal of Chronic Diseases, 25,* 665–672.

Cooper, C. L. (1985, Feb 24). Survey of occupations rated on a nine point scale for stressfulness, your place in the stress league. *Sunday Times.*

Cooper, H., Okamura, L., & Gurka, V. (1992). Social activity and subjective well-being. *Personality and Individual Differences, 13,* 573–583.

Costa, P. T., & McCrae, R. R. (1980). Influence of extraversion and neuroticism on subjective well-being: happy and unhappy people. *Journal of Personality and Social Psychology, 38,* 668–678.

Costa, P. T., McRae, R. R., & Norris, A. H. (1981). Personal adjustment to aging: longitudinal prediction from neuroticism and extraversion. *Journal of Gerontology, 36,* 78–85.

Costa, P. T., Zonderman, A. B., & McCrae, R. R. (1985). Longitudinal course of social support among men in the Baltimore longitudinal study of aging. In I. G. Sarason & B. R. Sarason (Eds.), *Social Support: Theory, Research and Applications* (pp. 137–154). Dordrecht, The Netherlands: Nijhoff.

Coyne, J. C. (1976). Depression and the response of others. *Journal of Abnormal Psychology, 85,* 28–40.

Crandall, J. E. (1984). Social interest as a moderator of life stress. *Journal of Personality and Social Psychology, 47,* 164–174.

Crews, D. J., & Landers, D. M. (1987). A meta-analytic review of aerobic fitness and reactivity to psychosocial stressors. *Medicine and Science in Sports and Exercise, 19*(5, Suppl.), S114–S120.

Csikszentmihalyi, M. (1975). *Beyond Boredom and Anxiety.* San Francisco: Jossey-Bass.

Cummins, R. A. (1995). On the trail of the gold standard for life satisfaction. *Social Indicators Research, 35,* 179–200.

Cunningham, M. R. (1979). Weather, mood, and helping behaviour: quasi experiments with the sunshine Samaritans. *Journal of Personality and Social Psychology, 37,* 1947–1956.

Cunningham, M. R. (1988). What do you do when you're happy or blue? Mood, expectancies, and behavioral interest. *Motivation and Emotion, 12,* 309–331.

Davidson, R. J. (1993). The neuropsychology of emotion and affective style. In M. Lewis & J. M. Haviland (Eds.), *Handbook of Emotion* (pp. 143–154). New York: Guilford Press.

Davis, J. M., & Farina, A. (1970). Humor appreciation as social communication. *Journal of Personality and Social Psychology, 15,* 175–178.

Davis, P. A., & Leonard, B. G. (1999). Influence of emotional intensity and frequency of positive and negative events on depression. *European Journal of Personality Assessment, 15,* 106–116.

Davitz, J. R. (1964). *The Communication of Emotional Meaning.* New York: McGraw-Hill.

Decker, W. H., & Rotondo, D. M. (1999). Use of humor at work: predictors and implications. *Psychological Reports, 84,* 961–968.

Deckers, L., & Ruch, W. (1992). Sensation seeking and the situational humour response questionnaire (SHRQ): its relationship in American and German samples. *Personality and Individual Differences, 13,* 1051–1054.

Deeg, D., & van Zonneveld, R. (1989). Does happiness lengthen life? In R. Veenhoven (Ed.), *How Harmful is Happiness?* (pp. 29–43). Rotterdam, The Netherlands: Rotterdam University Press.

De Jonge, J., & Schaufeli, W. B. (1998). Job characteristics and employee well-being: a test of Warr's Vitamin Model in health care workers using structural equation modelling. *Journal of Organizational Behavior*, *19*, 387–407.

DeNeve, K. M., & Cooper, H. (1998). The happy personality: a meta-analysis of 137 personality traits and subjective well-being. *Psychological Bulletin*, *124*, 197–229.

Diener, E. (1984). Subjective well-being. *Psychological Bulletin*, *95*, 542–575.

Diener, E. (1994). Assessing subjective well-being: progress and opportunities. *Social Indicators Research*, *31*, 103–157.

Diener, E. (1995). A value-based index for measuring national quality of life. *Social Indicators Research*, *36*, 107–127.

Diener, E., & Biswas-Diener, R. (2000). Income and subjective well-being: will money make us happy? University of Illinois, unpublished.

Diener, E., & Diener, C. (1996). Most people are happy. *Psychological Science*, *7*, 181–185.

Diener, E., & Diener, M. (1995). Cross-cultural correlates of life satisfaction and self-esteem. *Journal of Personality and Social Psychology*, *68*, 653–663.

Diener, E., Diener, M., & Diener, C. (1995). Factors predicting the subjective well-being of nations. *Journal of Personality and Social Psychology*, *69*, 851–864.

Diener, E., & Emmons, R. A. (1984). The independence of positive and negative affect. *Journal of Personality and Social Psychology*, *47*, 1105–1117.

Diener, E., Emmons, R. A., Larsen, R. J., & Griffin, S. (1985). The Satisfaction With Life Scale. *Journal of Personality Assessment*, *49*, 71–75.

Diener, E., & Fujita, F. (1995). Resources, personal strivings, and subjective well-being: a nomothetic and idiographic approach. *Journal of Personality and Social Psychology*, *68*, 926–935.

Diener, E., & Fujita, F. (1997). Social comparisons and subjective well-being. In B. Buunk & R. Gibbons (Eds.), *Health, Coping, and Social Comparison* (pp. 329–357). Mahwah, NJ: Lawrence Erlbaum Associates Inc.

Diener, E., Horowitz, J., & Emmons, R. A. (1985). Happiness of the very wealthy. *Social Indicators Research*, *16*, 263–274.

Diener, E., Larsen, E., Levine, S., & Emmons, R. A. (1985). Intensity and frequency: dimensions underlying positive and negative affect. *Journal of Personality and Social Psychology*, *48*, 1253–1265.

Diener, E., & Larsen, R. J. (1984). Temporal stability and cross-situational consistency of affective, behavioral, and cognitive responses. *Journal of Personality and Social Psychology*, *47*, 580–592.

Diener, E., & Lucas, R. (1999). Personality and subjective well-being. In D. Kahneman, E. Diener, & N. Schwarz (Eds.), *Foundations of Hedonic Psychology* (pp. 213–229). New York: Russell Sage.

Diener, E., & Oishi, S. (in press). Money and happiness: income and subjective well-being across nations. In E. Diener & E. M. Suh (Eds.), *Subjective Well-Being Across Cultures*. Cambridge, MA: MIT Press.

Diener, E., Sandvik, E., & Larsen, R. J. (1985). Age and sex effects for emotional intensity. *Developmental Psychology*, *21*, 542–546.

Diener, E., Sandvik, E., & Pavot, W. (1991). Happiness is the frequency, not the intensity, of positive versus negative affect. In F. Strack, M. Argyle, & N. Schwarz (Eds.), *Subjective Well-Being* (pp. 119–139). Oxford, UK: Pergamon.

Diener, E., Sandvik, E., Seidlitz, L., & Diener, M. (1993). The relationship between income and subjective well-being: relative or absolute? *Social Indicators Research*, *28*, 195–223.

Diener, E., & Suh, E. (1997a). Measuring quality of life: economic, social and subjective indicators. *Social Indicators Research*, *40*, 189–216.

Diener, E., & Suh, E. M. (1997b). Subjective well-being and age: an international analysis. In K. W. Schaie & M. P. Lawton (Eds.), *Annual Review of Gerontology and Geriatrics* (Vol. 17, pp. 304–324). New York: Springer.

Diener, E., Suh, E. M., Lucas, R. E., & Smith, H. L. (1999). Subjective well-being: three decades of progress. *Psychological Bulletin*, *125*, 276–302.

Diener, E., & Suh, E. M. (1999). National differences in subjective well-being. In D. Kahneman, E. Diener, & N. Schwartz (Eds.) *Well-Being: The Foundations of Hedonic Psychology*, pp 434–450. New York: Sage.

Dittmar, H. (1992). *The Social Psychology of Material Possessions*. Hemel Hempstead, UK: Harvester Wheatsheaf.

Dormann, C., & Zapf, D. (1999). Social support, social stress at work, and depressive symptoms: testing for main and moderating effects with structural equations in a three-wave longitudinal study. *Journal of Applied Psychology*, *84*, 874–884.

Douglas, M. (1968). The social control of cognition: some factors in joke perception. *Man*, *3*, 361–376.

Dull, V. T., & Skokan, L. A. (1995). A cognitive model of religion's influence on health. *Journal of Social Issues*, *51*, 49–64.

Dunn, J. (1988). *Beginnings of Social Understanding*. Oxford, UK: Blackwell.

du Pre, A. (1998). *Humor and the Healing Arts*. Mahwah, NJ: Lawrence Erlbaum Associates Inc.

Durkheim, E. (1897). *Suicide*. London: Routledge & Kegan Paul.

Eder, A. (1990). Risk factor loneliness: on the interrelations between social integration, happiness and health in 11-, 13- and 15-year old schoolchildren in 9 European countries. *Health Promotion International*, *5*(1), 19–83.

Edwards, J. N., & Klemmack, D. L. (1973). Correlations of life satisfaction: a re-examination. *Journal of Gerontology*, *28*, 497–502.

Ekman, P. (1982). *Emotion in the Human Face* (2nd ed.). Cambridge, UK: Cambridge University Press.

Ekman, P., & Friesen, W. V. (1975). *Unmasking the Face*. Englewood Cliffs, NJ: Prentice-Hall.

Elliot, D. H., & Elliot, J. L. (1990). Behavior and the life cycle: a consideration of the role of longitudinal time-use studies. *Social Indicators Research*, *23*, 395–414.

Ellison, C. G. (1991). Religious involvement and subjective well-being. *Journal of Health and Social Behavior*, *32*, 80–99.

Ellison, C. G., Gay, D. A., & Glass, T. A. (1989). Does religious commitment contribute to individual life satisfaction? *Social Forces*, *68*, 100–123.

Ellison, C. G., & George, L. K. (1994). Religious involvement, social ties, and social support in a Southeastern community. *Journal for the Scientific Study of Religion*, *33*, 46–61.

Emmons, R. A. (1999). *The Psychology of Ultimate Concerns: Motivation and Spirituality in Personality*. New York: Guilford Press.

Emerson, J. (1969). Negotiating the serious import of humor. *Sociometry*, *32*, 169–181.

Emery, R. E. (1982). Interparental conflict and the children of discord and divorce. *Psychological Bulletin, 92*, 310–330.

Emmons, R. A. (1986). Personal strivings: an approach to personality and subjective well-being. *Journal of Personality and Social Psychology, 51*, 1058–1068.

Esterlin, R. A. (2000). *Income and happiness: toward a unified theory.* Paper presented at the Nuffield College conference on Well-Being.

Eysenck, H. J. (1976). *The Measurement of Personality.* Lancaster, UK: MTP Press.

Eysenck, H. J., & Eysenck, S. B. G. (1975). *Manual of the Eysenck Personality Questionnaire.* London: Hodder & Stoughton.

Eysenck, H. J., Nias, D. K. B., & Cox, D. N. (1982). Sport and personality. *Advances in Behaviour Research and Therapy, 4*, 1–56.

Falkenburg, L. E. (1987). Employee fitness programs: their impact on the employee and the organization. *Academy of Management Review, 12*, 511–522.

Fava, G. A., Fafanelli, C., Cazzaro, M., Conti, S., & Grandi, S. (1998). Well-being therapy: a novel psychotherapeutic approach for residual symptoms of affective disorders. *Psychological Medicine, 28*, 475–480.

Feather, N. T. (1982). Unemployment and its psychological correlates: study of depressive symptoms, self-esteem, Protestant ethic values, attributional style and apathy. *Australian Journal of Psychology, 34*, 309–323.

Feather, N. T., & Bond, M. J. (1983). Time structure and purposeful activity among employed and unemployed university graduates. *Journal of Occupational Psychology, 56*, 241–250.

Feeney, J. A. (1994). Attachment styles, communication patterns and satisfaction across the life cycle of marriage. *Personal Relationships, 1*, 333–348.

Fehr, B. (1988). Prototype analysis of the concepts of love and commitment. *Journal of Personality and Social Psychology, 55*, 557–579.

Feist, G. J., Bodner, T. E., Jacobs, J. F., Miles, M., & Tan, V. (1995). Integrating top-down and bottom-up structural models of subjective well-being. *Journal of Personality and Social Psychology, 68*, 138–150.

Feist, J., & Brannon, L. (1988). *Health Psychology.* Belmont, CA: Wadsworth.

Fieve, R. R. (1994). *Prozac.* London: Thorson.

Fincham, F., Beach, S. R. H., Harold, G. T., & Osborne, L. N. (1997). Marital satisfaction and depression: different causal relations for men and women. *Psychological Science, 8*, 351–357.

Fincham, F. D., & Bradbury, T. N. (1993). Marital satisfaction, depression and attributions: a longitudinal analysis. *Journal of Personality and Social Psychology, 64*, 442–452.

Finegan, J. E., & Seligman, C. (1995). In defense of the Velten mood induction procedure. *Canadian Journal of Behavioural Science, 27*, 405–419.

Fitzgerald, M. J., Pinkofsky, H. B., Brannon, G., Dandridge, E., & Calhoun, A. (1999). Olanzap: inme-induced mania. *American Journal of Psychiatry, 156*, 1114.

Fleishman, E. A., & Harris, E. F. (1962). Patterns of leadership behavior related to employee grievances and turnover. *Personnel Psychology, 15*, 43–56.

Fletcher, B. (1988). *Work, Stress, Disease and Life Experience.* Chichester, UK; Wiley.

Foot, H. C., & Chapman, A. J. (1976). The social responsiveness of young children in humorous situations. In A. J. Chapman & H. C. Foot (Eds.), *Humour and Laughter: Theory, Research and Applications* (pp. 187–214). Chichester, UK: Wiley.

Fordyce, M. W. (1977). Development of a program to increase personal happiness. *Journal of Counseling Psychology, 24*, 511–520.

Fordyce, M. W. (1983). A program to increase happiness: further studies. *Journal of Counseling Psychology*, *30*, 483–498.

Fordyce, M. W. (1988). A review of research on the happiness measure: a sixty second index of happiness and mental health. *Social Indicators Research*, *20*, 355–381.

Forgas, J. P. (1998). On being happy and mistaken: mood effects on the fundamental attribution error. *Journal of Personality and Social Psychology*, *75*, 318–331.

Forgas, J. P. (1999). On feeling good and being rude: affective influences on language use and request formulations. *Journal of Personality and Social Psychology*, *76*, 928–939.

Forgas, J. P., Levinger, G., & Moylan, S. J. (1994). Feeling good and feeling close. *Personal Relationships*, *1*, 165–184.

Francis, L. J. (1999). Happiness is a thing called stable extraversion: A further examination of the relationship between the Oxford Happiness Inventory and Eysenck's dimensional model of personality and goals. *Personality and Individual Differences*, *26*, 5–11.

Frankl, V. E. (1959). *Man's Search for Meaning: An Introduction to Logotherapy*. London: Hodder & Stoughton.

Fredrickson, B. L. (1998). What good are positive emotions? *Review of General Psychology*, *2*, 300–319.

Freedman, J. L. (1978). *Happy People*. New York: Harcourt Brace Jovanovich.

Freiheit, S. R., Overholser, J. C., & Lehnert, K. L. (1998). The association between humor and depression in adolescent psychiatric inpatients and high school students. *Journal of Adolescent Research*, *13*, 32–48.

French, J. R. P., & Caplan, R. D. (1970). Psychosocial factors in coronary heart disease. *Industrial Medicine*, *39*, 383–397.

French, J. R. P., Caplan, R. D., & van Harrison, R. (1982). *The Mechanisms of Job Stress and Strain*. Chichester, UK: Wiley.

Freud, S. (1960). *Jokes and their Relation to the Unconscious*. New York: Norton. (Original work published 1905.)

Frey, B. S., & Stutzer, A. (2000). *Happiness, economy and institutions*. Paper presented at the Nuffield College conference on Well-Being.

Frey, R. S., & Song, F. (1997). Human well-being in Chinese cities. *Social Indicators Research*, *42*, 77–101.

Fridlund, A. J. (1991). Sociality of solitary smiling: potentiation by an implicit audience. *Journal of Personality and Social Psychology*, *60*, 229–240.

Friesen, W. V. (1972). *Cultural differences in facial expression: an experimental test of the concept of display rules*. Unpublished PhD dissertation, University of California, San Francisco.

Frost, R. O., & Green, M. L. (1982). Duration and post-experimental removal of Velten mood induction procedure effects. *Personality and Social Psychology Bulletin*, *8*, 341–347.

Fryer, D., & Payne, R. (1984). Proactive behaviour in unemployment. *Leisure Studies*, *3*, 273–295.

Fuchs, E., & Havighurst, R. (1973). *To Live on this Earth: American Indian Education*. Garden City, NY: Doubleday, Anchor Books.

Fukuyama, F. (1992). *The End of History and the Last Man*. Harmondsworth, UK: Penguin Books.

Furnham, A. (1997). Eysenck's personality theory and organizational psychology. In H. Nyborg (Ed.), *The Scientific Study of Human Nature: Tribute to Hans J. Eysenck at Eighty* (pp. 462–490). Oxford, UK: Pergamon/Elsevier.

Furnham, A., & Argyle, M. (1998). *The Psychology of Money*. London: Routledge.

Furnham, A., & Cheng, H. (1997). Personality and happiness. *Psychological Reports, 80*, 761–762.

Furnham, A., & Schaeffer, R. (1984). Person–environment fit, job satisfaction and mental health. *Journal of Occupational Psychology, 57*, 295–307.

Gallie, D., & Paugam, S. (Eds.). (2000). *Welfare Regimes and the Experience of Unemployment in Europe*. Oxford, UK: Oxford University Press.

Gallie, D., & Russell, H. (1998). Unemployment and life satisfaction: a cross-cultural comparison. *Archives of European Sociology, 39*, 248–280.

Gallie, D., White, M., Cheng, Y., & Tomlinson, M. (1998). *Restructuring the Employment Relationship*. Oxford, UK: Clarendon Press.

Gallup, G. H. (1976). Human needs and satisfaction: a global survey. *Public Opinion Quarterly, 40*, 459–467.

Garrity, T. F., & Stallones, L. (1998). Effects of pet contact on human well-being. In C. C. Wilson & D. C. Turner (Eds.), *Companion Animals in Human Health* (pp. 3–22). Thousand Oaks, CA: Sage.

Garvey, C. (1977). *Play*. Cambridge, MA: Harvard University Press.

Gavin, L. A., & Furman, W. (1996). Adolescent girls' relationships with mothers and best friends. *Child Development, 67*, 375–386.

Gay, P. (1998). *Getting into Work*. London: National Centre for Volunteering.

Genia, V. (1996). I. E., Quest, and fundamentalism as predictors of psychological and spiritual well-being. *Journal for the Scientific Study of Religion, 35*, 56–64.

Gerrards-Hesse, A., Spies, K., & Hesse, F. W. (1994). Experimental inductions of emotional states and their effectiveness. *British Journal of Psychology, 85*, 55–78.

Gershuny, J. (1992). Are we running out of time? *Futures*, January/February, 3–18.

Gershuny, J. (1994). The psychological consequences of unemployment: an assessment of the Jahoda thesis. In D. Gallie, C. Marsh, & C. Vogler (Eds.), *Social Change and the Experience of Unemployment* (pp. 231–263). Oxford, UK: Oxford University Press.

Gilbert, P., & Trower, P. (1990). The evolution and manifestation of social anxiety. In W. R. Crozier (Ed.), *Shyness and Embarrassment: Perspectives from Social Psychology* (pp. 144–177). Cambridge, UK: Cambridge University Press.

Glik, D. C. (1986). Psychosocial wellness among spiritual healing participants. *Social Science and Medicine, 22*, 579–586.

Glyptis, S. (1989). *Leisure and Unemployment*. Cambridge, UK: Polity Press.

Gohm, C. L., Oishi, S., Darlington, J., & Diener, E. (1998). Culture, parental conflict, parental marital status, and the subjective well-being of young adults. *Journal of Marriage and the Family, 60*, 319–334.

Goldberg, D. (1972). *The Detection of Psychiatric Illness by Questionnaire*. London: Oxford University Press.

Goldberg, D. (1978). *Manual of the General Health Questionnaire*. Windsor, UK: NFER.

Goldman, M. (1960). *The sociology of negro humor*. Unpublished. Cited by W. H. Martineau. A model of the social functions of humor. In J. H. Goldstein & P. E. McGhee (Eds.), *The Psychology of Humor* (pp. 101–125). New York: Academic Press.

Goldsmith, A. H., Veum, J. R., & Darity, W. (1997). Unemployment, joblessness, psychological well-being and self-esteem. *Journal of Socio-Economics, 26*, 133–158.

Gordon, S. L. (1989). The socialization of children's emotions: emotional culture, competence and exposure. In C. Saarni & P. L. Harris (Eds.), *Children's Understanding of Emotion* (pp. 319–349). Cambridge, UK: Cambridge University Press.

Gove, W. R. (1972). The relationship between sex roles, marital status, and mental illness. *Social Forces, 51*, 34–44.

Graef, R., Csikszentmihalyi, M., & Gianinno, S. N. (1983). Measuring intrinsic motivation in daily life. *Leisure Studies, 2*, 158–168.

Graham, E. E. (1995). The involvement of sense of humor in the development of social relationships. *Communication Reports, 8*, 158–169.

Grammer, K. (1990). Strangers meet: laughter and nonverbal signs of interest in opposite sex encounters. *Journal of Nonverbal Behavior, 14*, 209–236.

Gray, J. A. (1972). The psychophysiological nature of introversion–extraversion: a modification of Eysenck's theory. In V. D. Neblitsyn & J. A. Gray (Eds.), *Biological Bases of Individual Behavior* (pp. 182–205). New York: Academic Press.

Gray, J. A. (1982). *The Neurophysiology of Anxiety*. Oxford, UK: Clarendon Press.

Greeley, A. M. (1975). *The Sociology of the Paranormal*. London: Sage.

Greenberg, R. P., Bornstein, R. F., Zborowski, M. J., Fisher, S., & Greenberg, M. D. (1994). A meta-analysis of fluoxetine outcome in the treatment of depression. *Journal of Nervous and Mental Disease, 182*, 547–551.

Greene, T. R. & Noice, H. (1988). Influence of positive affect upon creative thinking and problem solving in children. *Psychological Reports, 63*, 895–898.

Grob, A., Little, T. D., Wanner, B., & Wearing, A. J. (1996). Adolescents' well-being and perceived control across 14 sociocultural contexts. *Journal of Personality and Social Psychology, 71*, 785–795.

Gruner, C. R. (1976). Wit and humour in mass communication. In A. J. Chapman & H. C. Foot (Eds.), *Humour and Laughter: Theory, Research and Application* (pp. 287–311). Chichester, UK: Wiley.

Hackman, J. R., & Oldham, G. R. (1976). Motivation through the design of work: test of a theory. *Organizational Behavior and Human Performance, 16*, 250–279.

Hagedorn, J. W. (1996). Happiness and self-deception: an old question examined by a new measure of subjective well-being. *Social Indicators Research, 38*, 139–160.

Haggard, L. M., & Williams, D. R. (1992). Identity affirmation through leisure activities. *Journal of Leisure Research, 24*, 1–18.

Hall, C. B., & Nelson, G. (1996). Social networks, social support, personal empowerment, and the adaptation of psychiatric consumers/survivors. *Social Science and Medicine, 43*, 1743–1754.

Hall, J. (1976). Subjective measures of quality of life in Britain, 1971 to 1975: some developments and trends. *Social Trends, 7*, 47–60.

Harding, S. (1985). Values and the nature of psychological well-being. In M. Abrams, D. Gerard, & N. Timms (Eds.), *Values and Social Change in Britain* (pp. 227–252). Basingstoke, UK: Macmillan.

Haring, M. J., Okun, M. A., & Stock, W. A. (1984). A quantitative synthesis of literature on work status and subjective well-being. *Journal of Vocational Behavior, 25*, 316–324.

Haring-Hidore, M., Stock, W. A., Okun, M. A., & Witter, R. A. (1985). Marital status and subjective well-being: a research synthesis. *Journal of Marriage and the Family, 47*, 947–953.

Harris, M. (1997). Monitoring optimism in South Africa. *Social Indicators Research, 41*, 279–304.

Harris, P., & Middleton, W. (1994). The illusion of control and optimism about health: on being less at risk but no more in control than others. *British Journal of Social Psychology, 33*, 369–386.

Harris, P. L., & Lipian, M. S. (1989). Understanding emotion and experiencing emotion. In C. Saarni & P. L. Harris (Eds.), *Children's Understanding of Emotion* (pp. 241–258). Cambridge, UK: Cambridge University Press.

Hatfield, E., & Rapson, R. L. (1996). *Love and Sex: Cross-Cultural Perspectives*. Boston, MA: Allyn & Bacon.

Haw, C. E. (1995). The family life cycle: a forgotten variable in the study of women's employment and well-being. *Psychological Medicine, 25,* 727–738.

Haworth, J. T., & Hill, S. (1992). Work, leisure and psychological well-being in a sample of young adults. *Journal of Community and Applied Social Psychology, 2,* 147–160.

Hay, D. (1990). *Religious Experience Today*. London: Mowbray.

Hazan, C., & Shaver, P. (1987). Romantic love conceptualized as an attachment process. *Journal of Personality and Social Psychology, 52,* 511–524.

Headey, B. (1999). Health benefits and health cost saving due to pets: preliminary estimates from an Australian national survey. *Social Indicators Research, 47,* 233–243.

Headey, B., & Veenhoven, R. (1989). Does happiness induce a rosy outlook? In R. Veenhoven (Ed.), *How Harmful is Happiness?* (pp. 106–127). Rotterdam, The Netherlands: Rotterdam University Press.

Headey, B., Veenhoven, R., & Wearing, A. (1991). Top-down versus bottom-up theories of subjective well-being. *Social Indicators Research, 24,* 81–100.

Headey, B. W., Holmstrom, E. L., & Wearing, A. J. (1984). Well-being and ill-being: different dimensions. *Social Indicators Research, 14,* 115–139.

Headey, B. W., Holmstrom, E. L., & Wearing, A. J. (1985). Models of well-being and ill-being. *Social Indicators Research, 17,* 211–234.

Headey, B. W., & Wearing, A. (1992). *Understanding Happiness*. Melbourne, Australia: Longman Cheshire.

Healy, D. (1997). *The Antidepressant Era*. Cambridge, MA: Harvard University Press.

Heaton, T. B., & Goodman, K. L. (1985). Religion and family formation. *Review of Religious Research, 26,* 343–359.

Helson, R., & Lohnen, E. C. (1998). Affective coloring of personality from young adulthood to midlife. *Personality and Social Psychology Bulletin, 24,* 241–252.

Henderson, M., & Argyle, M. (1985). Social support by four categories of work colleagues: relationships between activities, stress and satisfaction. *Journal of Occupational Behaviour, 6,* 229–239.

Henderson, M., Argyle, M., & Furnham, A. (1984). *The assessment of positive life events*. Oxford, UK: University of Oxford, Department of Experimental Psychology.

Henderson, S., Byrne, D. G., Duncan-Jones, P., Scott, R., & Adcock, S. (1980). Social relationships, adversity and neurosis: a study of associations in a general population sample. *British Journal of Psychiatry, 136,* 354–383.

Henley Centre for Forecasting. (1985). *Leisure Futures*. London: Quarterly.

Herringer, L. G. (1998). Facets of extraversion related to job satisfaction. *Personality and Individual Differences, 24,* 731–733.

Herzberg, F., Mausner, B., & Snyderman, B. (1959). *The Motivation to Work*. New York: Wiley.

Higgins, N. C., Michelle, D. St. A., & Poole, G. D. (1997). The controllability of negative life experiences mediates unrealistic optimism. *Social Indicators Research, 42,* 299–323.

Hills, P., & Argyle, M. (1998a). Musical and religious experiences and their relationship to happiness. *Personality and Individual Differences, 25,* 91–102.

Hills, P., & Argyle, M. (1998b). Positive moods derived from leisure and their relationship to happiness and personality. *Personality and Individual Differences, 25,* 523–535.

Hills, P., & Argyle, M. (2001). Happiness, introversion–extraversion and happy introverts. *Personality and Individual Differences, 30,* 595–608.

Hills, P., Argyle, M., & Reeves, R. (2000). Individual differences in leisure satisfactions: an investigation of four theories of leisure motivation. *Personality and Individual Differences, 28,* 763–779.

Hobfoll, S. E. (1989). Conservation of resources: a new attempt at conceptualizing stress. *American Psychologist, 44,* 513–524.

Hochschild, A. R. (1983). *The Managed Heart: The Commercialization of Human Feeling.* Berkeley, CA: University of California Press.

Hoffman, L. W., & Manis, J. D. (1982). The value of children in the United States. In F. I. Nye (Ed.), *Family Relationships* (pp. 143–170). Beverly Hills, CA: Sage.

Hofstede, G. (1980). *Culture's Consequences.* Beverly Hills, CA: Sage.

Holdaway, S. (1983) *Inside the British Police,* Oxford, UK: Blackwell.

Holden, R. (1998). *Happiness Now.* London: Hodder & Stoughton.

Hollin, C. R., & Trower, P. (1986). *Handbook of Social Skills Training* (2 vols.). Oxford, UK: Pergamon.

Holmes, T. H., & Rahe, R. H. (1967). The social readjustment rating scale. *Journal of Psychosomatic Research, 11,* 213–218.

Hood, R. W., Spilka, B., Hunsberger, B., & Gorsuch, R. (1996). *The Psychology of Religion: an Empirical Approach* (2nd ed.). New York: Guilford Press.

Hoppock, R. (1935). *Job Satisfaction.* New York: Harper.

Hops, H., & Lewinsohn, P. M. (1995). A course for the treatment of depression in adults and children. In K. D. Craig and K. S. Dobson (Eds.), *Anxiety and Depression in Adults and Children* (pp. 230–245). Thousand Oaks, CA: Sage.

Horwitz, A. V., White, H. R., & Howell-White, S. (1996). Becoming married and mental health: a longitudinal study of a cohort of young adults. *Journal of Marriage and the Family, 58,* 895–907.

House, J., Robbins, C., & Metzner, H. L. (1982). The association of social relationships and activities with mortality: prospective evidence from the Tucumsch Community Health Survey. *American Journal of Epidemiology, 116,* 123–140.

House, R. J. (1981). *Work Stress and Social Support.* Reading, MA: Addison-Wesley.

Houston, D. M., McKee, K. J., Carroll, L., & Marsh, H. (1998). Using humour to promote psychological wellbeing in residential homes for older people. *Aging and Mental Health, 2,* 328–332.

Howes, M. J., & Hokanson, J. E. (1979). Conversational and social responses to depressive interpersonal behavior. *Journal of Abnormal Psychology, 88,* 625–34.

Hsaiao, E. T., & Thayer, R. E. (1988). Exercising for mood regulation: the importance of experience. *Personality and Individual Differences, 24,* 829–836.

Hummer, R. A., Rogers, R. G., Nam, C. B., & Ellison, C. G. (1999). Religious involvement and US adult mortality. *Demography, 36,* 273–285.

Hurlock, E. B. (1929). Motivation in fashion. *Archives of Psychology, 3,* 1–72.

Iaffaldano, M. T., & Muchinsky, P. M. (1985). Job satisfaction and job performance: a meta analysis. *Psychological Bulletin, 97,* 251–273.

Idler, E. L. (1987). Religious involvement and the health of the elderly: some hypotheses and an initial test. *Social Forces, 66,* 226–238.

Idler, E. L. (1995). Religion, health, and non-physical sense of self. *Social Forces, 74,* 683–704.

Idler, E. L., & Benyamini, Y. (1997). Self-rated health and mortility: a review of twenty-seven community studies. *Journal of Health and Social Behavior, 38,* 21–37.

Inglehart, R. (1971). The silent revolution in Europe: intergenerational change in post-industrial societies. *American Political Science Review, 65,* 990–1017.

Inglehart, R. (1990). *Culture Shift in Advanced Industrial Society.* Princeton, NJ: Princeton University Press.

Inglehart, R., & Rabier, J.-R. (1986). Aspirations adapt to situations—but why are the Belgians so much happier than the French? In F. M. Andrews (Ed.), *Research on the Quality of Life* (pp. 1–56). Ann Arbor, MI: Institute for Social Research, University of Michigan.

Isen, A. M. (1987). Positive affect, cognitive processes, and social behavior. *Advances in Experimental Social Psychology, 20,* 203–253.

Isen, A. M., & Levin, P. F. (1972). Effect of feeling good on helping: cookies and kindness. *Journal of Personality and Social Psychology, 21,* 384–388.

Isen, A. M., & Simmonds, S. F. (1978). The effect of feeling good on a helping task that is incompatible with a good mood. *Social Psychology Quarterly, 41,* 345–349.

Iso-Ahola, S. E., & Park, C. J. (1996). Leisure-related social support and self-determination as buffers of stress–illness relationship. *Journal of Leisure Research, 28,* 169–187.

Izard, C. E. (1977). *Human Emotions.* New York: Plenum.

Jackson, S. E., & Schuler, R. S. (1985). A meta-analysis and conceptual critique of research on role ambiguity and role conflict in work settings. *Organizational Behavior and Human Decision Processes, 36,* 16–78.

Jahoda, M. (1982). *Employment and Unemployment.* Cambridge, UK: Cambridge University Press.

James, O. (1997). *Britain on the Couch.* London: Century.

Jarvis, G. K., & Northcott, H. C. (1987). Religion and differences in morbidity and mortality. *Social Science and Medicine, 25,* 813–824.

Jenkinson, C., & McGee, H. (1998). *Health Status Measurement.* Abingdon, UK: Radcliffe Medical Press.

Jones, W. H. (1985). The psychology of loneliness: some personality issues in the study of social support. In I. G. Sarason & B. R. Sarason (Eds.), *Social Support: Theory, Research and Applications* (pp. 225–241). Dordrecht, The Netherlands: Nijhoff.

Jordan, T. E. (1992). An index of the quality of life for Victorian children and youth: the VICY index. *Social Indicators Research, 27,* 257–277.

Jordan, T. E. (1993). "L'Homme moyen": estimating the quality of life for British adults, 1815–1914, an index. *Social Indicators Research, 29,* 183–203.

Joseph, S., & Lewis, C. A. (1998). The Depression–Happiness scale: reliability and validity of a bipolar self-report scale. *Journal of Clinical Psychology, 54,* 537–544.

Judge, T. A., & Watanabe, S. (1993). Another look at the job satisfaction–life satisfaction relationship. *Journal of Applied Psychology, 78,* 939–948.

Kahneman, D., Diener, E., & Schwarz, N. (Eds.). (1999). *Foundations of Hedonic Psychology.* New York: Russell Sage.

Kaldor, P. (1994). *Winds of Change.* Homebush West, NSW, Australia: Anzea.

Kalleberg, A. L., & Loscocco, K. A. (1983). Aging, values and rewards: explaining age differences in job satisfaction. *American Sociological Review, 35,* 78–90.

Kammann, R., & Flett, R. (1983). Affectometer 2: a scale to measure current level of general happiness. *Australian Journal of Psychology, 35*, 259–265.

Kandel, D. B., Davies, M., & Raveis, V. H. (1985). The stressfulness of daily roles for women: marital, occupational and household roles. *Journal of Health and Social Behavior, 26*, 64–78.

Kane, T. R., Suls, J., & Tedeschi, J. T. (1977). Humour as a tool of social interaction. In A. J. Chapman & H. C. Foot (Eds.), *It's a Funny Thing, Humour* (pp. 13–16). Oxford, UK: Pergamon.

Karasek, R. A. (1979). Job demands, job decision latitude, and mental strain: implications for job redesign. *Administrative Science Quarterly, 24*, 285–308.

Kasl, S. V. (1978). Epidemiological contributives to the study of work stress. In C. L. Cooper & R. Payne (Eds.), *Stress at Work* (pp. 3–48). Chichester, UK: Wiley.

Kasl, S. V. (1980). The impact of retirement. In C. L. Cooper & R. Payne (Eds.), *Current Concerns in Occupational Stress* (pp. 137–186). Chichester, UK: Wiley.

Kasser, T., & Ryan, R. M. (1993). A dark side of the American dream: correlates of financial success as a central life aspiration. *Journal of Personality and Social Psychology, 65*, 410–422.

Kelley, M. W. (1972). *Why Conservative Churches are Growing*. New York: Harper & Row.

Kelly, J. R. (1983). *Leisure Identities and Interactions*. London: Allen & Unwin.

Keltner, D., & Bonanno, G. A. (1997). A study of laughter and dissociation: distinct correlates of laughter and smiling during bereavement. *Journal of Personality and Social Psychology, 73*, 687–702.

Keltner, D., Locke, K. D., & Audrain, P. C. (1993). The influence of attributions on the relevance of negative feelings to satisfaction. *Personality and Social Psychology Bulletin, 19*, 21–29.

Keltner, D., Young, R. C., Heerey, E. A., Oermig, C., & Monarch, N. D. (1998). Teasing in hierarchical and intimate relations. *Journal of Personality and Social Psychology, 75*, 1231–1247.

Kessler, R. C. (1982). A dissaggregation of the relationship between socioeconomic status and psychological distress. *American Sociological Review, 47*, 757–764.

King, L. A., & Napa, C. K. (1998). What makes a life good? *Journal of Personality and Social Psychology, 75*, 156–165.

Kirkpatrick, L. A. (1992). An attachment-theory approach to the psychology of religion. *International Journal for the Psychology of Religion, 2*, 3–28.

Klein, M. H., Greist, J. H., & Gurtman, A. S. (1985). A comparative outcome study of group psychotherapy vs exercise treatments for depression. *International Journal of Mental Health, 13*, 148–177.

Klemmack, D. L., & Roff, L. L. (1984). Fear of personal aging and subjective well-being in later life. *Journal of Gerontology, 39*, 756–758.

Kobasa, S. C. (1982). The hardy personality: towards a social psychology of stress and health. In G. S. Sanders & J. Suls (Eds.), *Social Psychology of Health and Illness* (pp. 3–32). Hillsdale, NJ: Lawrence Erlbaum Associates Inc.

Kobrin, F. E., & Hendershot, G. E. (1977). Do family ties reduce mortality? Evidence from the United States 1966–1968. *Journal of Marriage and the Family, 39*, 737–745.

Kohn, M. L., & Schooler, C. (1982). Job conditions and personality: a longitudinal assessment of their reciprocal effects. *American Journal of Sociology, 87*, 1257–1286.

Konecni, V. J. (1982). Social interaction and musical preference. In D. Deutsch (Ed.), *The Psychology of Music* (pp. 497–516). New York: Academic Press.

Kornhauser, A. (1965). *Mental Health of the Industrial Worker.* New York: Wiley.

Korunka, C., Weiss, A., Huemer, K. H., & Karetta, B. (1995). The effect of new technologies on job satisfaction and psychosomatic complaints. *Applied Psychology: An International Review, 44,* 123–142.

Kossek, E. E., & Ozeki, C. (1998). Work–family conflict, policies and the job–life satisfaction relationship: a review and directions for organizational behavior–human resources research. *Journal of Applied Psychology, 83,* 139–149.

Krause, J. S., & Sternberg, M. (1997). Aging and adjustment after spinal cord injury: the roles of chronological age, time since injury, and environmental change. *Rehabilitation Psychology, 42,* 287–302.

Kraut, R. E., & Johnston, R. E. (1979). Social and emotional messages of smiling: an ethological approach. *Journal of Personality and Social Psychology, 37,* 1539–1553.

Krauze, M., Brandwein, T., & Fox, S. (1995). Work attitudes and emotional responses of permanent, voluntary, and involuntary temporary-help employees: an exploratory study. *Applied Psychology: An International Review, 44,* 217–232.

Kubey, R., & Csikszentmihalyi, M. (1990). *Television and the Quality of Life.* Hillsdale, NJ: Lawrence Erlbaum Associates Inc.

Kubovy, M. (1999). Pleasures of the mind. In D. Kahneman, E. Diener, & N. Schwarz (Eds.), *Well-Being: The Foundations of Hedonic Psychology* (pp. 134–154) New York: Sage.

Kuiper, N. A., & Martin, R. A. (1998). Laughter and stress in daily life: relation to positive and negative affect. *Motivation and Emotion, 22,* 133–153.

Kuiper, N. A., Martin, R., Oliknger, L. J., Kazarian, S. S., & Jette, J. L. (1998). Sense of humor, self-concept, and psychological well-being in psychiatric inpatients. *Humor: International Journal of Humor Research, 11,* 357–381.

Kuiper, N. A., Martin, R. F. A., & Dance, K. A. (1992). Sense of humour and enhanced quality of life. *Personality and Individual Differences, 13,* 1273–1283.

Lachman, M. E., & Weaver, S. L. (1998). The sense of control as a moderator of social class differences in health and well-being. *Journal of Personality and Social Psychology, 74,* 763–773.

La Fave, L., Haddad, J., & Maeson, A. (1976). Superiority, enhanced self-esteem, and perceived incongruity. In A. J. Chapman & H. C. Foot (Eds.), *Humour and Laughter: Theory, Research and Applications* (pp. 63–91). Chichester, UK: Wiley.

Lai, J. C. L., & Wong, W. S. (1998). Optimism and coping with unemployment among Hong Kong Chinese women. *Journal of Research in Personality, 32,* 454–479.

Laird, J. D. (1984). Facial response and emotion. *Journal of Personality and Social Psychology, 47,* 909–937.

Landau, S. F., Beit-Hallahmi, B., & Levy, S. (1998). The personal and the political: Israelis' perception of well-being in times of war and peace. *Social Indicators Research, 44,* 329–365.

Langston, C. A. (1994). Capitalizing on and coping with daily-life events: expressive responses to positive events. *Journal of Personality and Social Psychology, 67,* 1112–1125.

Larsen, R. J., & Diener, E. (1987). Emotional response intensity as an individual difference characteristic. *Journal of Research in Personality, 21,* 1–39.

Larsen, R. J., Diener, E., & Emmons, R. A. (1985). An evaluation of subjective well-being measures. *Social Indicators Research, 17,* 1–18.

Larsen, R. J., & Ketelaar, T. (1991). Personality and susceptibility to positive and negative emotional states. *Journal of Personality and Social Psychology, 61,* 132–140.

Larson, R. (1978). Thirty years of research on the subjective well-being of older Americans. *Journal of Gerontology, 33*, 109–125.

Larson, R., Csikszentmihalyi, M., & Freeman, M. (1984). Alcohol and marihuana use in adolescents' daily lives: a random sample of experiences. *International Journal of the Addictions, 19*, 367–381.

Larson, R. W. (1990). The solitary side of life: an examination of the time people spend alone from childhood to old age. *Developmental Review, 10*, 155–183.

Lawler, E. E., & Porter, L. W. (1963). Percentions regarding management compensation. *Industrial Relations, 3*, 41–49.

LeDoux, J. E. (1993). Emotional networks in the brain. In M. Lewis & J. M. Haviland (Eds.), *Handbook of Emotions* (pp. 109–118). New York: Guilford Press.

Lee, Y.-T., & Seligman, M. E. P. (1997). Are Americans more optimistic than the Chinese? *Personality and Social Psychology Bulletin, 23*, 32–40.

Lefcourt, H. M., Davidson, K., Prkachin, K. M., & Mills, D. E. (1997). Humor as a stress moderator in the prediction of blood pressure obtained during five stressful tasks. *Journal of Research in Personality, 31*, 523–542.

Leicht, K. T., & Shepelak, N. (1994). Organizational justice and satisfaction with economic rewards. *Research in Social Stratification and Mobility, 13*, 175–202.

Lepper, H. S. (1998). Use of other reports to validate subjective well-being measures. *Social Indicators Research, 44*, 367–379.

Lester, D. (2000). National differences in neuroticism and extraversion. *Personality and Individual Differences, 28*, 35–39.

Levin, J. S. (1994). Religion and health: is there an association, is it valid, and is it causal? *Social Science and Medicine, 38*, 1475–1482.

Levine, R. V., & Norenzayan, A. (1999). The pace of life in 31 countries. *Journal of Cross-Cultural Psychology, 30*, 178–205.

Lewinsohn, P. M., & Gotlib, I. H. (1995). Behavioral theory and treatment of depression. In E. E. Beckham & W. R. Leber (Eds.), *Handbook of Depression* (2nd ed., pp. 352–375). New York: Guilford Press.

Lewinsohn, P. M., & Graf, M. (1973). Pleasant activities and depression. *Journal of Consulting and Clinical Psychology, 41*, 261–268.

Lewinsohn, P. M., Sullivan, J. M., & Grosscup, S. J. (1982). Behavioral therapy: clinical applications. In A. J. Rush (Ed.), *Short-Term Therapies for Depression* (pp. 50–87). New York: Guilford Press.

Lichter, S., Haye, K., & Kammann, R. (1980). Increasing happiness through cognitive training. *New Zealand Psychologist, 9*, 57–64.

Lindenfield, G. (1997). *Emotional Confidence.* London: Thorsons.

Livingstone, S. M. (1988). Why people watch soap opera: analysis of the explanations of British viewers. *European Journal of Communication, 3*, 55–80.

Loewentstein, G., & Schkade, D. (1999). Wouldn't it be nice? Predicting future feelings. In D. Kahneman, E. Diener, & N. Schwarz (Eds.), *Well-Being: The Foundations of Hedonic Psychology* (pp. 85–105). New York: Russell Sage Foundation.

Loher, B. T., Noe, R. A., Moeller, N. L., & Fitzgerald, M. P. (1985). A meta-analysis of the relation of job characteristics to job satisfaction. *Journal of Applied Psychology, 70*, 280–289.

Lorenz, K. (1963). *On Aggression.* New York: Bantam.

Lu, L. (1997). Social support, reciprocity and well-being. *Journal of Social Psychology, 137*, 618–628.

Lu, L. (2000). Gender and conjugal differences. *Journal of Social Psychology*, *140*, 132–141.

Lu, L., & Argyle, M. (1992a). Happiness and cooperation. *Personality and Individual Differences*, *12*, 1019–1030.

Lu, L., & Argyle, M. (1992b). Receiving and giving support: effects on relationships and well-being. *Counselling Psychology Quarterly*, *5*, 123–133.

Lu, L., & Argyle, M. (1993). TV watching, soap opera and happiness. *Kaohsiung Journal of Medical Sciences*, *9*, 501–507.

Lu, L., & Argyle, M. (1994). Leisure satisfaction and happiness as a function of leisure activity. *Kaohsiung Journal of Medical Sciences*, *10*, 89–96.

Lu, L., & Lin, Y.-Y. (1998). Family roles and happiness in adulthood. *Personality and Individual Differences*, *25*, 195–207.

Lu, L., Shih, J. B., Lin, Y., & Ju, L. S. (1997). Personal and environmental correlates of happiness. *Personality and Individual Differences*, *23*, 453–462.

Lucas, R. E., Diener, E., & Suh, E. (1996). Discriminant validity of well-being measures. *Journal of Personality and Social Psychology*, *71*, 616–628.

Lundy, D. E., Tan, J., & Cunningham, M. R. (1998). Heterosexual romantic preferences: the importance of humor and physical attractiveness for different types of relationships. *Personal Relationships*, *5*, 311–325.

Lutz, C. A. (1988). *Unnatural Emotions: Everyday Sentiments on a Micronesian Atoll and their Challenge to Western Theory*. Chicago: University of Chicago Press.

Lykken, D., & Tellegen, A. (1996). Happiness is a stochastic phenomenon. *Psychological Science*, *7*, 186–189.

Lynch, J. J. (1977). *The Broken Heart*. New York: Basic Books.

Lynn, P., & Smith, J. D. (1991). *Voluntary Action Research*. London: The Volunteer Centre.

Lynn, R. (1971). *Personality and National Character*. Oxford, UK: Pergamon.

Lynn, R. (1981). Cross-cultural differences in neuroticism, extraversion and psychoticism. In R. Lynn (Ed.), *Dimensions of Personality* (pp. 263–286). Oxford, UK: Pergamon.

Lynn, R., & Martin, T. (1995). National differences for thirty-seven nations in extraversion, neuroticism, psychoticism and economic, demographic and other variables. *Personality and Individual Differences*, *19*, 401–406.

Lyubomirsky, S., & Ross, L. (1997). Hedonic consequences of social comparison: a contrast of happy and unhappy people. *Journal of Personality and Social Psychology*, *73*, 1141–1157.

Lyubomirsky, S., & Tucker, K. L. (1998). Implications of individual differences in subjective happiness for perceiving, interpreting, and thinking about life events. *Motivation and Emotion*, *22*, 155–186.

Magnus, K., Diener, E., Fujita, F., & Payot, W. (1993). Extraversion and neuroticism as predictors of objective life events: a longitudinal analysis. *Journal of Personality and Social Psychology*, *65*, 1046–1053.

Maio, G. R., Olson, J. M., & Bush, J. E. (1997). Telling jokes that disparage other groups: effects on the joke teller's stereotypes. *Journal of Applied Social Psychology*, *27*, 1986–2000.

Maletasta, C. Z., Grigoryev, P., Lamb, C., Albin, M., & Culver, C. (1986). Emotion socialization and expressive development in preterm and full-term infants. *Child Development*, *57*, 316–330.

Mallard, A. G., Lance, C. E., & Michalos, A. C. (1997). Culture as a moderator of overall life satisfaction–life facet relationships. *Social Indicators Research*, *40*, 259–284.

Maltby, J., Lewis, C. A., & Day, L. (1999). Religious orientation and psychological well-being: the role of the frequency of personal prayer. *British Journal of Health Psychology*, *4*, 363–378.

Manucia, G. K., Baumann, D. J., & Cialdini, R. B. (1984). Mood influences on helping: direct effects or side effects? *Journal of Personality and Social Psychology*, *46*, 357–364.

Markham, S. F. (1942). *Climate and the Energy of Nations*. London: Oxford University Press.

Markland, D., & Hardy, L. (1993). The exercise motivations inventory: preliminary development and validity of a measure of individuals' reasons for participation in regular physical exercise. *Personality and Individual Differences*, *15*, 289–296.

Markus, H. R., & Kitayama, S. (1991). Culture and the self: implications for cognition, emotion and motivation. *Psychological Review*, *98*, 224–253.

Marmot, M. G., Rose, G., Shipley, M., & Hamilton, P. J. S. (1978). Employment grade and coronary heart disease in British civil servants. *Journal of Epidemiology and Community Health*, *32*, 244–249.

Marmot, M. G., Shipley, M. J., & Rose, G. (1984). Inequalities in death—specific explanations of a general pattern. *Lancet*, *1*, 1003–1006.

Maroukalis, E., & Zervas, Y. (1993). Effects of aerobic exercise on mood of adult women. *Perceptual and Motor Skills*, *76*, 795–801.

Marsella, A. J. (1980). Depressive experience and disorder across cultures. In H. Triandis & J. Draguns (Eds.), *Handbook of Cross-Cultural Psychology, (Vol. 6)*. Boston, MA: Allyn & Bacon.

Martin, R. A. (1996). The Situational Humor Response Questionnaire (SHRQ) and Coping Humor Scale (CHS): a decade of research. *Humor: International Journal of Humor Research*, *9*, 251–272.

Martin, R. A., & Kuiper, N. A. (1999). Daily occurrence of humor: relationships with age, gender, and Type A personality. *Humor: International Journal of Humor Research*, *12*, 355–384.

Martin, R. A., & Lefcourt, H. M. (1983). Sense of humor as a moderator of the relation between stresses and moods. *Journal of Personality and Social Psychology*, *45*, 1313–1324.

Martineau, F. W. H. (1972). A model of the social functions of humor. In J. H. Goldstein & P. E. McGhee (Eds.), *The Psychology of Humor* (pp. 101–125). New York: Academic Press.

Maslach, C., & Jackson, S. E. (1982). Burnout in health professions: a social psychological analysis. In G. S. Sanders & J. Suls (Eds.), *Social Psychology of Health and Illness* (pp. 227–251). Hillsdale, NJ: Lawrence Erlbaum Associates Inc.

Maslow, A. H. (1954). *Motivation and Personality*. New York: Harper & Row.

Maslow, A. H. (1968). *Toward a Psychology of Being*. Princeton, NJ: Van Nostrand.

Mastekaasa, A. (1993). Marital status and subjective well-being: a changing relationhip? *Social Indicators Research*, *29*, 249–276.

Matlin, M. W., & Gawron, V. J. (1979). Individual differences in Pollyannaism. *Journal of Personality Assessment*, *43*, 411–412.

Matthews, K. A. (1988). Coronary heart disease and Type A behaviors: update on and alternative to the Booth-Kewley and Friedman (1987) quantitative review. *Psychological Bulletin*, *104*, 373–380.

Mayer, J. D. (1994). Emotion over time within a religious culture: a lexical analysis of the Old Testament. *Journal of Prehistory*, *22*, 235–248.

McAdams, D. P. (1988). Personal needs and personal relationships. In S. Duck (Ed.), *Handbook of Personal Relationships* (pp. 7–22). Chichester, UK: Wiley.

McClelland, D. C. (1987). *Human Motivation.* Cambridge, UK: Cambridge University Press.

McFadden, S. H., & Levin, J. S. (1996). Religion, emotions and health. In C. Magai & S. H. McFadden (Eds.), *Handbook of Emotion, Adult Development and Aging* (pp. 349–365). San Diego, CA: Academic Press.

McGhee, P. E. (1971). The development of the humor response: a review of the literature. *Psychological Bulletin, 76,* 328–348.

McGhee, P. E. (1979). *Humor: its Origin and Development.* San Francisco: W. H. Freeman.

McGoldrick, A. (1982). Early retirement: a new leisure opportunity. *Work and Leisure, 15,* 73–89.

McGregor, I., & Little, B. R. (1998). Personal projects, happiness and meaning. *Journal of Personality and Social Psychology, 74,* 494–512.

McIntosh, D. N., Silver, R. C., & Wortman, C. B. (1993). Religion's role in adjusting to a negative life event: coping with the loss of a child. *Journal of Personality and Social Psychology, 65,* 812–821.

McLeod, J. D., & Kessler, R. C. (1990). Socioeconomic status differences in vulnerability to undesirable life events. *Journal of Health and Social Behavior, 31,* 162–172.

Meehan, M. P., Duriak, J. A., & Bryant, F. B. (1993). The relationship of social support to perceived control and subjective mental health in adolescents. *Journal of Community Psychology, 21,* 49–55.

Mehnert, T., Krauss, H. H., Nadler, R., & Boyd, M. (1990). Correlates of life satisfaction in those with disabling conditions. *Rehabilitation Psychology, 35,* 3–17.

Melhuish, A. H. (1981). The doctor's role in educating managers about stress. In J. Marshall & C. L. Cooper (Eds.), *Coping with Stress at Work* (pp. 3–40). Andover, UK: Gower.

Melton, R. J. (1995). The role of positive affect in syllogism performance. *Personality and Social Psychology Bulletin, 21,* 788–794.

Mettee, D. R., Hrelec, E. J., & Wilkens, P. C. (1971). Humor as an interpersonal asset and liability. *Journal of Social Psychology, 85,* 51–64.

Michalos, A. C. (1985). Multiple discrepancies theory. *Social Indicators Research, 16,* 347–413.

Middleton, R. (1959). Negro and white reactions to racial humor. *Sociometry, 22,* 175–182.

Mishra, S. (1992). Leisure activities and life satisfaction in old age: a case study of retired government employees living in urban areas. *Activities, Adaptation and Aging, 16*(4), 7–26.

Mitchell, W. B., DiBartolo, P. M., Brown, T. A., & Barlow, D. H. (1998). Effects of positive and negative mood on sexual arousal in sexually functional males. *Archives of Sexual Behavior, 27,* 197–207.

Moberg, D. O., & Taves, M. J. (1965). Church participation and adjustment in old age. In A. M. Rose & W. A. Peterson (Eds.), *Older People and their Social World* (pp. 113–124). Philadelphia: F. A. Davis.

Morrison, D. R., & Cherlin, A. J. (1995). The divorce process and young children's well-being: a prospective analysis. *Journal of Marriage and the Family, 57,* 800–812.

Moser, K. A., Fox, A. J., & Jones, D. R. (1984). Unemployment and mortality in the OPCS longitudinal study. *Lancet, 2,* 1324–1329.

Moses, J., Steptoe, A., Mathews, A., & Edwards, S. (1989). The effects of exercise training on mental well-being in the normal population. *Journal of Psychosomatic Research, 33,* 47–61.

Mottaz, C. (1986). Gender differences in work satisfaction, work-related rewards and values, and the determinants of work satisfaction. *Human Relations, 39,* 359–376.

Moyle, P. (1995). The role of negative affectivity in the stress process: tests of alternative models. *Journal of Organizational Behavior, 16,* 647–668.

Mroczak, D. K., & Kolanz, C. M. (1998). The effect of age on positive and negative affect: a developmental perspective on happiness. *Journal of Personality and Social Psychology, 75,* 1333–1349.

Mulkay, M. (1988). *On Humour.* Cambridge, UK: Polity Press.

Mullis, R. J. (1992). Measures of economic well-being as predictors of psychological well-being. *Social Indicators Research, 26,* 119–135.

Murphy, G. C., & Athanasou, J. A. (1999). The effect of unemployment on mental health. *Journal of Occupational and and Organizational Psychology, 72,* 83–99.

Murphy, L. R. (1994). Workplace interventions for stress reduction and prevention. In C. L. Cooper & R. Payne (Eds.), *Causes, Coping and Consequences of Stress at Work* (pp. 301–339). Chichester, UK: Wiley.

Murray, S. L., & Holmes, J. G. (1997). A leap of faith? Positive illusions in romantic relationships. *Personality and Social Psychology Bulletin, 23,* 586–604.

Myers, D. G. (1999). Close relationships and quality of life. In D. Kahneman, E. Diener, & N. Schwarz (Eds.), *Well-Being: The Foundations of Hedonic Psychology* (pp. 374–391). New York: Russell Sage.

Myers, D. M. (1992). *The Pursuit of Happiness.* New York: Morrow.

Near, J. P., Smith, C., Rice, R. W., & Hunt, R. G. (1980). The relationship between work and nonwork domains. *Academy of Management Review, 5,* 415–429.

Needles, D. J., & Abramson, L. Y. (1990). Positive life events, attributional style, and hopefulness: testing a model of recovery from depression. *Journal of Abnormal Psychology, 99,* 156–165.

Neulinger, J. (1981). *The Psychology of Leisure* (2nd ed.). Springfield, IL: Charles C. Thomas.

Nevo, O. (1994). The psychological contribution of humor in Israel during the Gulf War. *Psychologia: Israel Journal of Psychology, 4,* 41–50.

Nevo, O., Aharonson, H., & Klingman, A. (1998). The development and evaluation of a systematic program for improving sense of humor. In W. Ruch (Ed.), *The Sense of Humor: Explorations of a Personality Characteristic. Humor Research* (Vol. 3, pp. 385–404). Berlin, Germany: De Gruyter.

Nolen-Hoeksema, S. (1991). Responses to depression and their effects on the duration of depressive episodes. *Journal of Abnormal Psychology, 100,* 569–585.

Nolen-Hoeksema, S., & Rusting, C. L. (1999). Gender differences in well-being. In D. Kahneman, E. Diener, & N. Schwarz (Eds.), *Foundations of Hedonic Psychology* (pp. 330–350). New York: Russell Sage.

Noor, N. (1995). Work and family roles in relation to women's well-being: a longitudinal study. *British Journal of Social Psychology, 34,* 87–106.

Noor, N. M. (1997). The relationship between wives' estimates of time spent doing housework, support and wives' well-being. *Journal of Community and Applied Social Psychology, 7,* 413–423.

O'Brien, G. E. (1986). *Psychology of Work and Employment.* Chichester; UK: Wiley.

Oettingen, G. (1992). Prerequisites for the power of positive thinking. Berlin, Germany: Max Plank Institute.

Offer, A. (2001). On economic welfare measurement and human well-being over the long run. In P. A. David, P. Solar & M. Thomas (Eds) *The Economic Future in Historical Perspective*. Oxford, UK: Oxford University Press.

Oishi, S., Diener, E. F., Lucas, R. E., & Suh, E., M. (1999). Cross-cultural variations in predictors of life satisfaction: perspectives from needs and values. *Personality and Social Psychology Bulletin, 25,* 980–990.

Okun, M. A., & George, L. K. (1984). Physician and self-ratings of health, neuroticism and subjective well-being among men and women. *Personality and Individual Differences, 5,* 533–539.

Okun, M. A., Stock, W. A., Haring, M. J., & Witten R. A. (1984). Health and subjective well-being: a meta-analysis. *International Journal of Aging and Human Development, 19,* 111–132.

Olds, J. (1958). Self-stimulation of the brain. *Science, 127,* 315–324.

Olson, G. L., & Schober, B. I. (1993). The satisfied poor. *Social Indicators Research, 28,* 173–193.

O'Malley, M. N., & Andrews, L. (1983). The effects of mood and incentives on helping: are there some things that money can't buy? *Motivation and Emotion, 7,* 179–189.

Osarchuk, M., & Tate, S. J. (1973). Effect of induced fear of death on belief in afterlife. *Journal of Personality and Social Psychology, 27,* 256–260.

Ostroot, N. M., & Snyder, W. W. (1985). Measuring cultural bias in a cross-cultural study. *Social Indicators Research, 17,* 243–251.

Oswald, A. J. (1997). Happiness and economic performance. *The Economic Journal, 107,* 1815–1831.

Ouweneel, P., & Veenhoven, R. (1994). *Nation Characteristics and Average Happiness,* Rotterdam, The Netherlands: Erasmus University.

Pacini, R., Muir, F., & Epstein, S. (1998). Depressive realism from the perspective of cognitive experiential self-theory. *Journal of Personality and Social Psychology, 74,* 1056–1068.

Paffenbarger, R. S., Hyde, R. T., & Dow, A. (1991). Health benefits of physical activity. In B. L. Driver, P. J. Brown, & G. L. Peterson (Eds.), *Benefits of Leisure* (pp. 49–57). State College, PA: Venture Publishing.

Paffenbarger, R. S., Wing, A. L., & Hyde, R. T. (1978). Physical activity as an index of heart attack in college alumni. *American Journal of Epidemiology, 108,* 161–175.

Pahnke, W. H. (1966). Drugs and mysticism. *International Journal of Parapsychology, 8,* 295–314.

Palinkas, L. A., Wingard, D. L., & Barrett, C. E. (1990). The biocultural context of social networks and depression among the elderly. *Social Science and Medicine, 30,* 441–447.

Paloutzian, R. F. (1981). Purpose in life and value changes following conversion. *Journal of Personality and Social Psychology, 41,* 1153–1160.

Paloutzian, R. F., & Ellison, C. W. (1982). Loneliness, spiritual well-being, and the quality of life. In L. A. Peplau & D. Perlman (Eds.), *Loneliness: A Sourcebook of Current Theory, Research and Therapy* (pp. 224–237). New York: Wiley.

Pargament, K. I. (1997). *The Psychology of Religion and Coping.* New York: Guilford Press.

Park, C., Cohen, L. M., & Herb, L. (1990). Intrinsic religiousness and religious coping as life stress moderators for Catholics versus Protestants. *Journal of Personality and Social Psychology, 59,* 562–574.

Park, C. L., Cohen, L. H., & Murch, R. L. (1996). Assessment and prediction of stress-related growth. *Journal of Personality, 64,* 71–105.

Parker, S. (1982). *Work and Retirement.* London: Allen & Unwin.

Paykel, E. S., Emms, E. M., Fletcher, J., & Rassaby, E. S. (1980). Life events and social support in puerperal depression. *British Journal of Psychiatry, 136*, 339–346.

Payne, R. (1988). A longitudinal study of the psychological well-being of unemployed men and the mediating effect of neuroticism. *Human Relations, 41*, 119–138.

Peale, N. V. (1953). *The Power of Positive Thinking*. Kingswood, UK: World's Work.

Pearce, J. L. (1993). *Volunteers*. London: Routledge.

Pearce, P. L. (1982). *The Social Psychology of Tourist Behaviour*. Oxford, UK: Pergamon.

Pennebaker, J. W. (1989). Confession, inhibition, and disease. *Advances in Experimental Social Psychology, 22*, 211–244.

Petty, M. M., McGee, G. W., & Cavender, J. W. (1984). A meta-analysis of the relationships between individual job satisfaction and individual performance. *Academy of Management Review, 9*, 712–721.

Petty, R. E., & Wegener, D. T. (1998). Attitude change: multiple roles for persuasion variables. In D. T. Gilbert, S. T. Fiske, & G. Lindzey (Eds.), *The Handbook of Social Psychology* (4th ed., Vol. 1, pp. 323–390). Boston: McGraw-Hill.

Plancherel, B., & Bolognini, M. (1995). Coping and mental health in early adolescence. *Journal of Adolescence, 18*, 459–474.

Platt, S. (1986). Recent trends in parasuicide ("attempted suicide") among men in Edinburgh. In S. Allen et al. (Eds.), *The Experience of Unemployment* (pp. 150–167). Basingstoke, UK: Macmillan Education.

Pollio, H. R., & Edgerly, J. W. (1976). Comedians and comic style. In A. J. Chapman & H. C. Foot (Eds.), *Humour and Laughter: Theory, Research and Applications* (pp. 215–242). Chichester, UK: Wiley.

Pollner, M. (1989). Divine relations, social relations, and well-being. *Journal of Health and Social Behavior, 30*, 92–104.

Poloma, M. M., & Pendleton, B. F. (1991). *Exploring Neglected Dimensions of Religion in Quality of Life Research*. Lewiston, NY: Edwin Mellon Press.

Prager, K. J., & Buhrmester, D. (1998). Intimacy and need fulfilment in couple relationships. *Journal of Social and Personal Relationships, 15*, 435–469.

Preuschoft, S., & Van Hooff, J. A. R. A. M. (1997). The social function of "smile" and "laughter": variations across primate species and societies. In U. C. Segestrale & P. Molnar (Eds.), *Non-verbal Communication: Where Nature Meets Culture* (pp. 171–190). Mahwah, NJ: Lawrence Erlbaum Associates Inc.

Privette, G. (1983). Peak experience, peak performance, and peak flow: a comparative analysis of positive human experiences. *Journal of Personality and Social Psychology, 45*, 1361–1368.

Putnam, R. D. (1996). The strange disappearance of civic America. *American Prospect*, Winter, 34–48.

Putman, R. D. (2000) *Bowling Alone*. New York: Simon and Schuster.

Radcliffe-Brown, A. R. (1940). On joking relationships. *Africa, 13*, 195–210.

Rahman, T. and Khaléque, A. (1996). The purpose in life and academic behavior of problem students in Bangladesh. *Social Indicators Research, 39*, 59–64.

Ransford, H., & Palisi, B. J. (1996). Aerobic exercise, subjective health and psychological well-being within age and gender subgroups. *Social Science and Medicine, 42*, 1555–1559.

Raphael, D., Renwick, R., Brown, I., & Rootman, I. (1996). Quality of life indicators and health: current status and emerging conceptions. *Social Indicators Research, 39*, 65–88.

Rehm, L. P. (1990). Cognitive and behavioral theories. In B. B. Wolman & C. Stricker (Eds.), *Depressive Disorders* (pp. 64–91). New York: Wiley.

Reich, J. W., & Zautra, A. (1981). Life events and personal causation. *Journal of Personality and Social Psychology, 41,* 1002–1012.

Reis, H. R., & Franks, P. (1994). The role of intimacy and social support in health outcomes: two processes or one? *Personal Relationships, 1,* 185–197.

Reis, H. T. (1984). Social interaction and well-being. In S. Duck (Ed.), *Personal Relationships* (Vol. 5, pp. 21–45). London: Academic Press.

Reis, H. T., Nezlek, J., Kernis, M. H., & Spiegel, N. (1984). On specificity in the impact of social participation on physical and mental health. *Journal of Personality and Social Psychology, 48,* 1018–1034.

Reynolds, J. R. (1997). The effects of industrial employment conditions on job-related stress. *Journal of Health and Social Behavior, 38,* 105–116.

Riddick, C. C., & Stewart, D. G. (1994). An examination of the life satisfaction and importance of leisure in the lives of older female retirees: a comparison of Blacks to Whites. *Journal of Leisure Research, 26,* 75–87.

Rimland, B. (1982). The altruism paradox. *Psychological Reports, 51,* 521–522.

Robert, S. A. (1998). Community-level socioeconomic status effects on adult health. *Journal of Health and Social Behavior, 39,* 18–37.

Robinson, J. P. (1977). *How Americans Use Time.* New York: Praeger.

Robinson, J. P. (1990). Television's effects on families' use of time. In J. Bryant (Ed.), *Television and the American Family* (pp. 195–209). Hillsdale, NJ: Lawrence Erlbaum Associates Inc.

Robinson, M. D., & Ryff, C. D. (1999). The role of self-deception in perceptions of past, present, and future happiness. *Personality and Social Psychology Bulletin, 25,* 595–606.

Robinson, T. E., & Berridge, K. C. (1993). The neural basis of drug craving: an incentive-sensitization theory of addiction. *Brain, 18,* 247–291.

Robinson-Wheeler, S., Kim, C., MacCallum, R. C., & Kiecolt-Glaser, J. K. (1997). Distinguishing optimism from pessimism in older adults: is it more important to be optimistic or not pessimistic? *Journal of Personality and Social Psychology, 73,* 1345–1353.

Rogers, S. J., & White, L. K. (1998). Satisfaction with parenting: the role of marital happiness, family structure, and parents' gender. *Journal of Marriage and the Family, 60,* 293–308.

Rokeach, M. (1981). *The Three Christs of Ypsilanti.* New York: Columbia University Press.

Rolls, E. T. (1999). *The Brain and Emotion.* Oxford, UK: Oxford University Press.

Rosenberg, B., & Shapiro, G. (1958). Marginality and Jewish humor. *Midstream, 4,* 70–80.

Rosenberg, M. (1965). *Society and the Adolescent Self-Image.* Princeton, NJ: Princeton University Press.

Rosenberg, M., Schooler, C., Schoenbach, C., & Rosenberg, F. (1995). Global self-esteem and specific self-esteem: different concepts, different outcomes. *American Sociological Review, 60,* 141–156.

Rosenthal, R., & DePaulo, B. (1979). Sex differences in eavesdropping on nonverbal cues. *Journal of Personality and Social Psychology, 37,* 273–285.

Ross, C. E., & Drentea, P. (1998). Consequences of different retirement activities for distress and the sense of personal control. *Journal of Health and Social Behavior, 39,* 317–334.

Ross, M., Eyman, A., & Kishuck, N. (1986). Determinants of subjective well-being. In

J. M. Olson, C. P. Herman, & M. Zanna (Eds), *Relative Deprivation and Social Comparison*. Hillsdale, NJ: Lawrence Erlbaum Associates Inc.

Ross, C. E., & Milgram, J. L. (1982). Important variables in adult sibling relationships: a quantitative study. In M. E. Lamb & B. Sutton-Smith (Eds.), *Sibling Relationships* (pp. 225–249). Hillsdale, NJ: Lawrence Erlbaum Associates Inc.

Ross, C. E., & Mirowsky, J. (1989). Explaining the social patterns of depression: control and problem-solving—or support and talking. *Journal of Health and Social Behavior, 30*, 206–219.

Ross, C. E., & Mirowsky, J. (1995). Does employment affect health? *Journal of Health and Social Behavior, 36*, 230–243.

Ross, C. E., & Van Willigen, M. (1997). Education and the subjective quality of life. *Journal of Health and Social Behavior, 38*, 275–297.

Rothbart, M. K. (1976). Incongruity, problem-solving and laughter. In A. J. Chapman & H. C. Foot (Eds.), *Humour and Laughter: Theory, Research and Applications* (pp. 37–54). Chichester, UK: Wiley.

Rotter, J. B. (1966). Generalised expectancies for internal versus external control of reinforcement. *Psychological Monographs, 80*, 1–28.

Roy, D. (1959). Banana time: job satisfaction and informal interaction. *Human Organization, 18*, 158–168.

Rubenstein, C. (1980). Vacations. *Psychology Today, 13* (May), 62–76.

Ruch, W. (1993). Exhilaration and humor. In M. Lewis & J. M. Haviland (Eds.), *Handbook of Emotions* (pp. 605–616). New York: Guilford Press.

Ruch, W. (1997). To be in good or bad humor: construction of the state form of the State-Trait-Cheerfulness-Inventory—STCI. *Personality and Individual Differences, 22*, 477–491.

Ruch, W., & Carrell, A. (1998). Trait cheerfulness and the sense of humour. *Personality and Individual Differences, 24*, 551–558.

Ruch, W., & Hehl, F. J. (1986). Conservatism as a predictor of responses to humour: II. The location of sense of humour in a comprehensive attitude space. *Personality and Individual Differences, 7*, 861–874.

Ruch, W. D. (Ed.). (1998). *The Sense of Humor: Explorations of a Personality Characteristic*. Berlin, Germany: De Gruyter.

Runciman, W. G. (1966). *Relative Deprivation and Social Justice*. London: Routledge & Kegan Paul.

Russell, J. A. (1980). A circumplex model of affect. *Journal of Personality and Social Psychology, 39*, 1161–1178.

Russell, J. A., & Carroll, J. M. (1999). On the bipolarity of positive and negative affect. *Psychological Bulletin, 125*, 3–30.

Russell, R. J. H., & Wells, P. A. (1994). Predictors of happiness in married couples. *Personality and Individual Differences, 17*, 313–321.

Ryff, C. D. (1989). Happiness is everything, or is it? Explorations on the meaning of psychological well-being. *Journal of Personality and Social Psychology, 57*, 1069–1081.

Saarni, C. (1979). Children's understanding of display rules for expressive behavior. *Developmental Psychology, 15*, 424–429.

Saarni, C. (1989). Children's understanding of strategic control of emotional expression in social transactions. In C. Saarni & P. L. Harris (Eds.), *Children's Understanding of Emotion* (pp. 181–208). Cambridge, UK: Cambridge University Press.

Sackett, G. P. (1966). Monkeys reared in isolation with pictures as visual imput: evidence for an innate releasing mechanism. *Science, 154,* 1468–1473.

Sales, S. M., & House, J. (1971). Job satisfaction as a possible risk factor in coronary heart disease. *Journal of Chronic Diseases, 23,* 861–873.

Salovey, P., O'Leary, A., Stretton, M. S., Fishkin, S. A, & Drake, C. A. (1991). Influence of mood on judgements about health and illness. In J. P. Forgas (Ed.), *Affect and Social Judgements* (pp. 241–262). Oxford, UK: Pergamon.

Sandvik, E., Diener, E., & Seidlitz, L. (1993). Subjective well-being: the convergence and stability of self-report and non-self-report measures. *Journal of Personality, 61,* 317–342.

Saper, B. (1990). The therapeutic use of humor for psychiatric disturbances of adolescence. *Psychiatric Quarterly, 61,* 261–272.

Sastry, J., & Ross, C. E. (1998). Asian ethnicity and the sense of personal control. *Social Psychology Quarterly, 61,* 101–120.

Scambler, D. J., Harris, M. J., & Milich, R. (1998). Sticks and stones: evaluations of responses to childhood teasing. *Social Development, 7,* 234–249.

Schachter, S., & Singer, J. (1962). Cognitive, social and physiological determinants of emotional state. *Psychological Review, 69,* 379–399.

Scheier, M. F., & Carver, C. S. (1985). Optimism, coping and health. *Health Psychology, 4,* 219–247.

Scherer, K. R. (1986). Vocal affect expression: a review and model for further research. *Psychological Bulletin, 99,* 143–165.

Scherer, K. R., & Oshinsky, J. J. (1977). Cue utilization in emotion attribution from auditory stimuli. *Motivation and Emotion, 1,* 331–346.

Scherer, K. R., Summerfield, A. B., & Walbott, H. G. (1986). *Experiencing Emotion,* Cambridge: Cambridge University Press.

Schmitt, M., & Maes, J. (1998). Perceived injustice in unified Germany and mental health. *Social Justice Research, 11,* 59–78.

Schor, J. (1998). *The Overspent American.* New York: Basic Books.

Schultz, T. R. (1976). A cognitive-developmental analysis of humour. In A. J. Chapman & H. C. Foot (Eds.), *Humour and Laughter: Theory, Research and Applications* (pp. 11–36). Chichester, UK: Wiley.

Schultz, T. R., & Horibe, F. (1974). Development of the appreciation of verbal jokes. *Developmental Psychology, 10,* 13–20.

Schulz, R., & Decker, S. (1985). Long-term adjustment to physical disability: the role of social support, perceived control, and self-blame. *Journal of Personality and Social Psychology, 48,* 1162–1172.

Schwartz, C. E., & Sendor, M. (1999). Helping others helps oneself: response shift effects in peer support. *Social Science and Medicine, 48,* 1563–1575.

Schwartz, J. C., & O'Connor, C. J. (1984). The social ecology of memorable emotional experiences. Paper at Second International Conference on Personal Relationships, Madison.

Schwarz, N. (1990). Feelings as information: informational and motivational functions of affective states. In R. M. Sorrentino & E. T. Higgins (Eds.), *Handbook of Motivation and Cognition: Cognitive Foundations of Social Psychology* (Vol. 2, pp. 527–561). New York: Guilford Press.

Schwarz, N., & Clore, G. L. (1983). Mood, misattribution, and judgments of well-being: informative and directive functions of affective states. *Journal of Personality and Social Psychology, 45,* 513–523.

Schwarz, N., & Strack, F. (1991). Evaluating one's life: a judgement model of subjective well-being. In F. Strack, M. Argyle, & N. Schwarz (Eds.), *Subjective Well-Being* (pp. 27–47). Oxford, UK: Pergamon Press.

Schwarz, N., & Strack, F. (1999). Reports of subjective well-being: judgmental processes and their methodological implications. In D. Kahneman, E. Diener, & N. Schwarz (Eds.), *Well-Being: The Foundations of Hedonic Psychology* (pp. 61–84). New York: Russell Sage.

Schwarz, N., Strack, F., Kommer, F., & Wagner, D. (1987). Soccer, rooms, and the quality of your life: mood effects on judgements of satisfaction with life in general and with specific domains. *European Journal of Social Psychology, 17*, 69–79.

Schwarzer, R., & Leppin, A. (1989). Social support and health: a meta-analysis. *Psychology and Health, 3*, 1–15.

Schyns, P. (1998). Crossnational differences in happiness: economic and cultural factors explored. *Social Indicators Research, 43*, 3–26.

Scott, K. D., & Taylor, G. S. (1985). An examination of conflicting findings on the relationship between job satisfaction and absenteeism: a meta-analysis. *Academy of Management Journal, 28*, 599–612.

Sedikides, C. (1995). Central and peripheral self-conceptions are differentially affected by mood: tests of the differential sensitivity hypothesis. *Journal of Personality and Social Psychology, 669*, 759–777.

Segerstrom, S. C., Taylor, S. E., Kemeny, M. E., & Fahey, J. L. (1998). Optimism is associated with mood, coping and immune change in response to stress. *Journal of Personality and Social Psychology, 74*, 1646–1655.

Seidlitz, L., Wyer, R. S., & Diener, E. (1997). Cognitive correlates of subjective well-being: the processing of valenced life events by happy and unhappy persons. *Journal of Research in Personality, 31*, 240–256.

Sem-Jacobsen, C. W. (1976). Electrical stimulation and self-stimulation in man with chronic implanted electrodes. Interpretations and pitfalls of results. In A. Wauquier & E. T. Rolls (Eds.), *Brain-Stimulation Reward* (pp. 505–520). Amsterdam: Elsevier.

Sethi, S., & Seligman, M. E. (1993). Optimism and fundamentalism. *Psychological Science, 4*, 256–259.

Shammi, P., & Stuss, D. T. (1999). Humour appreciation: a role of the right frontal lobe. *Brain, 122*, 657–666.

Shapiro, A., & Lambert, J. D. (1999). Longitudinal effects of divorce on the quality of the father–child relationship and on fathers' psychological well-being. *Journal of Marriage and the Family, 61*, 397–408.

Shaver, P. R., & Hazan, C. (1988). A biased overview of the study of love. *Journal of Social and Personal Relationships, 5*, 473–501.

Sheldon, K. M., & Elliot, A. J. (1999). Goal-striving, need satisfaction, and longitudinal well-being: the self-concordance model. *Journal of Personality and Social Psychology, 76*, 481–497.

Sheldon, K. M., Ryan, R., & Reis, H. T. (1996). What makes a good day? Competence and autonomy in the day and in the person. *Personality and Social Psychology Bulletin, 22*, 1270–1279.

Shepherd, R. J. (1997). *Aging, Physical Activity and Health.* Champaign, IL: Human Kinetics.

Siegel, J. M., & Kendall, D. H. (1990). Loss, widowhood, and psychological distress among the elderly. *Journal of Consulting and Clinical Psychology, 58*, 519–524.

Simmel, G. (1904). Fashion. *International Quarterly*, *1*, 130–155.

Sinclair, R. C., Mark, M. M., Enzle, M. E., & Borkovec, T. D. (1994). Toward a multiple-method view of mood induction: the appropriateness of a modified Velten mood induction technique and the problems of procedures with group assignment to conditions. *Basic and Applied Social Psychology*, *15*, 389–408.

Skevington, S. M., MacArthur, P., & Somerset, M. (1997). Developing items for the WHOQOL: an investigation of contemporary beliefs about quality of life related to health in Britain. *British Journal of Health Psychology*, *2*, 55–72.

Sloane, P. J., & Williams, H. (1996). Are "overpaid" workers really unhappy? A test of the theory of cognitive dissonance. *Labour*, *10(1)*, 3–15.

Slottje, D. J. (1991). *Measuring the Quality of Life Across Countries: A Multidimensional Analysis*. Boulder, CO: Westview.

Smith, D. F., & Hoklund, M. (1988). Love and salutogenesis in late adolescence: a preliminary investigation. *Psychology: A Journal of Human Behavior*, *25*, 44–49.

Smith, P. C., Kendall, K. M., & Hulin, C. L. (1969). *The Measurement of Satisfaction in Work and Retirement*. Chicago: Rand McNally.

Smith, S., & Razzell, P. (1975). *The Pools Winners*. London: Caliban Books.

Smulders, P. G. W., Kompier, M. A. J., & Paoli, P. (1996). The work environment in the twelve EU countries: differences and similarities. *Human Relations*, *49*, 1291–1313.

Sonstroem, R. J., & Potts, S. A. (1996). Life adjustment correlates of physical self-concepts. *Medicine and Science in Sports and Exercise*, *28*, 619–625.

Spector, P. E. (1997). *Job Satisfaction*. Thousand Oaks, CA: Sage.

Stack, S., & Eshleman, J. R. (1998). Marital status and happiness: a 17-nation study. *Journal of Marriage and the Family*, *60*, 527–536.

Staw, B. M., & Ross, J. (1985). Stability in the midst of change: a dispositional approach to job attitudes. *Journal of Applied Psychology*, *70*, 469–480.

Stebbins, R. A. (1979). *Amateurs*. Beverly Hills, CA: Sage.

Steinberg, H., & Sykes, E. A. (1985). Introduction to symposium on endorphins and exercise. *Pharmacology, Biochemistry and Behavior*, *23*, 857–862.

Steptoe (1998). "Effects of exercise on mood". Seminar at Oxford.

St. George, A., & McNamara, P. H. (1984). Race and psychological well-being. *Journal for the Scientific Study of Religion*, *23*, 351–363.

Stock, W. A., Okun, M. A., Haring, M. J., & Witter, R. A. (1985). Race and subjective well-being in adulthood: a Black–White research synthesis. *Human Development*, *28*, 192–197.

Stone, A. A., Cox, D. S., Valdimarsdottir, H., Jandorf, L., & Neale, J. M. (1987). Evidence that secretory IgA is associated with daily mood. *Journal of Personality and Social Psychology*, *52*, 988–993.

Stone, A. A., & Neale, J. M. (1984). Effects of severe daily events on mood. *Journal of Personality and Social Psychology*, *46*, 137–144.

Stone, L. (1977). *The Family, Sex and Marriage in England, 1500–1800*. London: Weidenfeld and Nicolson.

Stone, S. (1934). The Miller delusion: a comparative study in mass psychology. *American Journal of Psychiatry*, *91*, 593–623.

Storr, A. (1996). *Feet of Clay: A Study of Gurus*. London: Harper Collins.

Strack, F., Schwarz, N., Chassein, B., Kern, D., & Wagner, D. (1990). The salience of comparison standards and the activation of social norms: consequences for judgments of happiness and their communication. *British Journal of Social Psychology*, *29*, 303–314.

Strack, F., Schwarz, N., & Gschneidinger, E. (1985). Happiness and reminiscing: the role of time perspective, affect and mode of thinking. *Journal of Personality and Social Psychology*, *49*, 1460–1469.

Stroebe, W., & Stroebe, M. S. (1987). *Bereavement and Health*. Cambridge, UK: Cambridge University Press.

Strozier, C. B. (1994). *Apocalypse: On the Psychology of Fundamentalism in America*. Boston: Beacon Press.

Stull, D. E. (1988). A dyadic approach to predicting well-being in later life. *Research on Aging*, *10*, 81–101.

Suh, E., Diener, E., Oishi, S., & Triandis, H. (1997). The shifting basis of life satisfaction judgments across cultures: emotions versus norms. *Journal of Personality and Social Psychology*, *74*, 482–493.

Suh, E. M. (in press). Self, the hyphen between culture and subjective well-being. In E. Diener & E. M. Suh (Eds.), *Subjective Well-Being Across Cultures*. Cambridge, MA: MIT Press.

Sweetman, M. E., Munz, D. C., & Wheeler, R. J. (1993). Optimism, hardiness, and explanatory style as predictors of general well-being among attorneys. *Social Indicators Research*, *29*, 153–161.

Swenson, W. M. (1961). Attitudes towards death in an aged population. *Journal of Gerontology*, *16*, 49–52.

Tait, M., Padgett, M. Y., & Baldwin, T. T. (1989). Job satisfaction and life satisfaction: a reexamination of the strength of the relationship and gender effects as a function of the date of the study. *Journal of Applied Psychology*, *74*, 502–507.

Taussig, M., & Fenwick, R. (1999). Recession and well-being. *Journal of Health and Social Behavior*, *40*, 1–16.

Taylor, S. E., & Brown, J. D. (1988). Illusion and well-being: a social-psychological perspective on mental health. *Psychological Bulletin*, *103*, 193–210.

Taylor, S. E., & Gollwitzer, P. M. (1995). Effects of mindset on positive illusions. *Journal of Personality and Social Psychology*, *69*, 213–226.

Teasdale, J. D., & Russell, M. L. (1983). Differential effect of induced mood on the recall of positive, negative, and neutral words. *British Journal of Clinical Psychology*, *22*, 163–171.

Tellegen, A., Lykken, D. T., Bouchard, T. J., Wilcox, K. J., Segal, N. L. & Rich, S. (1988) Personality similarity in twins reared apart and together. *Journal of Personality and Social Psychology*, *54*, 1031–1039.

Thaut, M. H. (1989). The influence of music therapy interventions on self-rated changes in relaxation, affect, and thought in psychiatric prisoner-patients. *Journal of Music Therapy*, *26*, 155–166.

Thayer, R. E. (1989). *The Biopsychology of Mood and Arousal*. New York: Oxford University Press.

Thoits, P., & Hannan, M. (1979). Income and psychological distress: the impact of an income-maintenance experiment. *Journal of Health and Social Behavior*, *20*, 120–138.

Thoits, P. A. (1985). Social support and psychological well-being: theoretical possibilities. In I. G. Sarason & B. R. Sarason (Eds.), *Social Support: Theory, Research and Applications* (pp. 51–72). Dordrecht, The Netherlands: Nijkhoff.

Thorne, A. (1987). The press of personality: a study of conversation between introverts and extroverts. *Journal of Personality and Social Psychology*, *53*, 718–726.

Tomkins, S. S. (1962). *Affect, Imagery, Consciousness: Vol. 1. The Positive Affects.* New York: Springer.

Trew, K., & Kilpatrick, R. (1984). *The Daily Life of the Unemployed.* Belfast, Northern Ireland: Dept. of Psychology, Queen's University.

Triandis, H. C. (1995). *Individualism and Collectivism.* Boulder, CO: Westview Press.

Triandis, H., Bontempo, R., Villareal, M. J., Asai, M., & Lucca, N. (1988). Individualism and collectivism: cross-cultural perspectives on self-ingroup relationships. *Journal of Personality and Social Psychology, 54,* 323–338.

Trope, Y., Ferguson, M., & Raghumathan, R. (2000). Mood as a resource in processing self-relevant information. In J. P. Forgas (Ed.) *Handbook of Affect and Social Cognition,* pp. 256–274. Mahwah, NJ: Lawrence Erlbaum Associates Inc.

Tucker, L. A. (1990). Physical fitness and psychological distress. *International Journal of Sport Psychology, 21,* 185–201.

Turner, J. B. (1995). Economic context and the health effects of unemployment. *Journal of Health and Social Behavior, 36,* 213–229.

Turner, R. W., Ward, M. F., & Turner, D. J. (1979). Behavioral treatment for depression: an evaluation of therapeutic components. *Journal of Clinical Psychology, 35,* 166–175.

Turner, V. W. (1969). *The Ritual Process.* London: Routledge & Kegan Paul.

Ullman, C. (1982). Cognitive and emotional antecedents of religious conversion. *Journal of Personality and Social Psychology, 43,* 183–192.

Ulrich, R. S., Dimberg, U., & Driver, B. L. (1991). Psychophysiological indicators of leisure benefits. In B. L. Driver, P. J. Brown, & G. L. Peterson (Eds.), *Benefits of Leisure* (pp. 73–89). State College, PA: Venture Publishing.

Umberson, D. (1987). Family status and health behaviors: social control as a dimension of social integration. *Journal of Health and Social Behavior, 28,* 306–319.

Umberson, D., Chen, M. D., House, J. S., & Hopkins, K. (1996). The effect of social relationships on psychological well-being: are men and women really so different? *American Sociological Review, 61,* 837–857.

United Nations Development Programme (1990). *Human Development Report,* Oxford, UK: Oxford University Press.

Ushino, B. N., Cacioppo, J. T., & Kiecolt-Glaser, J. K. (1996). The relationship between social support and physiological processes: a review with emphasis on underlying mechanisms and implications for health. *Psychological Bulletin, 119,* 488–531.

van der Doef, M., & Maes, S. (1999). The Job Demands-Control (-Support) Model and psychological well-being: a review of 20 years of empirical research. *Work and Stress, 13,* 87–115.

Vanfossen, B. E. (1981). Sex differences in the mental health effects of spouse support and equity. *Journal of Health and Social Behavior, 22,* 130–143.

Van Hooff, J. A. R. A. M. (1972). A comparative approach to the phylogeny of laughter and smiling. In R. H. Hinde (Ed.), *Non-Verbal Communication* (pp. 209–241). Cambridge, UK: Cambridge University Press.

van Ranst, N., & Marcoen, A. (1997). Meaning in life of young and elderly adults: an examination of the factorial validity and invariance of the Life Regard Index. *Personality and Individual Differences, 22,* 877–884.

Veblen, T. (1899). *The Theory of the Leisure Class.* New York: Viking.

Veenhoven, R. (1988). The utility of happiness. *Social Indicators Research, 20,* 333–354.

Veenhoven, R. (1989). *Did the Crisis Really Hurt?* Rotterdam, The Netherlands: Rotterdam University Press.

Veenhoven, R. (1993). *Happiness in Nations: Subjective Appreciation of Life in 56 Nations.* Rotterdam, The Netherlands: RISBO.

Veenhoven, R. (1994). *Correlates of Happiness* (3 Vols.). Rotterdam, The Netherlands: RISBO, Center for Socio-Cultural Transformation.

Veenhoven, R. (1995). The cross-national pattern of happiness: test of predictions implied in three theories of happiness. *Social Indicators Research, 34,* 33–68.

Veenhoven, R. (2000). *Freedom and happiness.* Paper presented at the Nuffield College conference on Well-Being.

Veenhoven, R., & Ehrhardt, J. (1995). Test of predictions implied in three theories of happiness: the cross-national pattern of happiness. *Social Indicators Research, 34,* 33–68.

Vella, B. D. A., & White, V. (1997). Response set of social desirability in relation to the mental, physical and spiritual well-being scale. *Psychological Reports, 81,* 127–130.

Velten, E. (1968). A laboratory task for induction of mood states. *Behaviour Research and Therapy, 6,* 473–482.

Verkley, H., & Stolk, J. (1989). Does happiness lead into idleness? In R. Veenhoven (Ed.), *How Harmful is Happiness?* (pp. 79–93). Rotterdam, The Netherlands: Rotterdam University Press.

Veroff, J., Douvan, E., & Kulka, R. A. (1981). *The Inner American.* New York: Basic Books.

Vollenweider, F. X., Gamma, A., Liechti, M., & Huber, T. (1998). Psychological and cardiovascular effects and short-term sequelae of MDMA ("Ecstasy") in MDMA-naive healthy volunteers. *Neuropsychopharmacology, 19,* 241–251.

Wadsworth, M. E. J., Montgomery, S. M., & Bartley, M. J. (1999). The persisting effect of unemployment on health and social well-being in men early in working life. *Social Science and Medicine, 48,* 1491–1499.

Walker, C. (1977). Some variations in marital satisfaction. In R. Chester & J. Peel (Eds.), *Equalities and Inequalities in Family Life* (pp. 127–139). London: Academic Press.

Wanberg, C. R. (1997). Antecedents and outcomes of coping behaviors among unemployed and reemployed individuals. *Journal of Applied Psychology, 82,* 731–744.

Wanberg, C. R., Griffiths, R. F., & Gavin, M. B. (1997). Time structure and unemployment: a longitudinal study. *Journal of Occupational and Organizational Psychology, 70,* 75–90.

Wannamethee, G., Shaper, A. G., & Macfarlane, P. W. (1993). Heart rate, physical activity, and mortality from cancer and other noncardiovascular diseases. *American Journal of Epidemiology, 137,* 735–748.

Wanous, J. P., Reichers, A. E., & Hudy, M. J. (1997). Overall job satisfaction: how good are single item measures? *Journal of Applied Psychology, 82,* 247–252.

Warm, T. R. (1997). The role of teasing in development and vice versa. *Journal of Developmental and Behavioral Pediatrics, 18,* 97–101.

Warr, P. (1999). Well-being and the work place. In D. Kahneman, E. Diener, & N. Schwarz (Eds.), *Well-Being: The Foundations of Hedonic Psychology* (pp. 392–412). New York: Sage.

Warr, P. B. (1978). A study of psychological well-being. *British Journal of Psychology, 69,* 111–121.

Warr, P. B. (1982). A national study of non-financial employment commitment. *Journal of Occupational Psychology, 55,* 297–312.

Warr, P. B. (1984). Work and unemployment. In P. J. D. Drenth et al. (Eds.), *Handbook of Work and Organizational Psychology* (Vol. 1, pp. 413–443). Chichester, UK: Wiley.

Warr, P. B., & Payne, R. (1982). Experience of strain and pleasure among British adults. *Social Science and Medicine, 16,* 1691–1697.

Waterman, A. S. (1993). Two conceptions of happiness: contrasts of personal expressiveness (eudomania) and hedonic enjoyment. *Journal of Personality and Social Psychology, 64,* 678–691.

Watson, D., & Clark, L. A. (1984). Negative affectivity: the disposition to experience negative emotions. *Psychological Bulletin, 96,* 465–490.

Weisenberg, M., Raz, T., & Hener, T. (1998). The influence of film-induced mood on pain perception. *Pain, 76,* 365–375.

Weiss, R. S. (1973). *Loneliness: The Experience of Emotional and Social Isolation.* Cambridge, MA: MIT Press.

Welsford, E. (1961). *The Fool: His Social and Literary History.* New York: Anchor Books.

Wessman, A. E., & Ricks, D. F. (1966). *Mood and Personality.* New York: Holt, Rinehart & Winston.

West, C. G., Reed, D. M., & Gildengorin, G. L. (1998). Can money buy happiness? Depressive symptoms in an affluent older population. *Journal of the American Geriatrics Society, 46,* 49–57.

West, M. A., Borrill, C. S., & Unsworth, K. L. (1998). Team effectiveness in organizations. In C. Cooper & I. T. Robertson (Eds.), *International Review of Industrial and Organizational Psychology* (Vol. 13, pp. 1–48). Chichester, UK: Wiley.

Westermann, R., Spies, K., Stahl, G., & Hesse, F. W. (1996). Relative effectiveness and validity of mood induction procedures: a meta-analysis. *European Journal of Social Psychology, 26,* 557–580.

Wheeler, J. A., Gorey, K. M., & Greenblatt, B. (1998). The beneficial effects of volunteering for older volunteers and the people they serve: a meta analysis. *International Journal of Aging and Human Development, 47,* 69–79.

Wheeler, L., Reis, H., & Nezlek, J. (1983). Loneliness, social interaction and social roles. *Journal of Personality and Social Psychology, 45,* 943–953.

Whyte, M. K. (1990). *Dating, Mating, and Marriage.* New York: Aldine de Gruyter.

Wickrama, K., Conger, R. D., Lorenz, F. O., & Matthews, L. (1995). Role identity, role satisfaction, and perceived physical health. *Social Psychology Quarterly, 58,* 270–283.

Wickrama, K. A. S., Lorenz, F. O., Conger, R. D., Matthews, L., & Elder, G. H. (1997). Linking occupational conditions to physical health through the marital, social and interpersonal processes. *Journal of Health and Social Behavior, 38,* 363–370.

Williams, A. W., Ware, J. E., & Donald, C. A. (1981). A model of mental health, life events, and social support applicable to general populations. *Journal of Health and Social Behavior, 22,* 324–336.

Willmott, P. (1987). *Social Networks and Social Support.* London: Policy Studies Institute.

Wills, T. A. (1981). Downward comparison principles in social psychology. *Psychological Bulletin, 90,* 245–271.

Wilson, W. (1967). Correlates of avowed happiness. *Psychological Bulletin, 67,* 294–306.

Winefield, A. H. (1995). Unemployment: its psychological costs. In C. L. Cooper & I. T. Robertson (Eds.), *International Review of Industrial and Organizational Psychology* (Vol. 10, pp. 169–212). Chichester, UK: Wiley.

Winefield, A. H., Tiggemann, M., & Winefield, H. R. (1992). Spare time use and psychological well-being in employed and unemployed young people. *Journal of Occupational and and Organizational Psychology, 65,* 307–313.

Witter, R. A., Okun, M. A., Stock, W. A., & Haring, M. J. (1984). Education and subjective well-being: a meta-analysis. *Educational Evaluation and Policy Analysis, 6,* 165–173.

Witter, R. A., Stock, W. A., Okun, M. A., & Haring, M. J. (1985). Religion and subjective well-being in adulthood: a quantitative synthesis. *Review of Religious Research, 26,* 332–342.

Wood, W., Rhodes, N., & Whelan, M. (1989). Sex differences in positive well-being: a consideration of emotional style and marital status. *Psychological Bulletin, 106,* 249–264.

Wood, J. V., Taylor, S. E., & Lichtman, R. R. (1985). Social comparison in adjustment to breast cancer. *Journal of Personality and Social Psychology, 49,* 1169–1183.

Worcester, R. M. (1998). More than money. In I. Christie & L. Nash (Eds.), *The Good Life* (pp. 19–25). London: Demos.

World Values Study Group. (1994). *World Values Survey, 1981–1984 and 1990–1993.* Ann Arbor, MI: Institute for Social Research, University of Michigan.

Wright, S. J. (1985). Health satisfaction: a detailed test of the multiple discrepancies theory model. *Social Indicators Research, 17,* 299–313.

Wyer, R. S., & Collins, J. E. (1992). A theory of humor elicitation. *Psychological Review, 99,* 663–688.

Young, M., Benjamin, B., & Wallis, C. (1963). Mortality of widowers. *Lancet, 2,* 454–456.

Zillmann, D., & Cantor, J. R. (1976). A disposition theory of humour and mirth. In A. J. Chapman & H. C. Foot (Eds.), *Humour and Laughter: Theory, Research and Applications* (pp. 93–115). Chichester, UK: Wiley.

Zuckerman, M. (1979). *Sensation Seeking.* Hillsdale, NJ: Lawrence Erlbaum Associates Inc.

Author index

Subject index